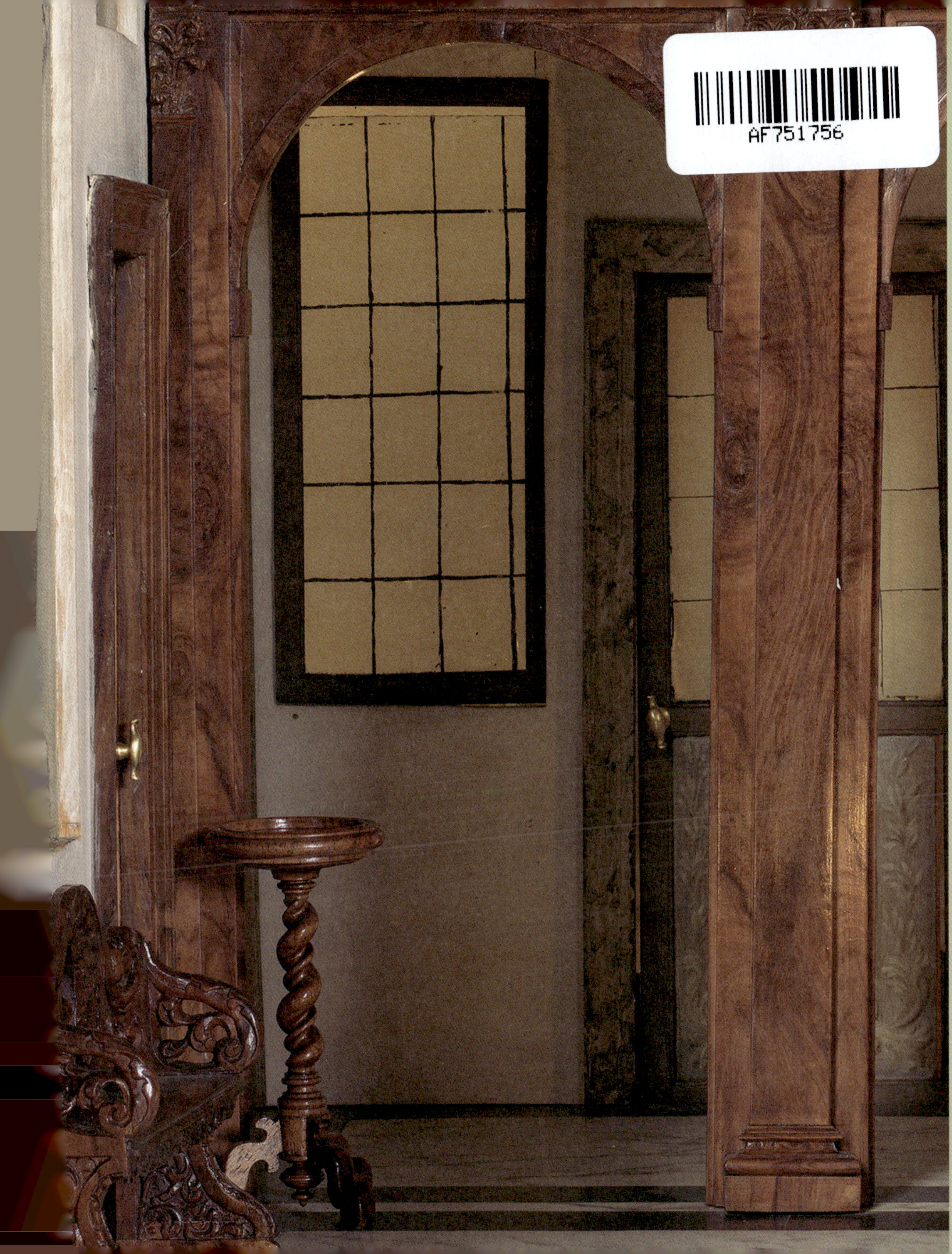

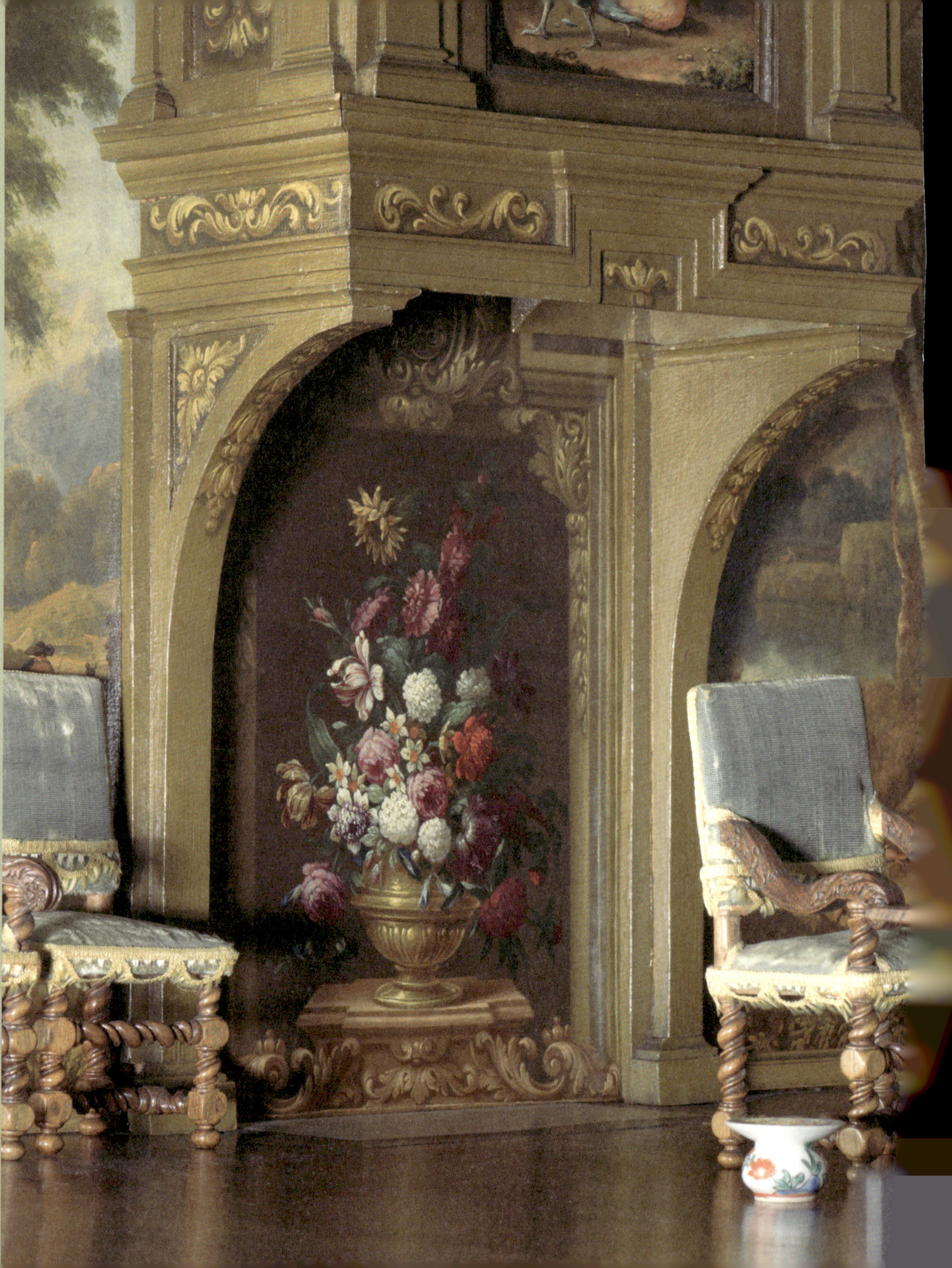

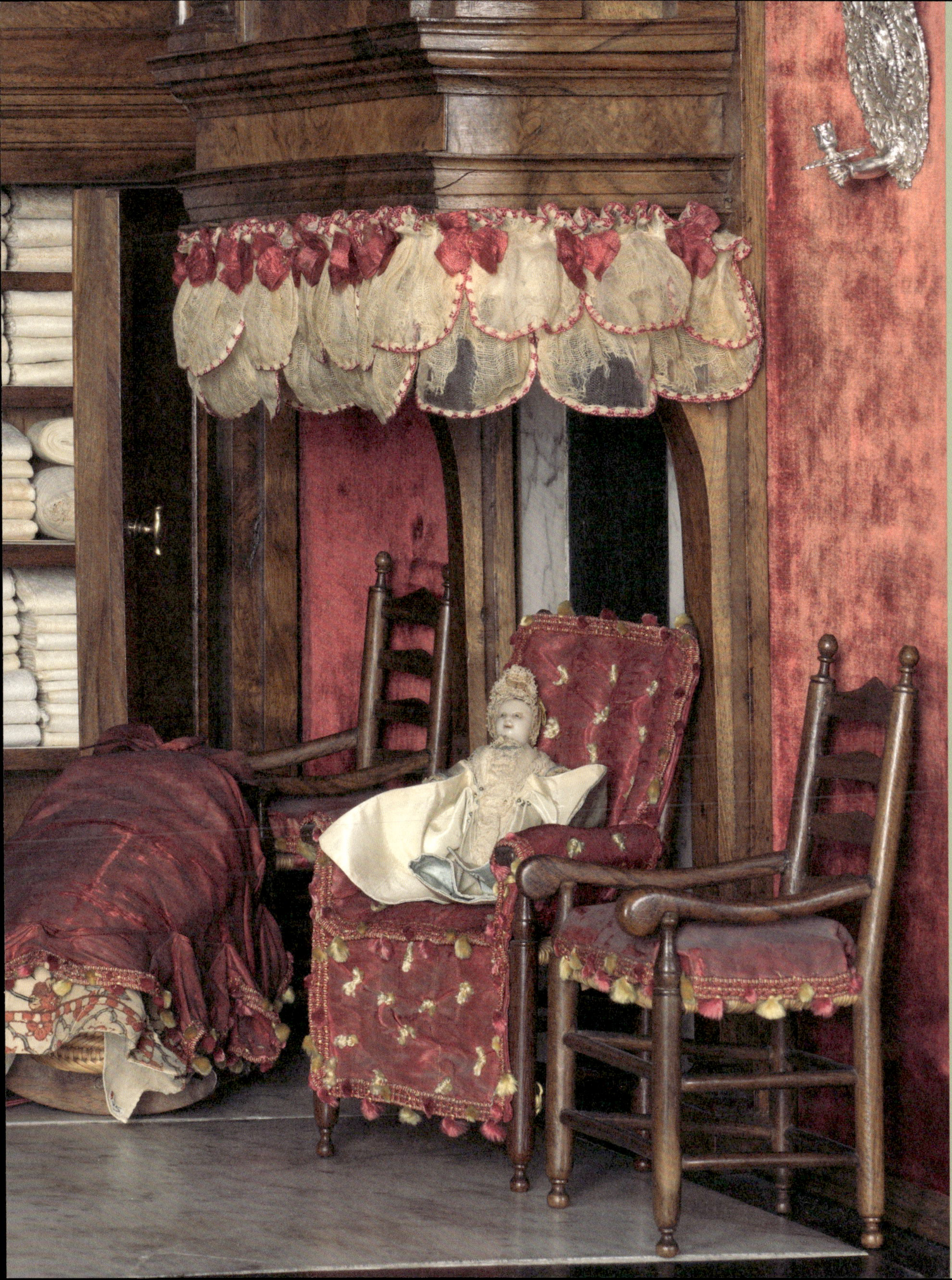

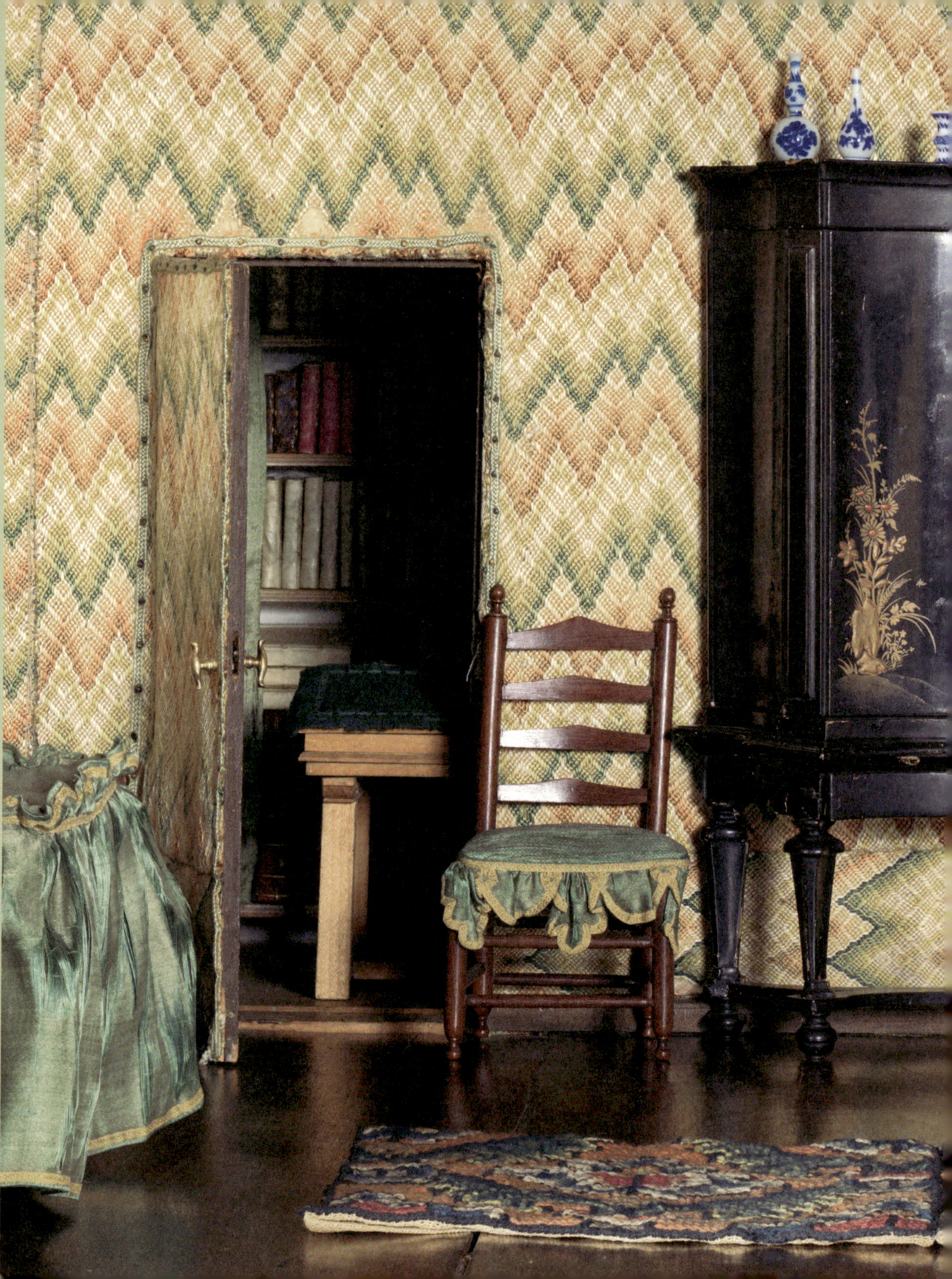

PETRONELLA OORTMAN'S DOLL'S HOUSE

SARA VAN DIJK AND ALEXANDER DENCHER

RIJKS MUSEUM

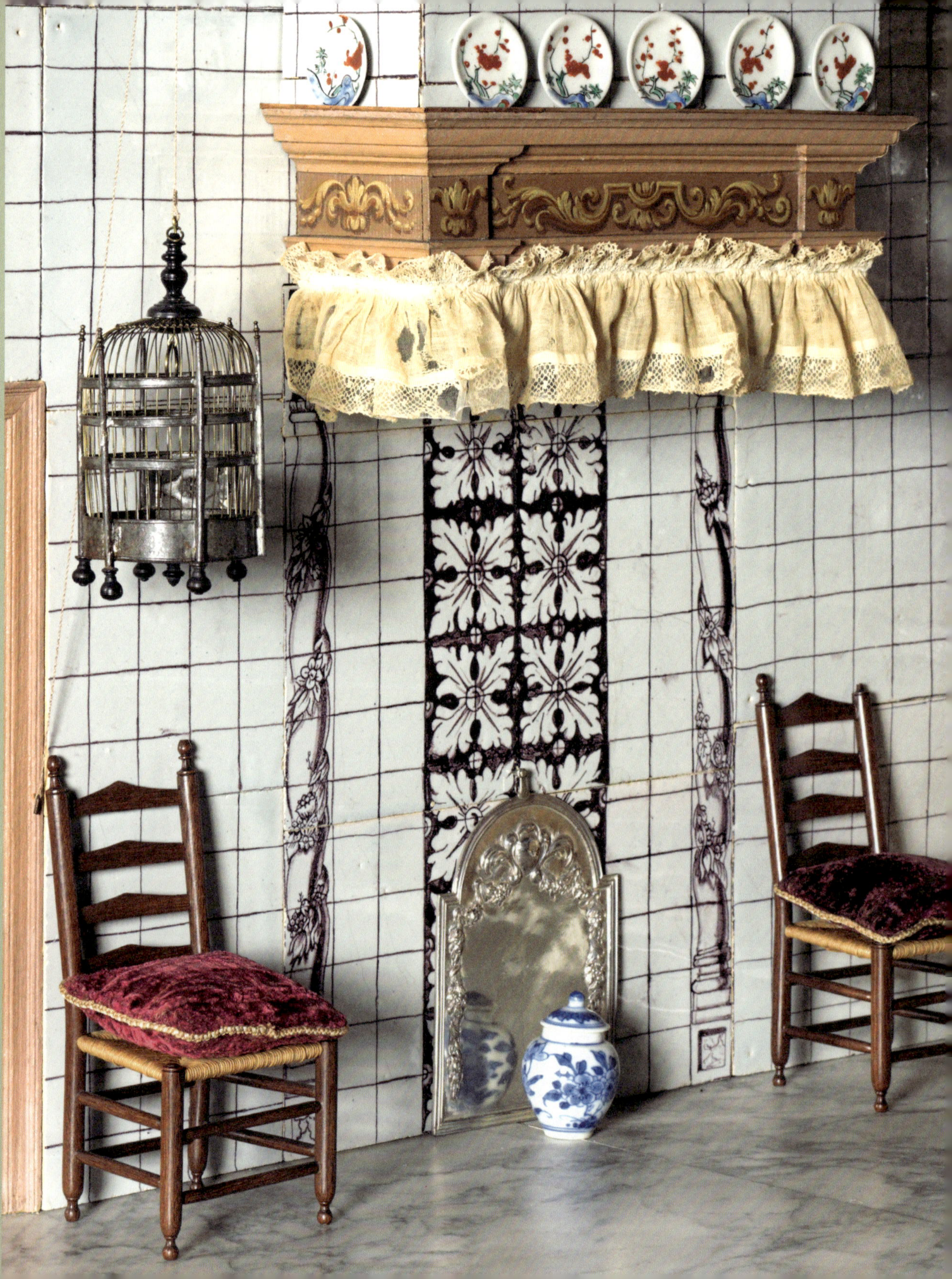

A LOOK INSIDE THE 17TH CENTURY

One of the greatest masterpieces in the Rijksmuseum is a miniature world. For more than two centuries, visitors young and old have been captivated by Petronella Oortman's impressive doll's house. This wealthy Amsterdam woman commissioned the cabinet and the interior, with its more than 700 miniature objects, to be crafted to scale by the finest artisans in Amsterdam and far beyond. The craftsmanship, attention to detail and exquisite finishing are breathtaking. A costly doll's house such as this was not intended as a plaything; it represents the ideal household – a microcosm where the lady of the house reigned supreme.

Although the household was a popular subject of seventeenth-century Dutch writings and paintings, this doll's house holds unique insights into domestic life. With regard to historical interiors and furnishings alone, it forms an inexhaustible source of knowledge. While most painters and writers were men, the owners of Dutch dolls' houses were, without exception, women. As patrons, they coordinated the activities of artists and artisans, bringing together the whole range of crafts from woodworking and painting to glass-blowing and silversmithing. These women collectors managed not only their real-life households, but also the miniature versions. Their work thus provides rare glimpses of a female perspective.

Two other more or less complete Dutch dolls' houses from this period have been preserved: Petronella Dunois's, also in the Rijksmuseum, and Petronella de la Court's, in the Centraal Museum in Utrecht [FIGS. 72, 73]. Parts of three other houses, two furnished by Cornelia van der Gon and one by Rachel van Dantsich, were reused by Sara Rothé in the eighteenth century for her own two doll cabinets, now in the Kunstmuseum Den Haag and the Frans Hals Museum in Haarlem. Historical sources tell of still other dolls' houses and cabinets of miniature furnishings. But none of these were as rich or superbly executed as Oortman's.

In the 1990s, the Rijksmuseum embarked on a major restoration project to preserve this doll's house, as well as Petronella Dunois's, for future generations. All the miniatures underwent cleaning and conservation, as did the cabinets. In the year 2000, this project culminated in the publication of *Het Hollandse pronkpoppenhuis*, Jet Pijzel-Dommisse's authoritative study of seventeenth- and eighteenth-century Dutch dolls' houses, in which the two houses in the Rijksmuseum play a leading role. Thanks to her meticulous research and detailed inventory of all the objects in each room, it remains a superlative reference work even now, a quarter century later, although unfortunately it has gone out of print.

In 2024, the museum decided to reopen the doors of its dolls' houses, this time for digital photography. It has made the houses more accessible than ever: 360-degree views are available online, and you can zoom in on each tiny object (www.rijksmuseum.nl/en/dollshouse). This represents a huge step forward, especially in the case of Oortman's doll's house, which has rooms that remain concealed from museum visitors. It enables us to examine this artwork with fresh eyes. We hope this book will take readers on an even more immersive journey into the doll's house, offering a look inside everyday life in the seventeenth century, the culture of collecting, and women's role in it.

Taco Dibbits
General Director, Rijksmuseum

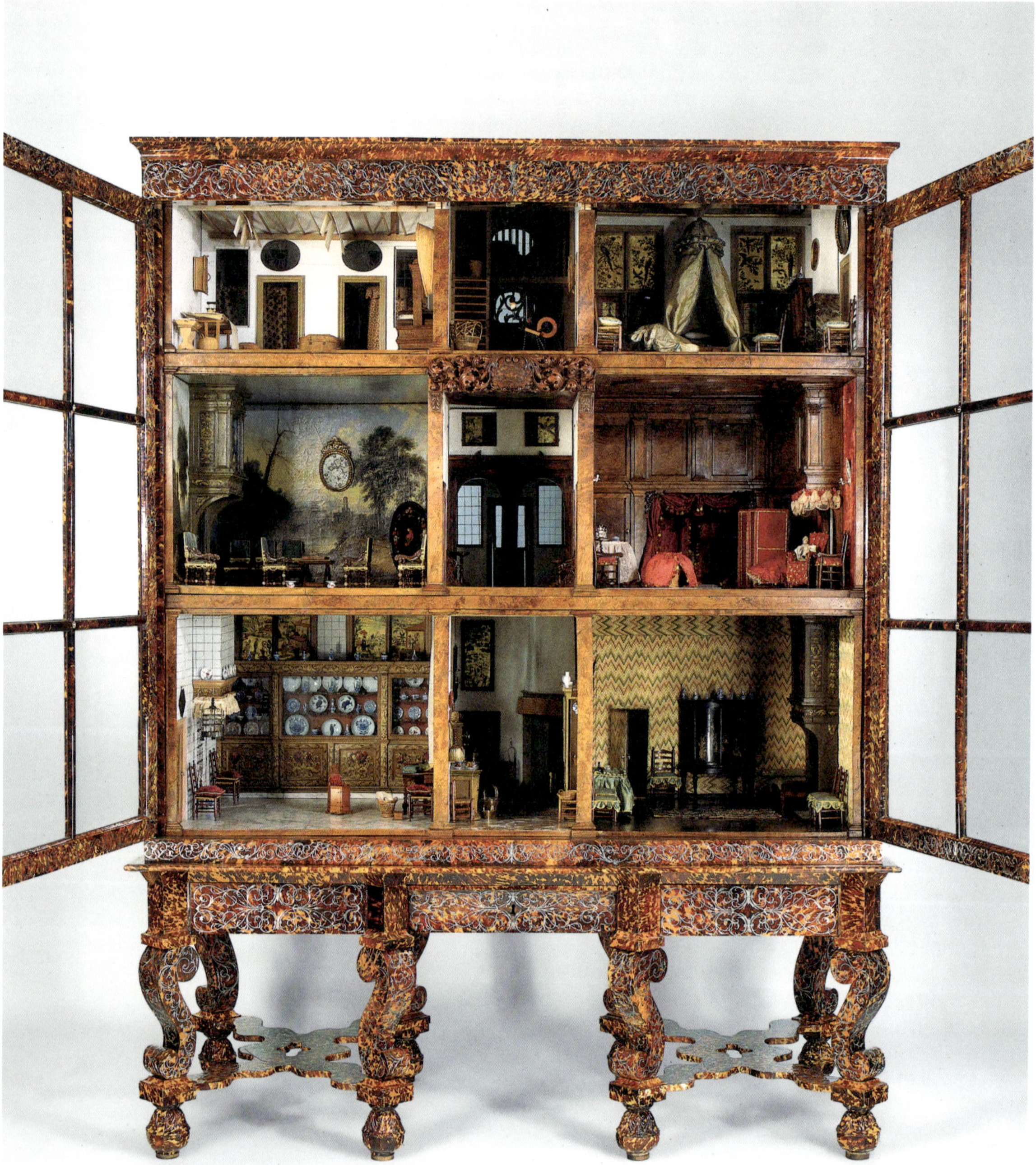

1
Petronella Oortman's doll's house was designed to impress. Of the three surviving seventeenth-century Dutch dolls' houses, this is the largest and most luxurious

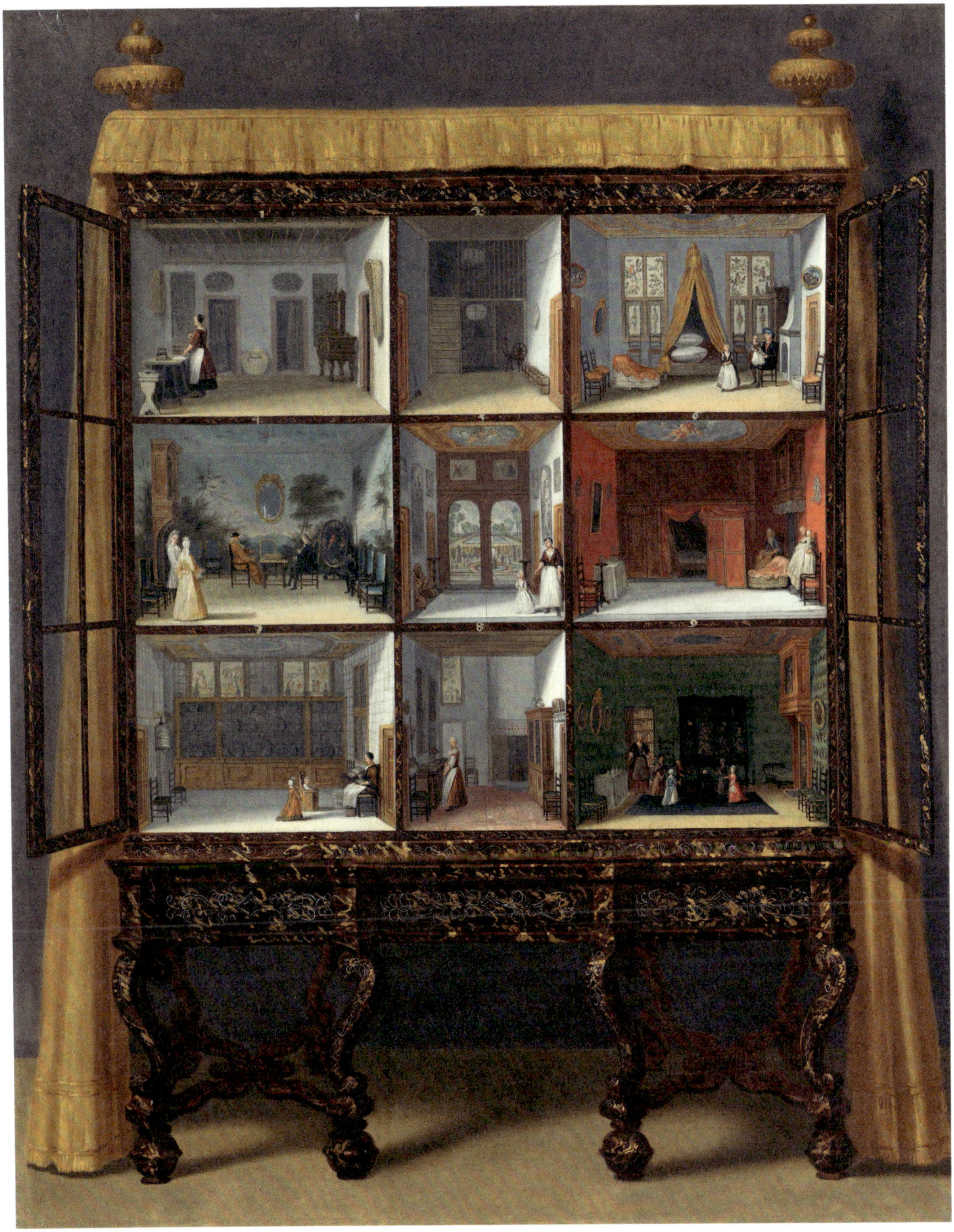

2
This painting by Jacob Appel shows that the doll's house was originally concealed by curtains and an impressive canopy. The dolls, now lost, are also visible here

AN ARTWORK WITHOUT EQUAL

In the late afternoon of 19 July 1718, nine German tourists entered the home of silk merchant Johannes Brandt on Warmoesstraat in Amsterdam. Among them were the brothers Zacharias and Friedrich von Uffenbach, both scientists and collectors. They had visited a variety of European collections, but none had prepared them for what they were about to see.

The brothers were touring the Low Countries for pleasure, together with their wives, some other family members and their friend Johann Adolph von Glauburg, who wrote an account of the entire journey. These holidaymakers *avant la lettre* explored castles and country estates in Gelderland, Het Loo Palace and the city of Utrecht, before travelling by barge along the Vecht to Amsterdam. There they experienced one of the highlights of their journey: a visit to Petronella Oortman's doll's house [FIG. 1].

In the seventeenth century, dolls' houses were not mere children's toys. They represented an ideal household, filled with hundreds of miniature objects, and were simultaneously unique works of art, decorated and furnished by wealthy women. Oortman's was already famous among specialists during her lifetime, but arranging to see it could be quite a challenge. Prince Eugene of Savoy, a collector who was also one of Europe's foremost military commanders, had been denied entry in 1716 because the owner was on her deathbed. A Frisian princess had twice requested to visit, unsuccessfully, and gained entry only on her third attempt, when she showed up on the doorstep unannounced.

The Uffenbachs were more fortunate, however, receiving a warm welcome from the widower Johannes Brandt. His daughter Hendrina had already made tea and gave the German visitors a three-hour guided tour of her mother's doll's house. Glauburg devoted no fewer than twenty pages to it in his account of his travels, far more than to anything else they saw on their trip, and for good reason: the doll's house was an unparalleled specimen. Oortman had spent twenty-five years working on it. As Glauburg remarks, she had invested a total of 20,000 to 30,000 guilders in the project – a veritable fortune, the price of a distinguished full-scale canal house in Amsterdam. This made it the most expensive and exquisite doll's house in all of Europe.

Its value lay, first of all, in the cabinet, which is made of oak but entirely veneered with tortoise-shell and inlaid with pewter. The technique is known as boulle work, after the French cabinetmaker André-Charles Boulle, who perfected this form of marquetry [FIGS. 3, 4]. On the sides, amid the abundant foliate and arabesque decoration, is the mirror monogram 'BO', for Brandt–Oortman [FIG. 5]. This stunning exterior deeply impressed the German travellers, who – like many later authors – mistook the gleaming polished pewter for silver. The high degree of refinement bespeaks the exceptional talent of the cabinet's creator. According to Hendrina Brandt, this anonymous cabinetmaker came to her mother's home over a period of three years to construct the cabinet, including the marquetry and locks. The craftsman was said to have worked for the French court, and both the decoration and the technique bear a strong resemblance to French royal furniture. There were probably only a few Dutch cabinetmakers familiar with this style. Possible candidates include two craftsmen from the family of the famous *ébéniste* (ebony worker) Pierre Gole: his son Corneille or his younger brother Adriaan. Both had worked in French court circles and fled to the Dutch Republic when King Louis XIV revoked religious freedom for Protestants in 1685.

But Glauburg lavishes the most attention on the cabinet's contents, marvelling at the precision of their execution. For instance, the dolls could be dressed and undressed, and the napkins were woven to scale. The textiles could even be washed, a process that took a full two weeks. An anonymous late eighteenth-century catalogue waxes just as lyrical about the lifelike quality of the objects. The wooden furniture is not glued or carved from single pieces of wood, but assembled with correct joinery. The wall hangings are even affixed to the walls with minuscule nails.

Such attention to detail was unique. For example, in a second seventeenth-century doll's house in the Rijksmuseum, belonging to Petronella Dunois, the napkins are cut from full-sized ones, resulting in patterns that are too large and interrupted. She also had many silver miniatures. There was a large market for these; a range of miniature silver household items were readily available, from spinning wheels to mousetraps [FIGS. 59, 61]. In Oortman's doll's house, such objects are executed in the same materials as their full-sized counterparts [FIGS. 60, 62]. This may seem simpler and cheaper at first glance, but

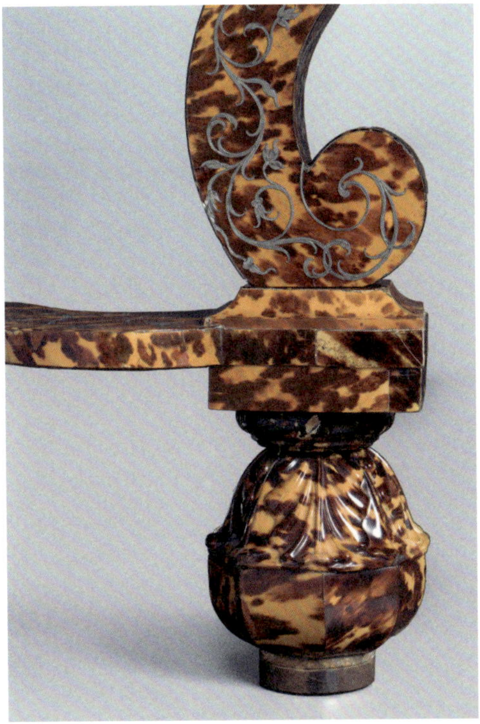

3
The cabinet has elegant scrolled legs. Even the feet are veneered with tortoiseshell pressed into foliate shapes in a mould

these miniatures were far more labour-intensive to create, and Oortman must have commissioned many pieces. The anonymous eighteenth-century catalogue sums it up: the cabinet is 'an outstanding WORK OF ART which in all probability has no equal anywhere in Europe or beyond' and offers an impression of 'a neat, orderly and well-organized household'.

Originally, that household buzzed with activity: the master of the house played a game of tric-trac (a form of backgammon) in the reception room, while in the entrance hall a maid led one of the children into the garden on leading strings. In the laundry attic, clothes were ironed, and in the best kitchen, a maid repaired a garment while keeping an eye on the children. Today, these dolls are missing (except for one baby), but we know of them not only from Glauburg's account but also thanks to a 'portrait' of the doll's house painted by the Amsterdam artist Jacob Appel around 1710 [FIG. 2]. Just as when he worked on his real portraits, Appel did not always have his model before him; he probably painted in his studio from sketches made on site. That accounts for some conspicuous discrepancies, for example, in the colours of the wall hangings. Even so, the picture remains a fantastic source of information. It depicts the cabinet in all its splendour, with not only its occupants but also its lost baldachin: a canopy adorned with plumes and curtains, which made the doll's house resemble a luxurious state bed. Each room may also have been fitted with a separate curtain that could be drawn aside. The combination of doors with curtains in front closed off the rooms in two different ways, lending the presentation of the doll's house a theatrical quality. For the curious visitor, the contents were revealed step by step: first the curtains were opened, then the doors – and finally the performance could begin.

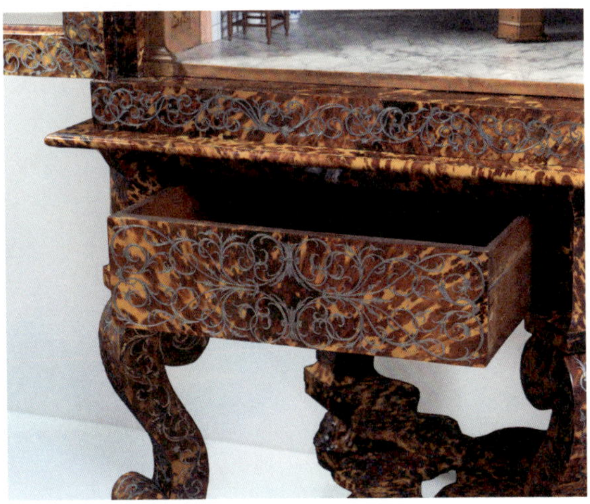

4
The cabinet has three removable drawers. The inside of each drawer is lined with cedar, which repels pests

PETRONELLA OORTMAN

The Uffenbach family viewed the doll's house in 1718, nearly two years after Petronella Oortman's death. She was buried on 27 November 1716 in Amsterdam's Nieuwe Lutherse Kerk. As detailed as her doll's house is, very little is known about its owner's life.

Her father, Hendrik Oortman, was born in Essen, Germany, and worked as a gunsmith. He was one of many migrants who settled in Amsterdam. In 1649, he became a *poorter* (citizen). This was a sign of prosperity, as those who were not born citizens had to pay for the status. Two years later, he married Aeltje Jans Steur and the couple moved to the Singel, an even clearer indication that business was thriving. They had ten children; Petronella (also known as Pieternella) was their second, born in 1656. In 1675, at the age of nineteen, she married the silk merchant Carel Witte – another very prosperous German immigrant, and a Lutheran, like her father. They settled on the Herengracht, opposite Bergstraat. The next few years were difficult. Petronella's father passed away in 1680, followed by her daughter Hendrika – not yet two years old – in 1684 and, lastly, her husband in 1685.

Just seven months later, in 1686, Petronella Oortman was remarried, to Johannes Brandt from the German island of Fehmarn in the Baltic Sea. He, too, was a silk merchant, and Oortman joined his household in Warmoesstraat, a very prestigious street at the time, home to the city's finest fabric shops. Brandt's house, which included his shop, was named 'In de stad Frankfurt' (In the city of Frankfurt) and located near the Oude Kerk. The couple had four children: Hendrina (born in 1691), Jan (1694), Jacob (1695) and Olivier (1697), all of whom were baptized at home. The family were very active in the Evangelical Lutheran church, to which most German and Scandinavian migrants belonged, where sermons were often delivered in German. Brandt held a position in the church administration. Oortman's death left him with the three oldest children, by then adults. The youngest had probably already passed away. In his old age, the widower moved in with his son Jan on the Keizersgracht. Jan inherited the doll's house, as shown by his estate inventory from 1743, which mentions 'a doll's cabinet inlaid with tortoiseshell and pewter'.

This 'doll's cabinet' perhaps brings us closest to Petronella Oortman herself. It cannot have been long after her marriage to Johannes Brandt that she commissioned the cabinet and began to collect (and in many cases specially commission) the miniatures. Although her creation is an idealized representation and certainly not a direct reflection of her personal life or a miniature version of her own house, it does offer insight into the exemplary seventeenth-century household from the perspective of a female collector. This is exceedingly rare in a period when only men wrote on the subject. In the nine rooms visible at first sight, plus a few artfully concealed spaces, she grants us a glimpse into the workings of a prosperous Amsterdam household around 1700.

5
The furniture maker cut the graceful monogram BO (for Brandt–Oortman) out of pewter, finely engraved it and inlaid it in the tortoiseshell with its flamelike pattern

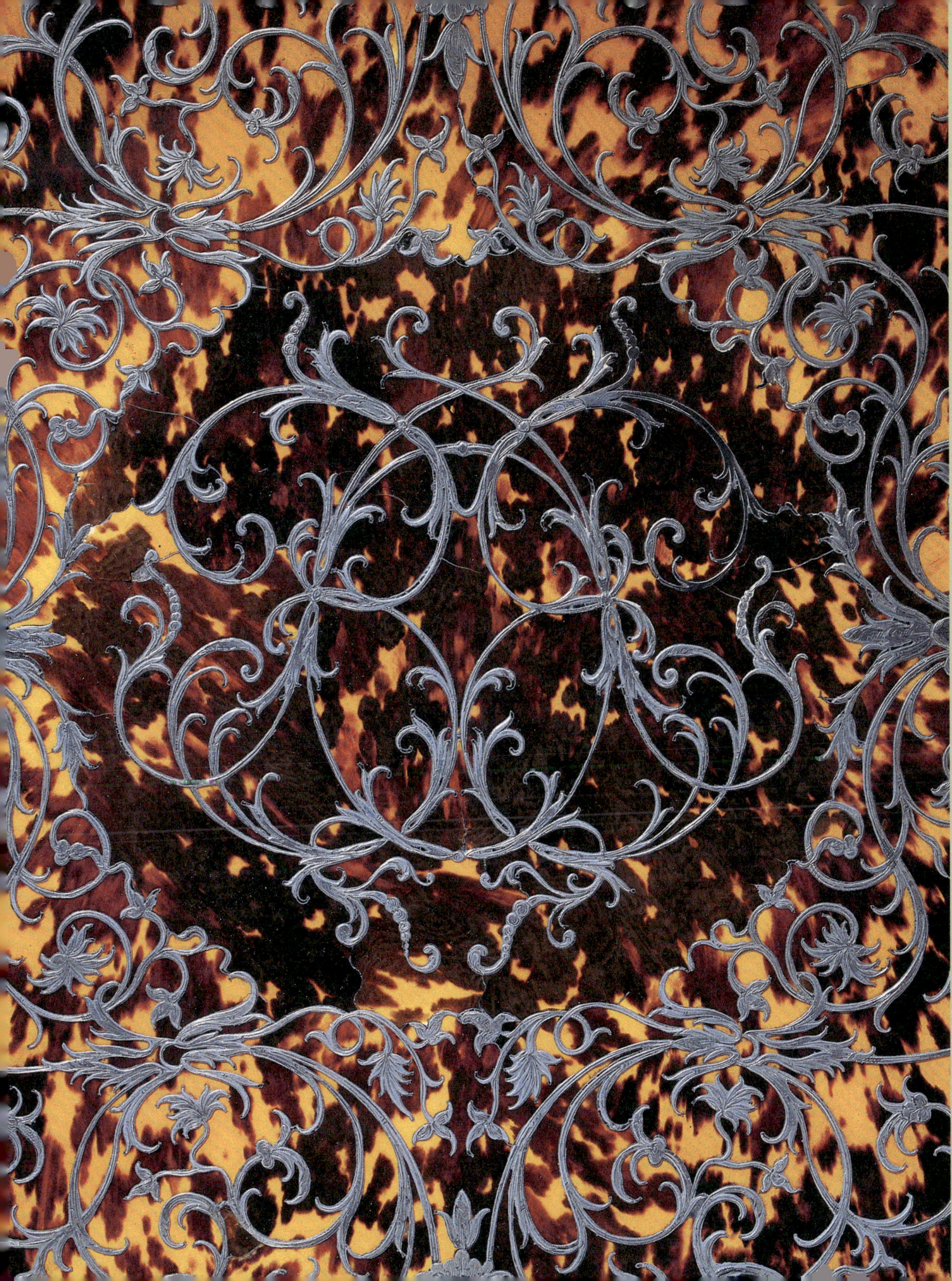

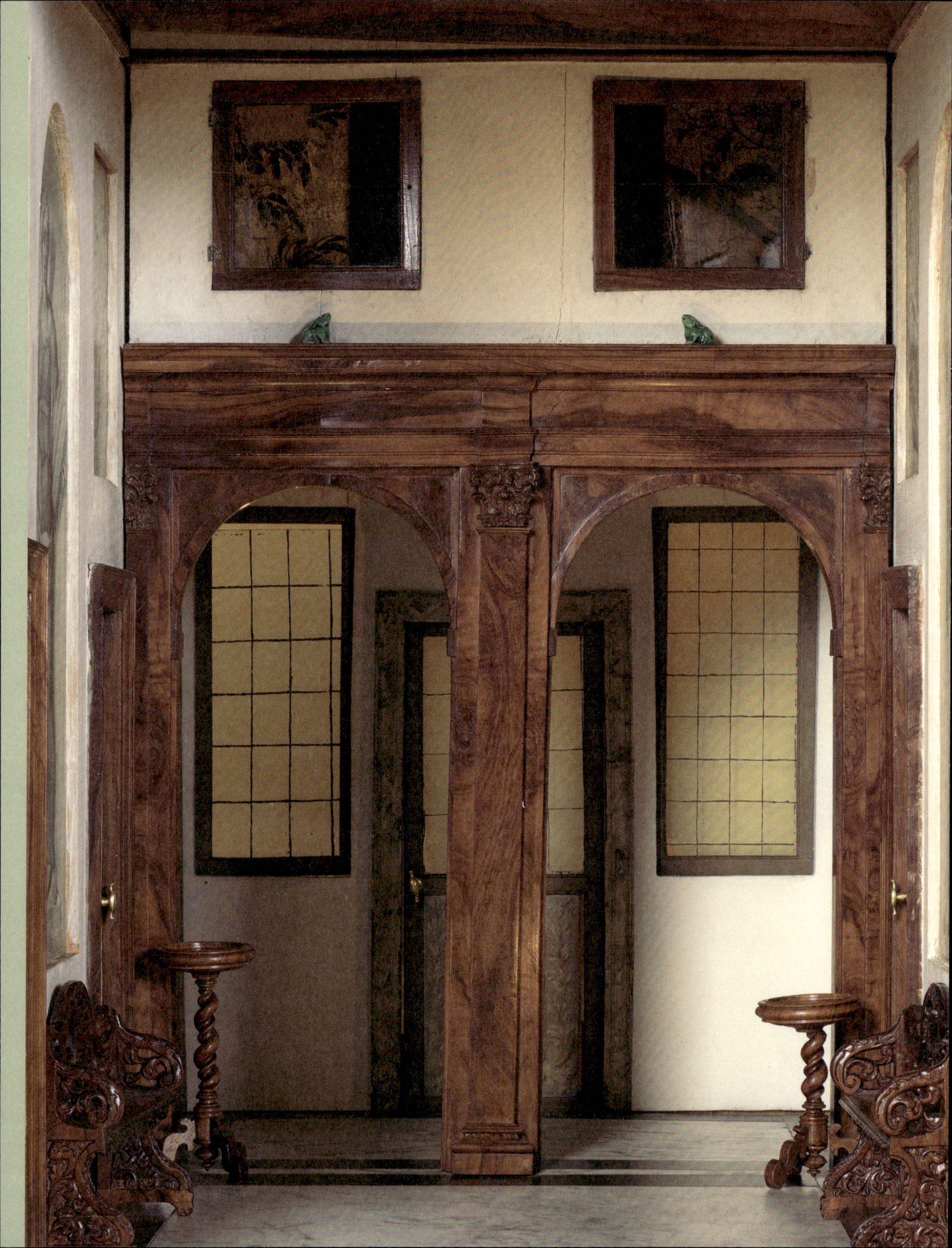

ENTRANCE HALL

Hendrina Brandt commenced her tour of the doll's house in the attic, rather than – as one might expect – in the entrance hall (*voorhuis*), where a visitor would enter a genuine seventeenth-century home. She must have wished to save the best for last. The entrance hall is full of surprises and encapsulates the essence of the entire house. Reason enough for us to begin there.

The entrance hall is sparsely yet elegantly furnished, forming a dignified introduction to the home [P. 14]. The floor is made of marble and the symmetrically placed doors are crafted from olive wood, as are the two carved hall benches and the two guéridons (a type of small, high table that was intended for a candlestick). Oortman seems to subtly emphasize that this is not her own home, but an idealized miniature version. The backrests of the hall benches are carved with a family crest of a fish with three crowned lozenges below it, which – unlike the recurring mirror monogram 'BO' – cannot be linked to Brandt or Oortman [FIG. 6]. It probably refers to the real Poppius family, whose crest comprised three red water-lily leaves under a golden sturgeon. That family name, a Latinized form of the Dutch 'Poppe', serves as a playful allusion to a *poppenhuis*, a doll's house.

The walls are decorated with monochrome paintings known as grisailles attributed to the Amsterdam painter Jan Cornelisz Hoogsaat. They depict personifications of well-known virtues: on the left wall Sapientia Divina (Divine Wisdom), and on the right wall Prudentia (Prudence [FIG. 8]), both flanked by allegorical scenes relating to Educatio (Education). Finally, the ceiling is radiant with the light of Aurora, the personification of dawn, holding a burning torch with the rising sun behind her [FIG. 7].

We know from Appel's painting that there was also originally a maid in this room with a child on leading strings, two broad straps of fabric attached to the shoulders of a child's clothing [P. 17]. They restrained young children from straying too far. This scene is the key to the entire room, and perhaps to the entire house. The rising sun represents young life, and the grisailles illustrate how to guide the young down the right path, as the maid literally does. All of the Republic's seventeenth-century writers on moral matters, from the bestselling author Jacob Cats to straight-laced clergymen like Petrus Wittewrongel, emphasized that the household was the

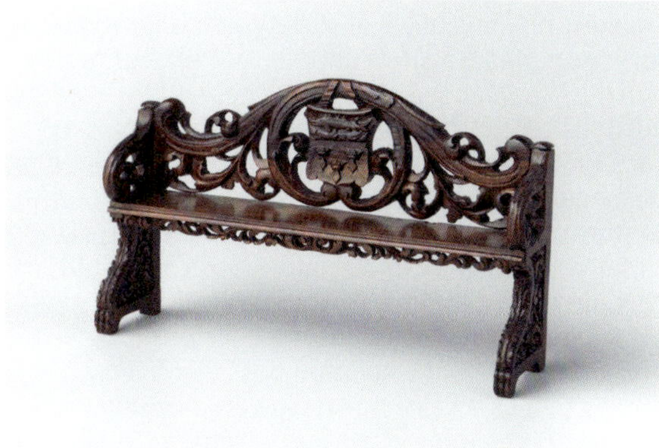

6
In the entrance hall, two identical benches face each other, in conformity with the strictly symmetrical, harmonious arrangement of the space

7
The ceiling, probably painted by Johannes Voorhout (I), depicts Aurora lighting the dawn with her torch

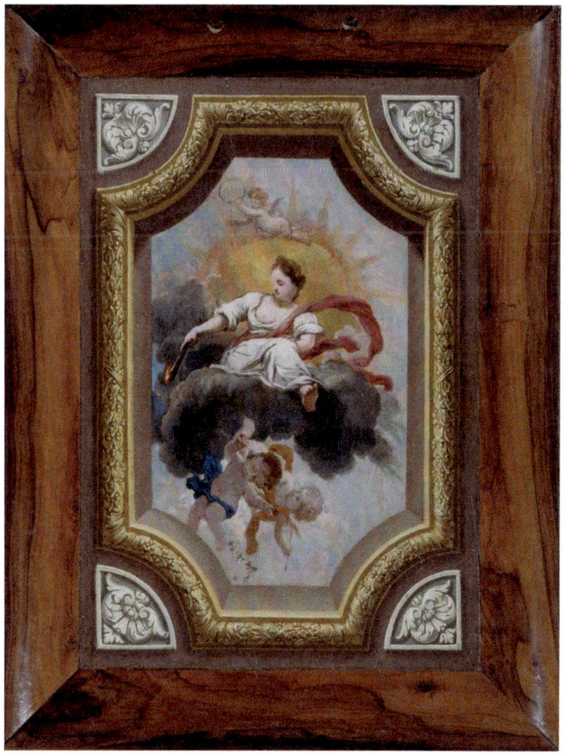

smallest building block of society – small, yet crucial, for it was a housewife's duty to care for her family and staff, and above all, to raise her children to be virtuous citizens, prepared to fulfil their roles in society. Accordingly, the doll's house is not merely a beautiful, opulent home. It is, as the late eighteenth-century catalogue states, an embodiment of 'Holland's cleanly and respectable Economy or Household'. This ideal household was not merely clean in the literal sense but also of unsullied virtue.

From the entrance hall, you pass through two arches to a small corridor. Its lowered ceiling, decorated with a painting of the god of commerce, Mercury, hints at the space above: the *comptoir* or office. Initially concealed from view, this workspace was revealed when the partition wall with the arches was slid upwards, appearing on a mezzanine level. Two internal windows overlooking the entrance hall provide additional light. In real houses, the *comptoir* was often suspended from the rafters near the entrance, so that business visitors would not have to pass through the entire house. Today, Oortman's *comptoir* is almost completely empty, save for some paperwork on the wall, but originally it was where the bookkeeper and his assistant kept track of the accounts, as can still be seen in other dolls' houses, such as Petronella de la Court's [FIG. 9].

In Oortman's day, the same corridor provided access to the garden. This was a separate structure, now lost, attached to the back of the doll's house. The terraces boasted geometrically designed borders, potted plants and garden sculptures. A mechanism made figures walk about there; these were somewhat smaller than the dolls in the house, in order to suggest depth. The garden even boasted a working fountain; in fact, its waters may well have been detrimental to the preservation of this spectacular feature. In Petronella de la Court's doll's house, the garden was treated as a discrete 'room'. This provides an impression of how Oortman's miniature garden may once have looked [FIG. 10].

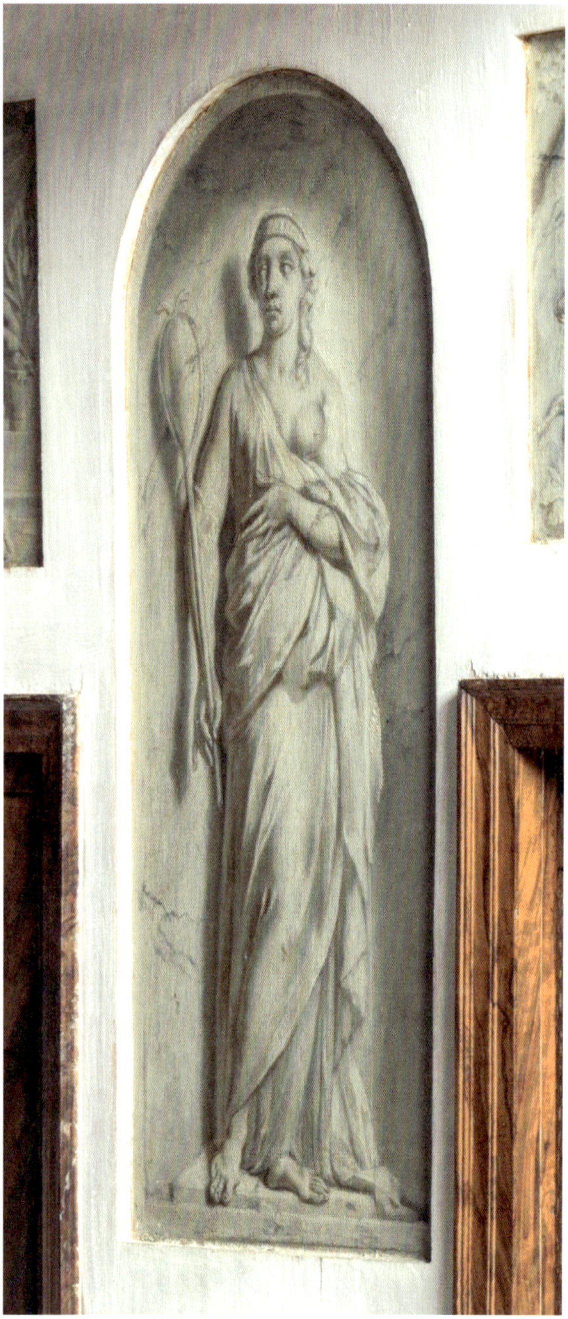

8
In this grisaille, Prudentia (Wisdom or Prudence) is identifiable by a mirror framed by winding snakes, in which she sees what is happening behind her. The snake represents the knowledge of good and evil

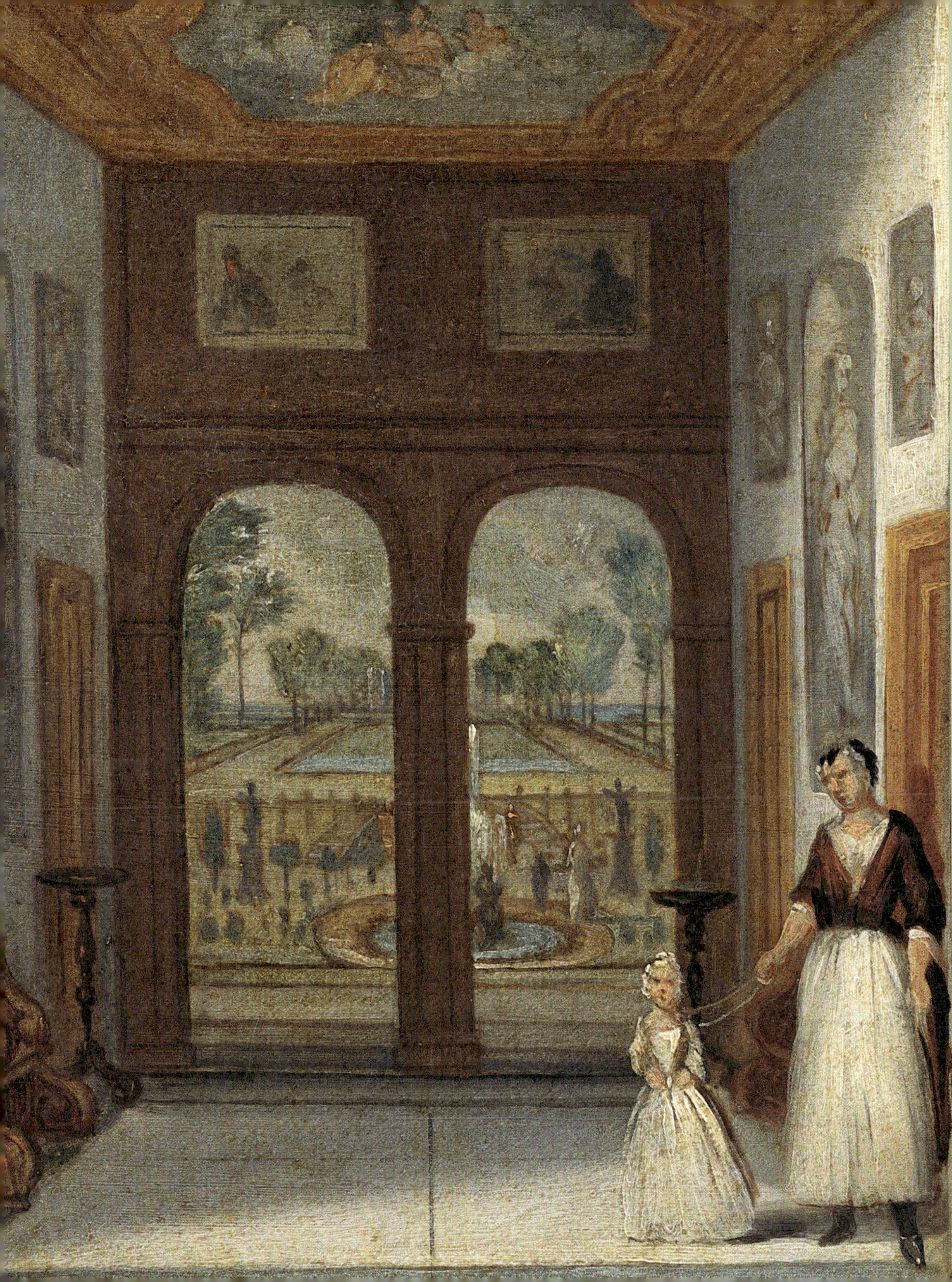

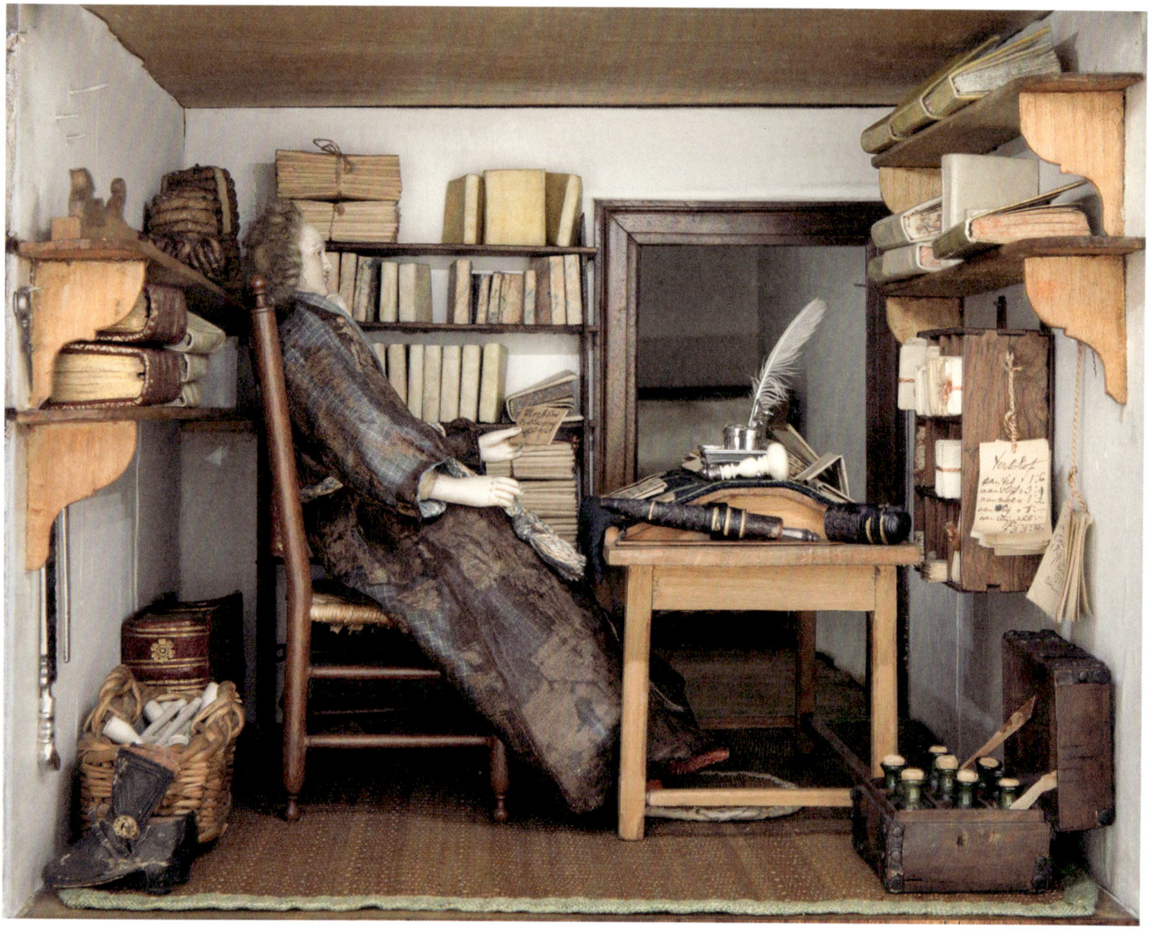

9
In the *comptoir* (office) of Petronella de la Court's doll's house, the master of the house sits comfortably at his writing desk in his dressing gown, surrounded by books and papers

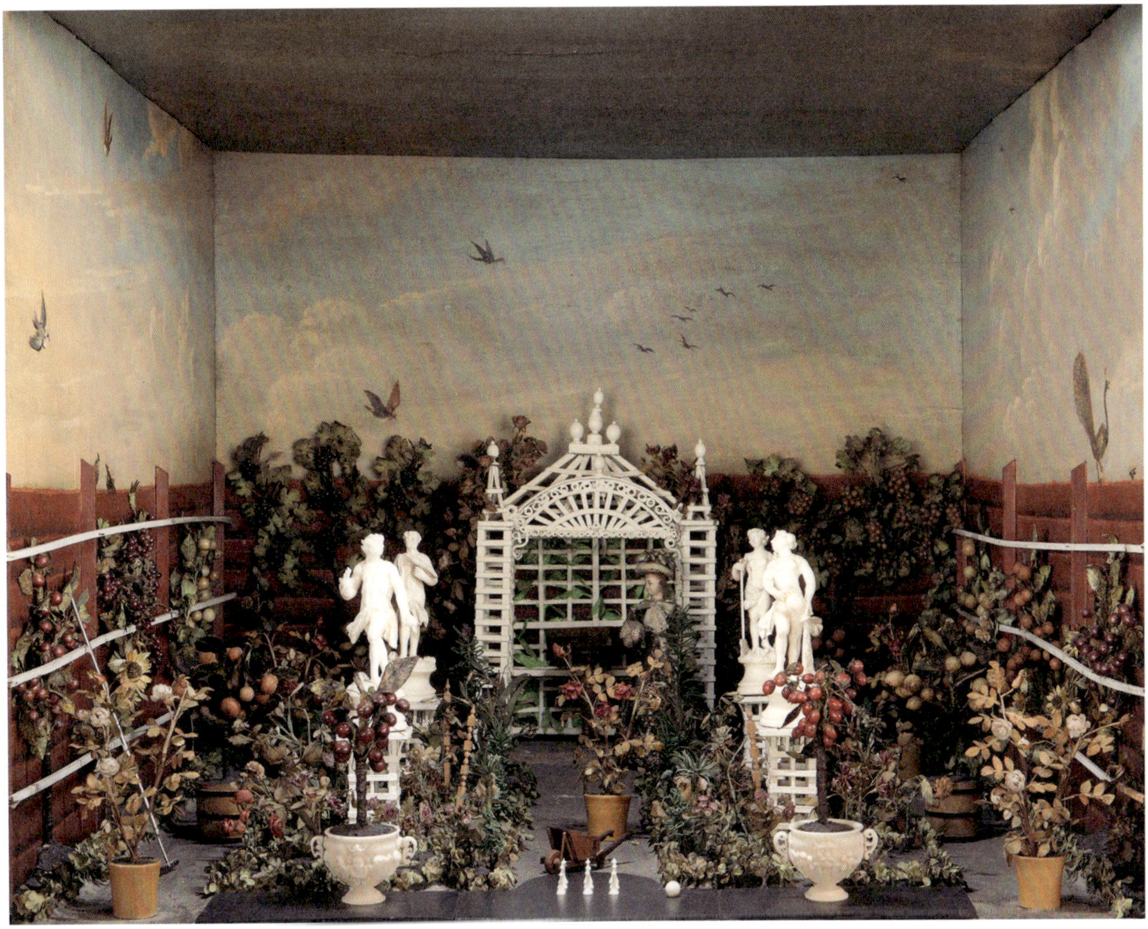

10
In the garden of Petronella de la Court's doll's house, a boy plays by a wooden gazebo amidst numerous plants and flowers made of wax, beads and paper

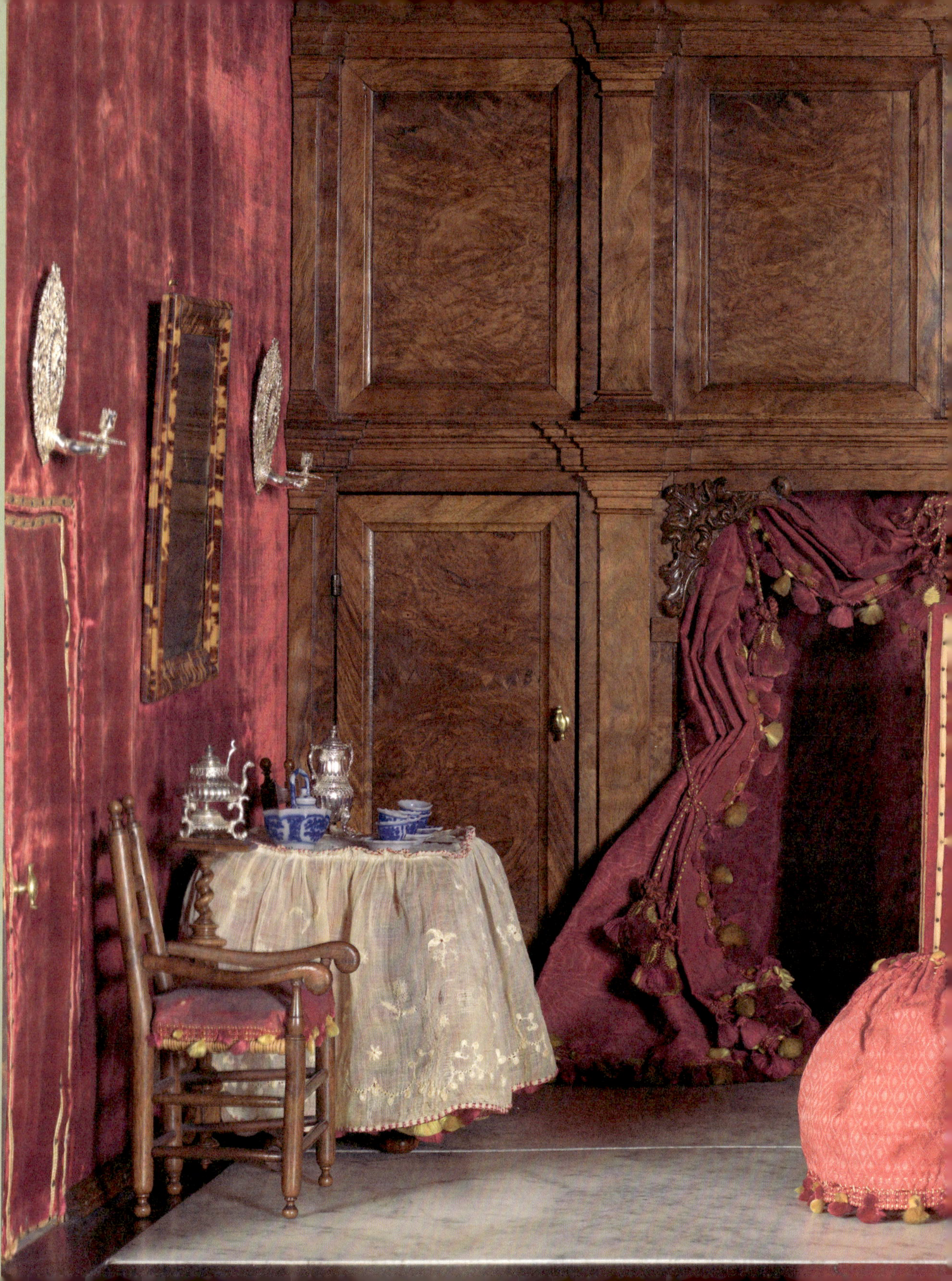

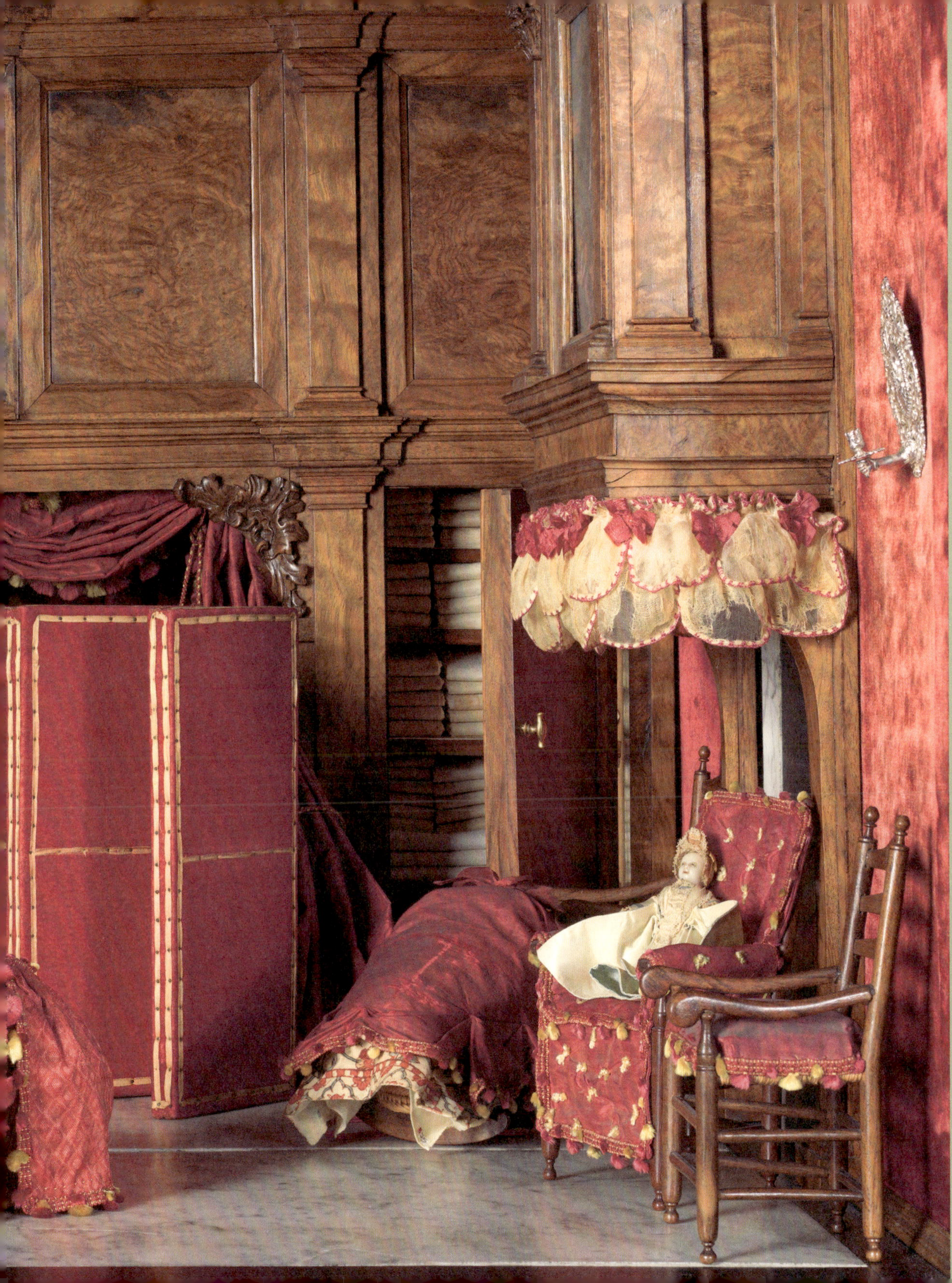

LYING-IN CHAMBER

Of the four doors in the entrance hall, only one can actually open and close. This door, located in the right foreground, leads to the lying-in chamber [PP. 20–21]. It forms an appropriate transition from the decorative paintings in the entrance hall, expressing an ideal vision of a child's upbringing, to childbirth and the daily practice of childrearing.

The Republic's affluent burghers had the custom of setting up a temporary lying-in chamber in one of the house's most distinguished rooms. A new mother would stay there for approximately six to eight weeks after giving birth to recuperate and receive guests. Such rooms are never found in the inventories of real houses, because after the confinement period they would return to their original use as reception areas. In the doll's house, however, the decoration is fully tailored to the room's purpose. The chimney piece by Johannes Voorhout (I) depicts Pharaoh's daughter finding Moses in the bulrush basket [FIG. 16]. The adult Moses is depicted on the ceiling, with the stone tablets bearing the Ten Commandments. The message is clear: these are the principles by which children must be raised if they are to become morally upright adult members of society.

The mortality rates for both mothers and infants were alarmingly high; before childrearing could truly begin, they had to safely navigate the first, risky weeks and months. The lying-in chamber was furnished with this in mind. The hearth provided light and warmth, while the folding screen, bed curtains and cradle cover protected the mother and child from draughts. The baby, now ensconced in the comfortable lying-in seat, is the only remaining inhabitant of the doll's house [FIG. 11]. This particular doll probably survived because it was safely nestled in the cradle under the cover [FIG. 14].

The lying-in chamber was not only functional; above all, it was meant to impress visitors. The rear wall has walnut panelling with pilasters and a central alcove holding a canopy bed. In the privileged classes, it was not unusual to furnish a stylish room where guests were received with a state bed, and to sleep there. This practice had been imported from France to the Dutch stadholder's court around 1650 and made its way into burghers' interiors in the following decades – with one difference: Oortman positioned the bed not with the headboard against the wall, as was the custom at court, but with one side against the rear wall of the alcove. This was the usual practice

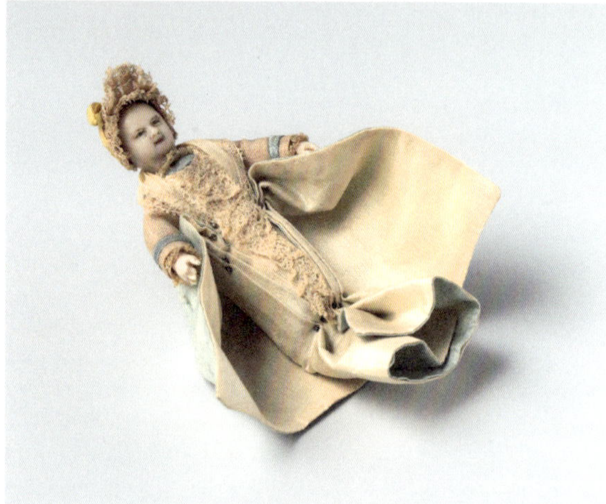

11
The baby is the only doll that has stood the test of time. The child is swaddled and warmly dressed in a jacket, a lace cap and an artfully pleated and pinned silk blanket

12
The *Japonse rok* ('Japanese robe') was a fashionable silk dressing gown that was warm and comfortable thanks to its padded lining

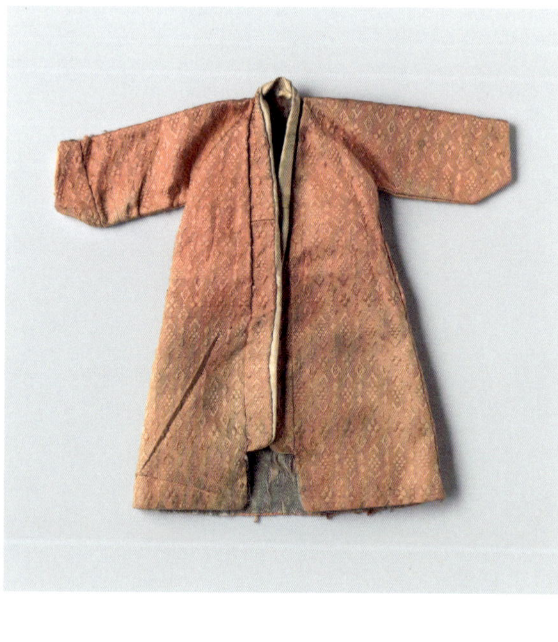

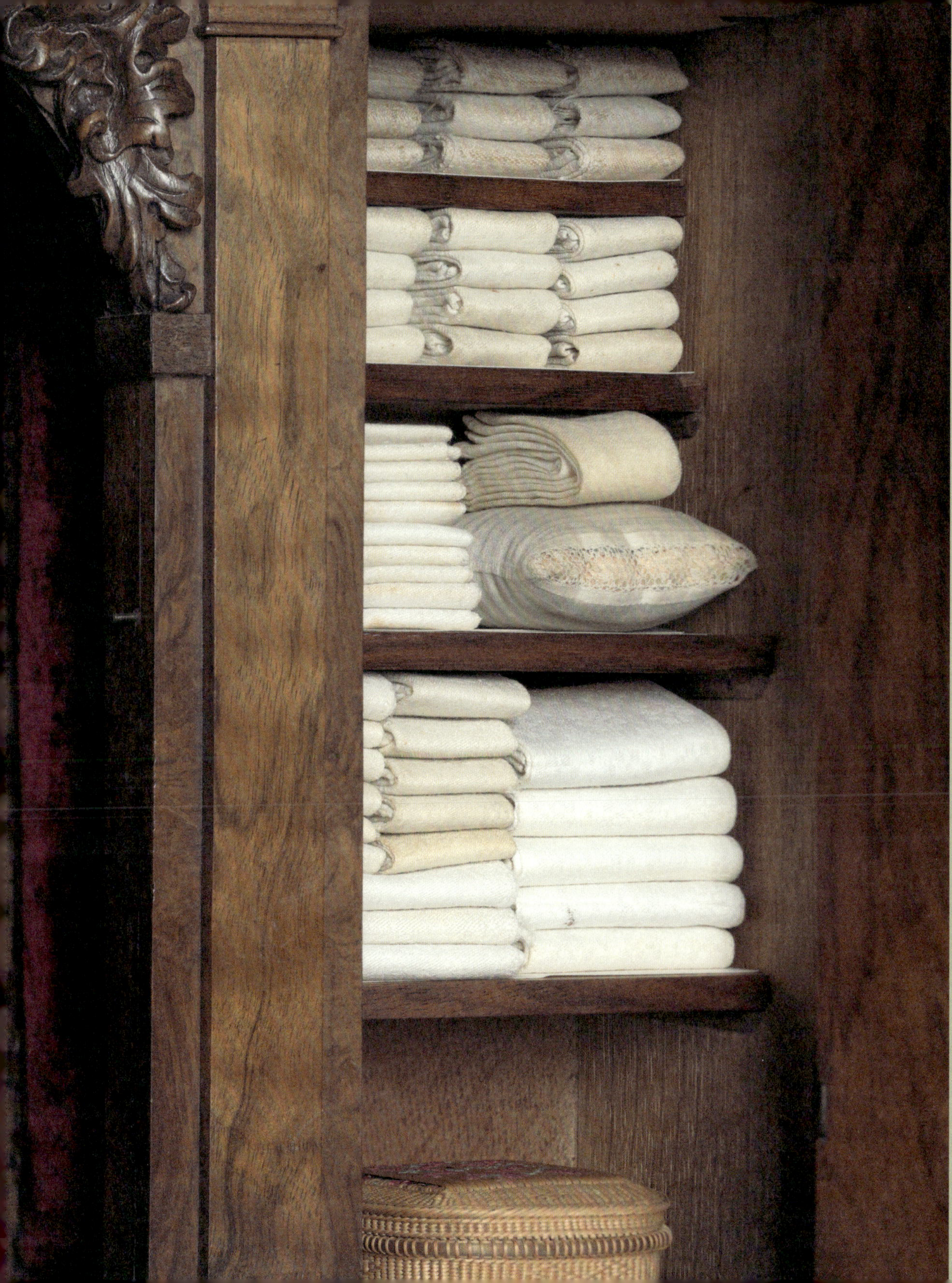

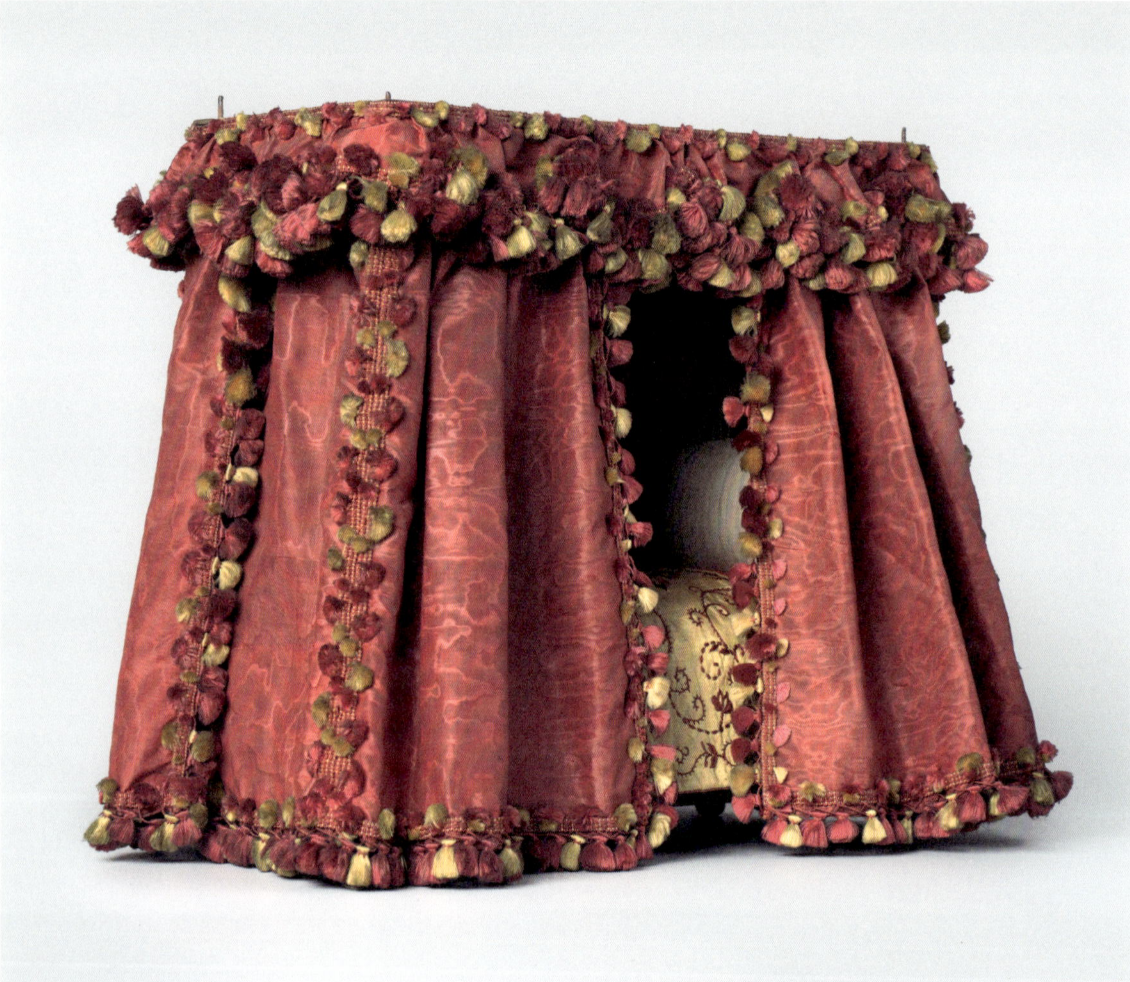

13
The walnut four-poster bed in the alcove exudes luxury and comfort. The heavy bedspread is beautifully embroidered, the curtains provide privacy and warmth, and the many tassels complete the ensemble

14, 15
The cradle is made up with a down mattress and pillow, a lace-trimmed sheet, a chintz blanket, and finally a red cradle cover. The fire basket has a matching red cover adorned with tassels

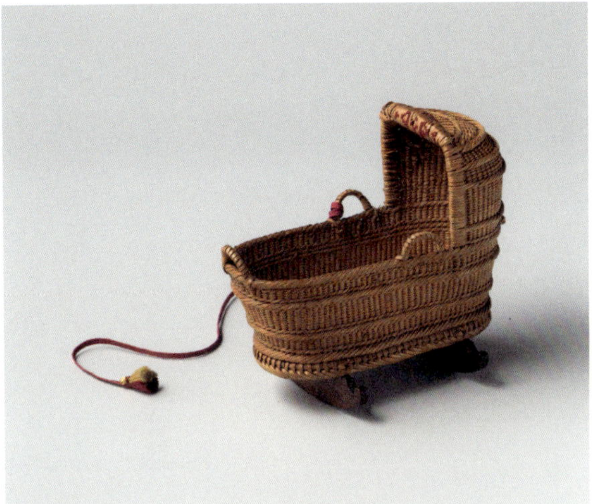
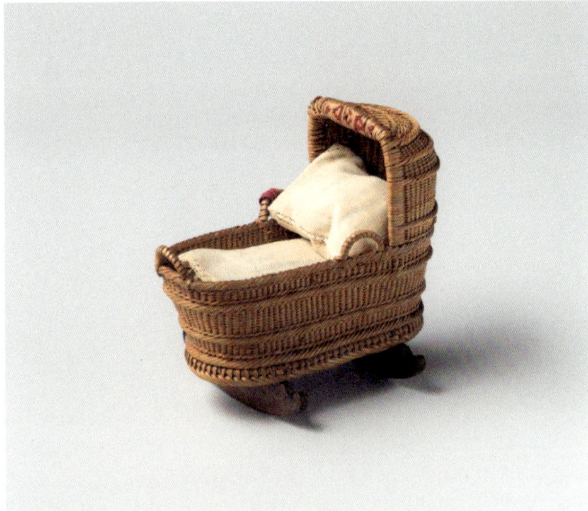
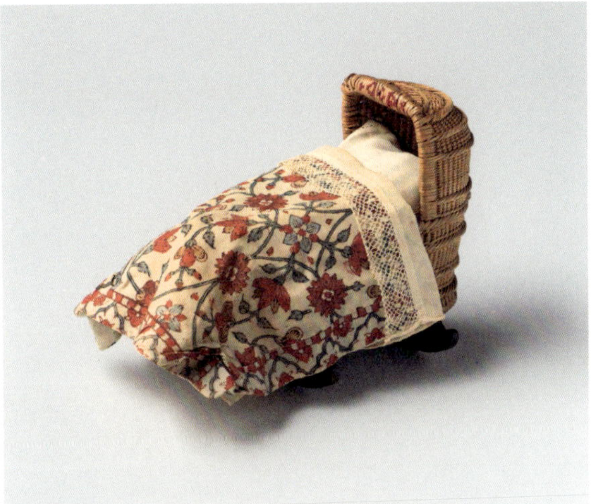
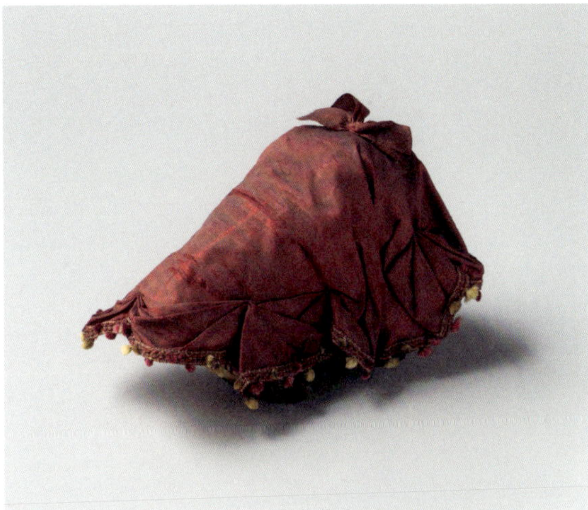
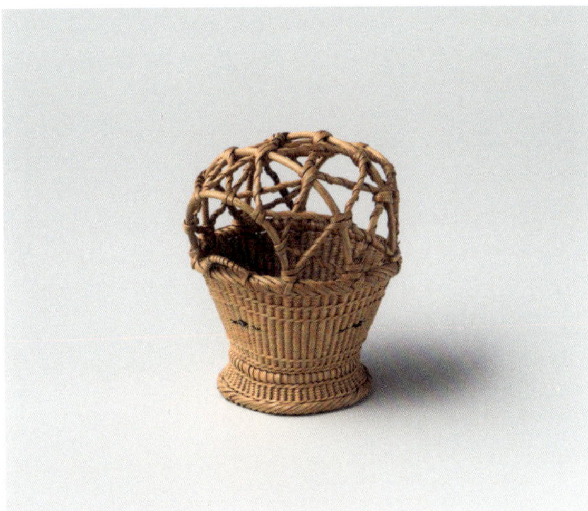
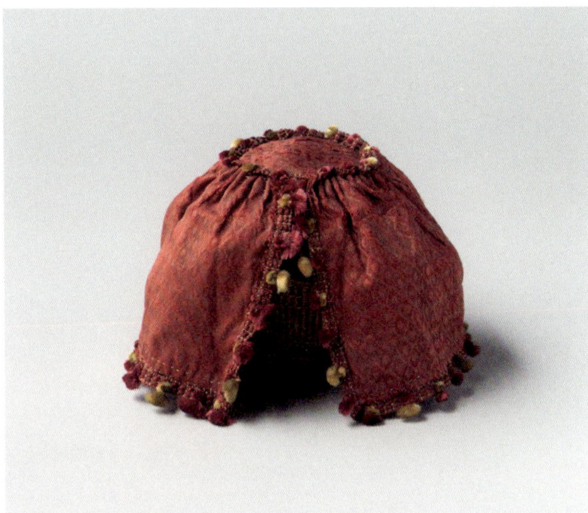

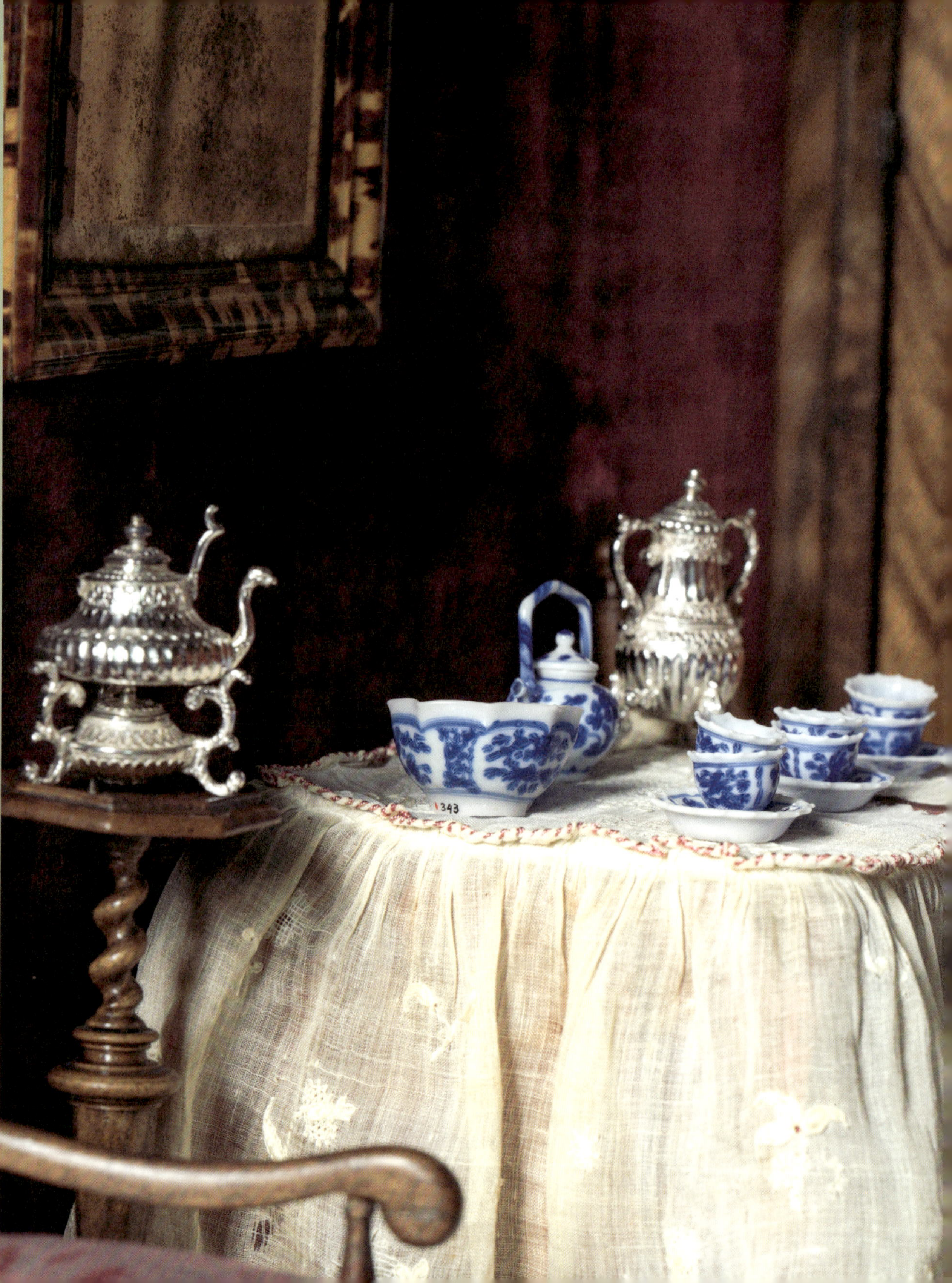

in burghers' real houses, as it meant the recess did not have to be as deep, and there was less lost space on either side of it. In the doll's house, that space is filled by two built-in cupboards: on the left a wardrobe for hanging comfortable dressing gowns, and on the right a well-stocked linen cupboard [FIG. 12 AND P. 23].

The upholstery of the canopy bed (partly concealed by the alcove curtains) is more valuable than the bed frame, which remains hidden beneath all the fabric, tassels and trimmings [FIG. 13]. The exterior is red with yellow accents, while the interior is the opposite: the ceiling of the canopy is yellow with red and yellow tassels, as are the inner curtains at the head of the bed. The bedspread is also yellow, embroidered in red with foliated scrolls and the initials 'BO', for Brandt–Oortman, which subtly hint at the continuation of the family line in the conjugal bed. The colour scheme perfectly complements the rest of the room, where deep red is a recurring theme in the wall upholstery, the chairs, the cradle cover, and even the bows on the drapery over the fireplace. This type of design, with fully coordinated colours, is referred to as *en suite* and was all the rage in the late seventeenth century.

The silver wall sconces illuminating the room are another elegant touch [FIG. 17]. Their decorations symbolically return to the theme of the cycle of life. Each plate represents one of the four seasons: a woman with a floral wreath for spring; ears of corn for summer; grapes for autumn; and an old man with a fur hat for winter. The seasons were associated with the stages of life, from infancy to old age.

Welcoming a new family member was a momentous occasion, and it could be done in style in the lying-in chamber. On a chest of drawers covered with a red silk cloth topped with a white linen tablecloth with white embroidery, the tea service is ready and waiting: a teapot, small cups (which were not yet made with handles in this period), and a bowl for rock candy [P. 26]. The silver urn was for coffee. A kettle on a chafing dish, for hot water to dilute the strong tea, has been placed on a guéridon beside the table.

All seventeenth- and eighteenth-century Dutch dolls' houses, unlike their German and most English counterparts, include richly furnished lying-in chambers such as this one, even if the owner herself had no children. The importance of the household and therefore of childbirth was a larger narrative that transcended individual lives. That story had to be told in every doll's house.

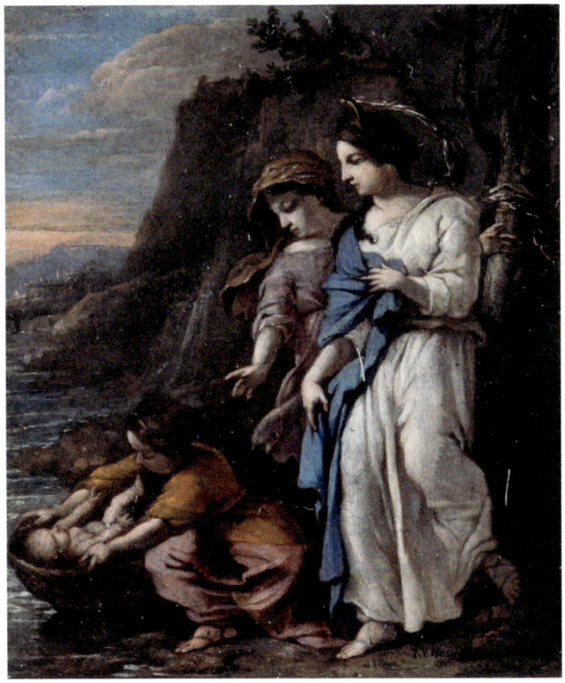

16
The painting above the mantelpiece depicts the biblical story of the prophet Moses being rescued as an infant by Pharaoh's daughter

17
This silver wall sconce is not only opulent but also functional: the wall plate, polished to a high lustre, optimally reflects the soft candlelight

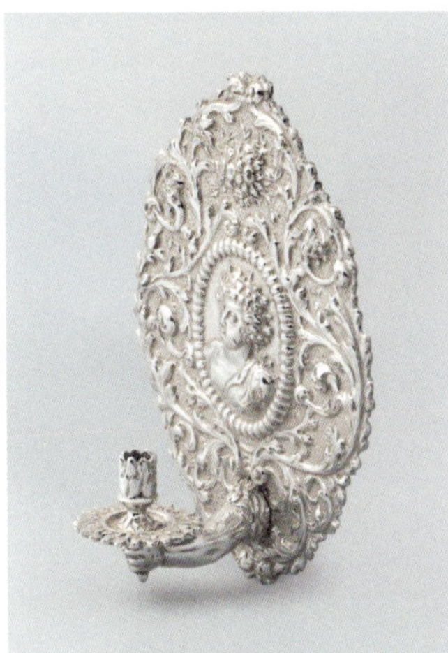

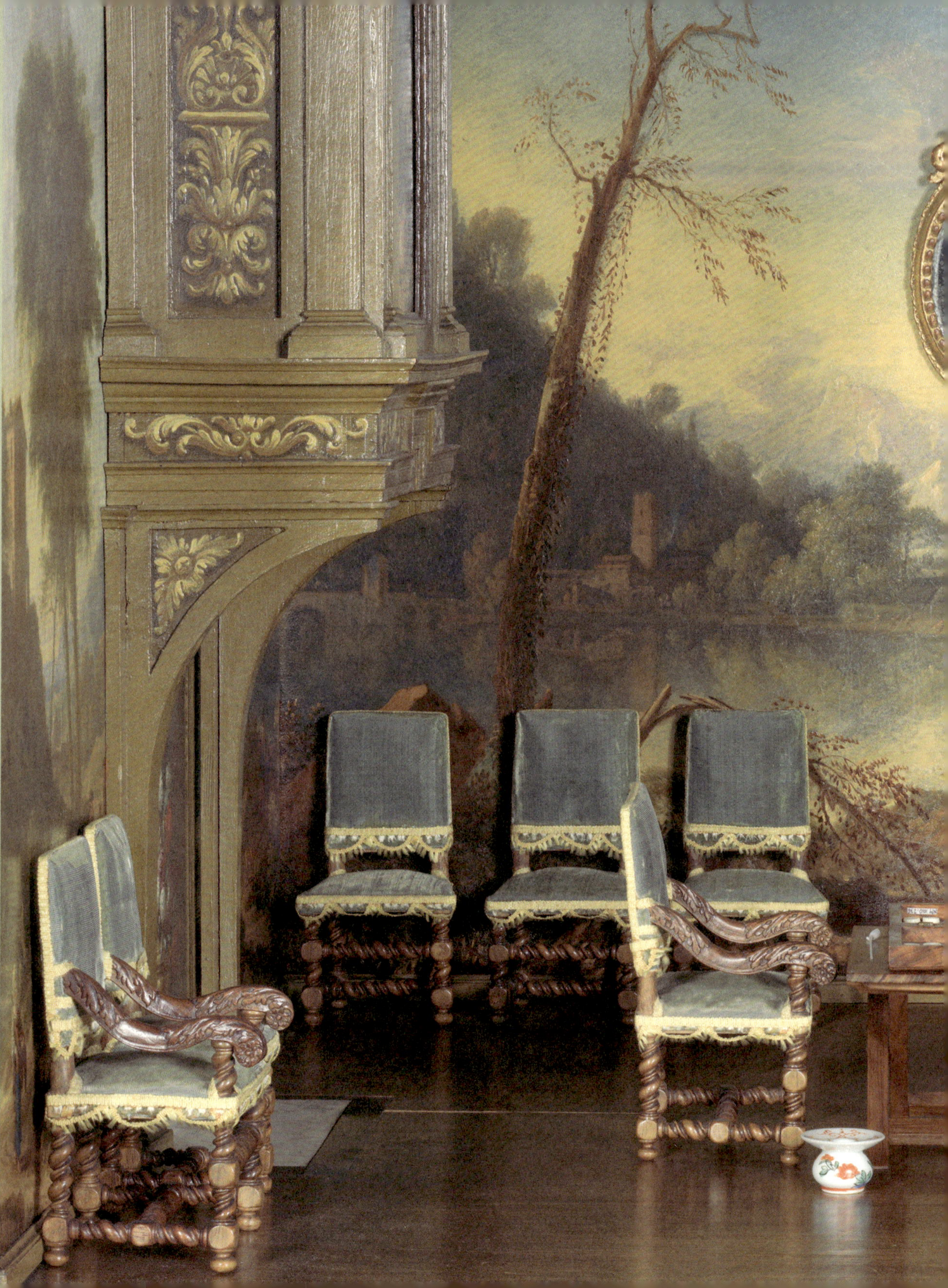

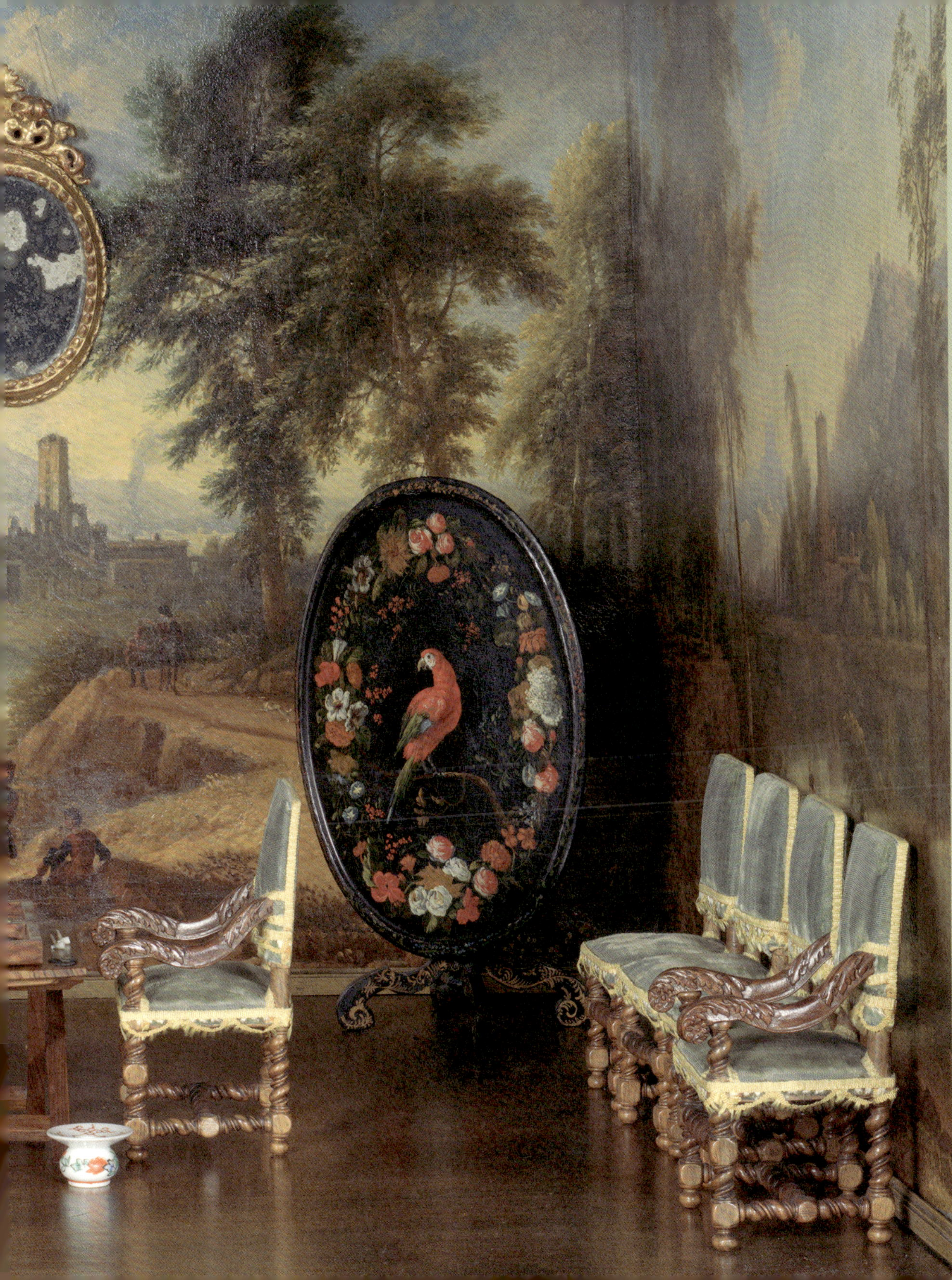

ZAAL

Oortman continues the storyline from the lying-in chamber in the *zaal*, a second elegant reception room located to the left of the entrance hall [PP. 28–29]. Glauburg notes that the new father was seated here; we can see him in Appel's painting [PP. 32–33], clad in a comfortable dressing gown. He has become unwell and sent for the doctor, who looks professional in his black garb. The remedy is a board game, which they are playing for money. The coins are genuine Russian silver kopeks, often used in dolls' houses because of their small size [FIG. 19]. The game board is multifunctional: on its outer sides are boards for chess and nine men's morris, and when opened, it can be used for playing tric-trac. Meanwhile, the gentlemen are smoking pipes, and they each have a Japanese porcelain spittoon at their feet [FIGS. 18, 20]. Such receptacles, a relative novelty in the late seventeenth century, were intended for phlegm and tobacco juice, which would leave unsightly stains on a wooden floor; hence the wide neck that neatly caught every drop.

The physician piqued the interest of the visiting travellers, and when asked where he had obtained his doctorate, Hendrina replied, 'In Harderwijk'. There, she told them, this doctor, 'Pirchel' (probably the real Johan Daniel Bilger from Strasbourg, who spent time in the Netherlands), had cured a woman who was too poor to pay the bill. Instead she had modelled a wax figure of the doctor in gratitude. It is unclear how much of this story is true, but some sources do indicate that single Catholic women provided for themselves by making wax altar figures and dolls. In any case, Oortman had no need to go as far as Harderwijk for hers. Just down the street, in Warmoesstraat, Hendrikje Cool ran a shop selling Catholic devotional items, wax dolls with clothing and other doll-related goods until her death in 1697.

Wherever the doctor had been purchased, it was, of course, amusing that he was looking after the man of the house rather than the recovering mother. The new father's flagging spirits were revived not only by the doctor's playful prescription but also by the room's decor. The walls are covered from floor to ceiling with an Italianate landscape on canvas, and the ceiling painting of birds in a cloudy sky heightens the sense of being outdoors [FIG. 21]. Poems from the period describe such decoration as 'an eternal spring' or 'summer for the eye', making the room a pleasant place to while away the hours.

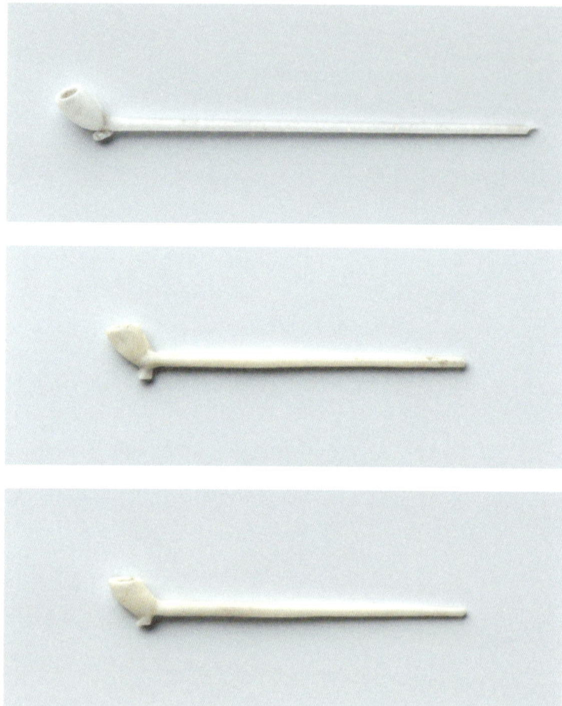

18
Pipes and other tobacco-related items are found in all dolls' houses. Smoking was popular – along with taking snuff and chewing tobacco – and was even considered healthy

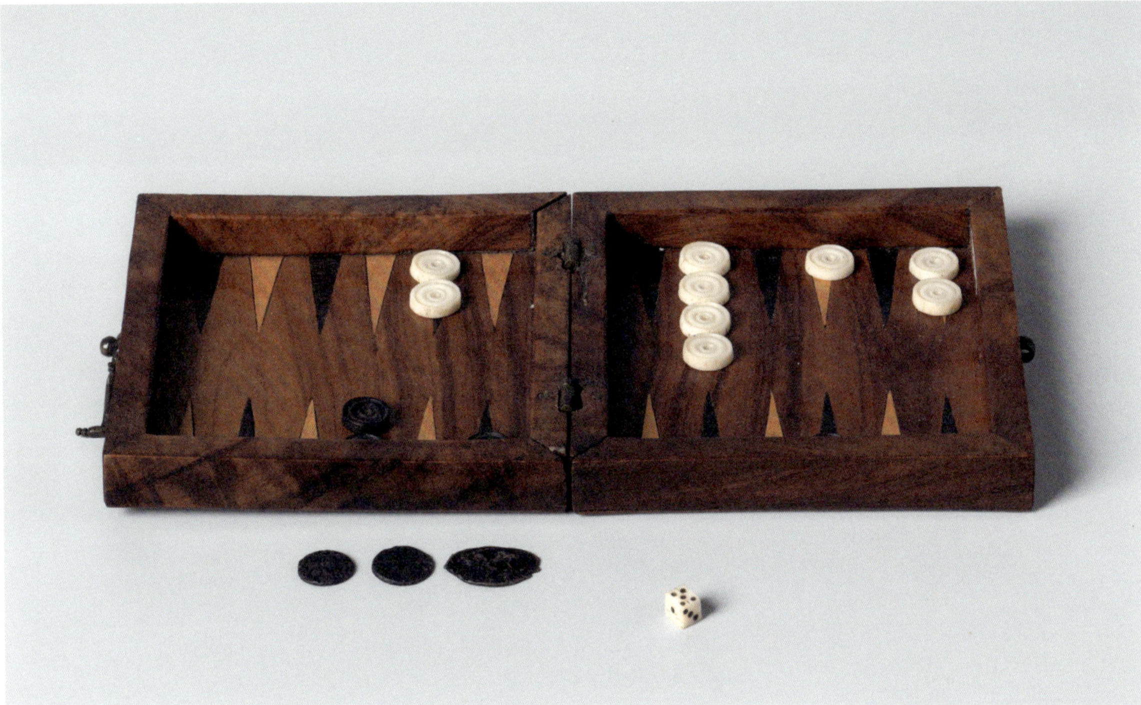

19
Tric-trac was a popular board game. The small, silver Russian coins (kopeks) were collected specifically for use as miniature gambling stakes in dolls' houses

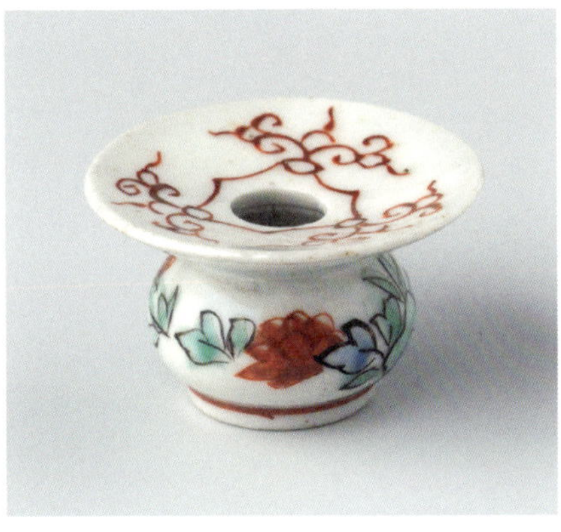

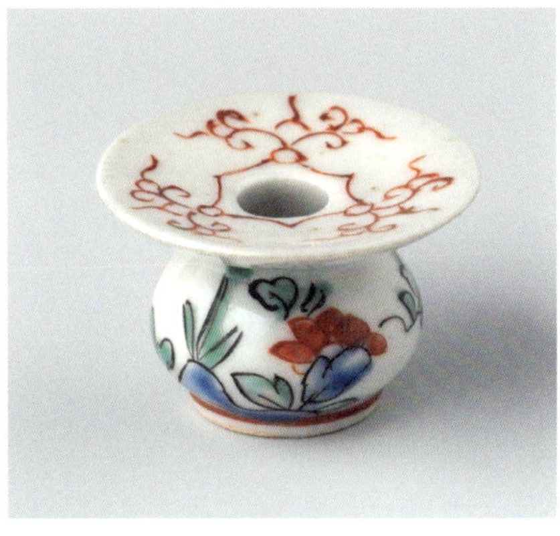

20
The two spittoons (for chewing tobacco) are made of precious Japanese porcelain in the Kakiemon style

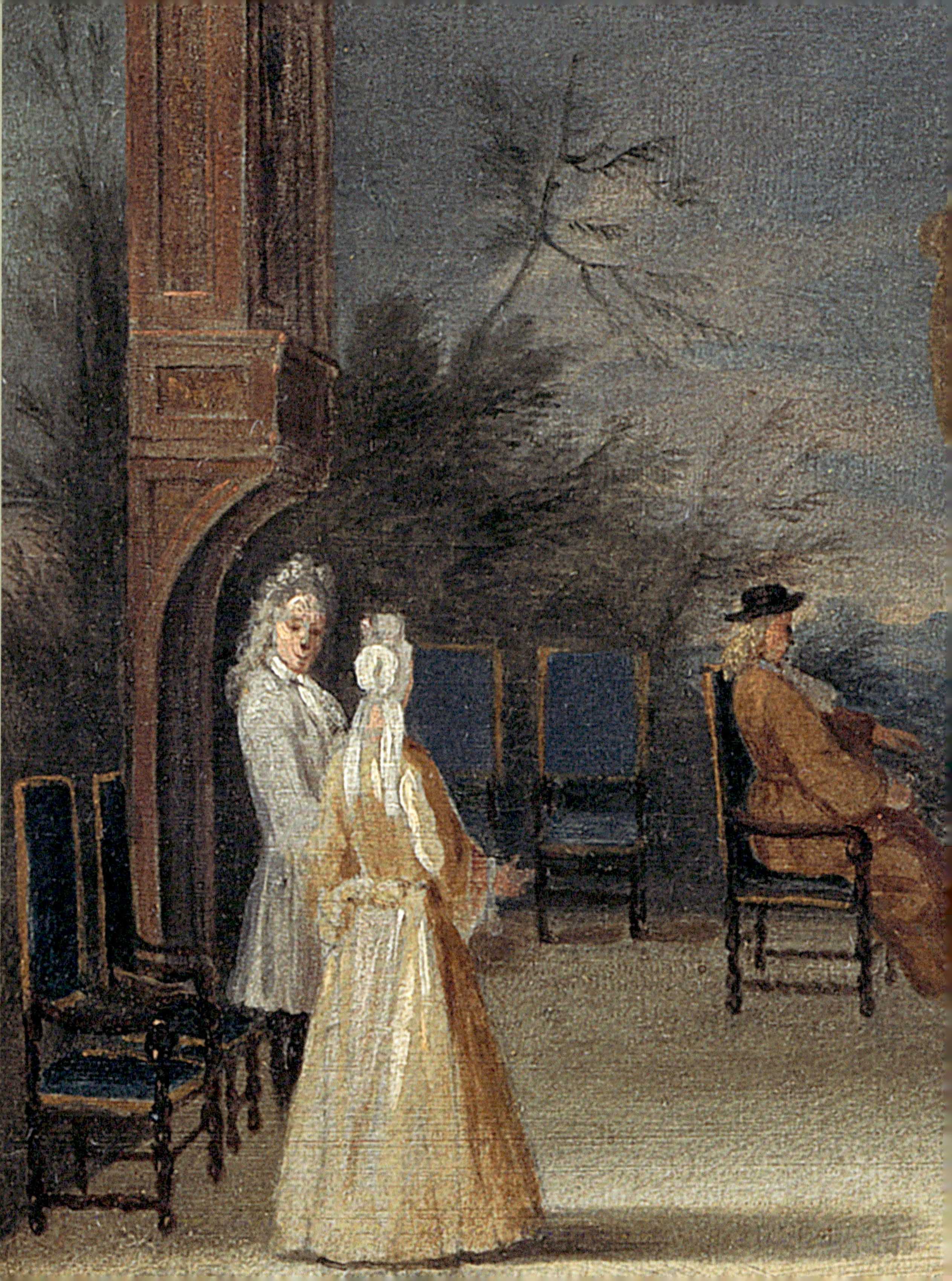

The large fireplace interrupts this illusionistic space [P. 2]. In the hearth is a flower still life on the same canvas used for the landscape. This represents a fireboard, a painted panel placed against the back of the hearth in summer, when the fire was not lit, to conceal the soot.

The relatively sparse furniture is superbly executed. The chairs are upholstered *en suite* in grey-green velvet and gold-yellow trim with ecru tassels, a colour scheme that harmonizes with the landscape. All the furniture was normally kept against the wall. Only what was needed was moved into place. For instance, the doctor and the new father sat at a trestle table that could be put away. For a tea party, the painted oval tea table in the corner could be unfolded and put in place [FIG. 22]. And for visitors who dropped in to admire the new baby, chairs could be quickly added.

In Appel's painting, a young Black servant welcomes the guests with his hat under his arm. His presence also contributed to the grandeur of the room. While most of the staff wore simple clothing and kept the household running behind the scenes, he stands in the most fashionable room in the house, wearing an expensive livery coat with gold braid, as well as a gleaming silver collar – a traditional symbol of slavery. Officially, slavery was prohibited in the Republic, but having a young man of colour as a servant elevated one's status. Oortman's 'ideal household' could not do without one.

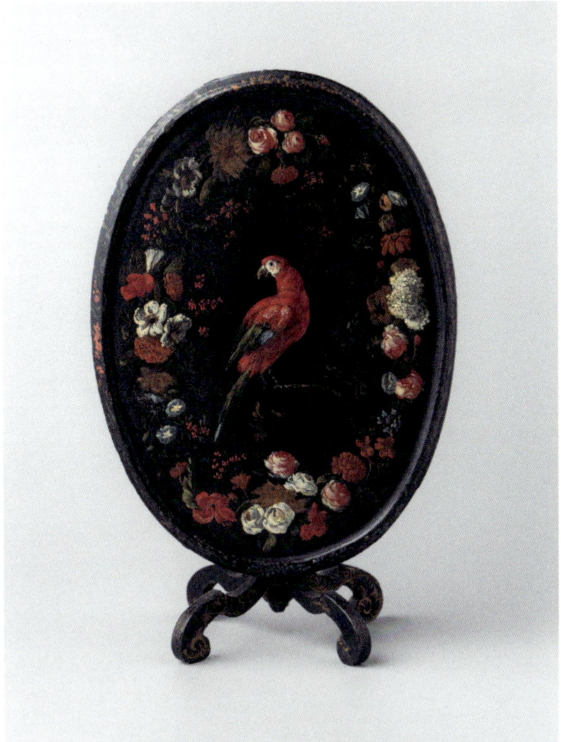

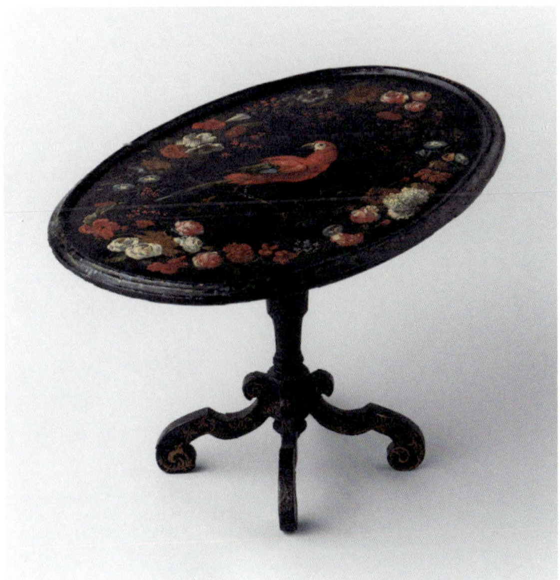

21
The illusionistic sky with clouds and birds, a ceiling painting by Nicolas Piemont, brings nature into the house

22
Folding tea tables became increasingly popular in affluent households in the late seventeenth century. When folded, the tabletop served as a decorative element in the room

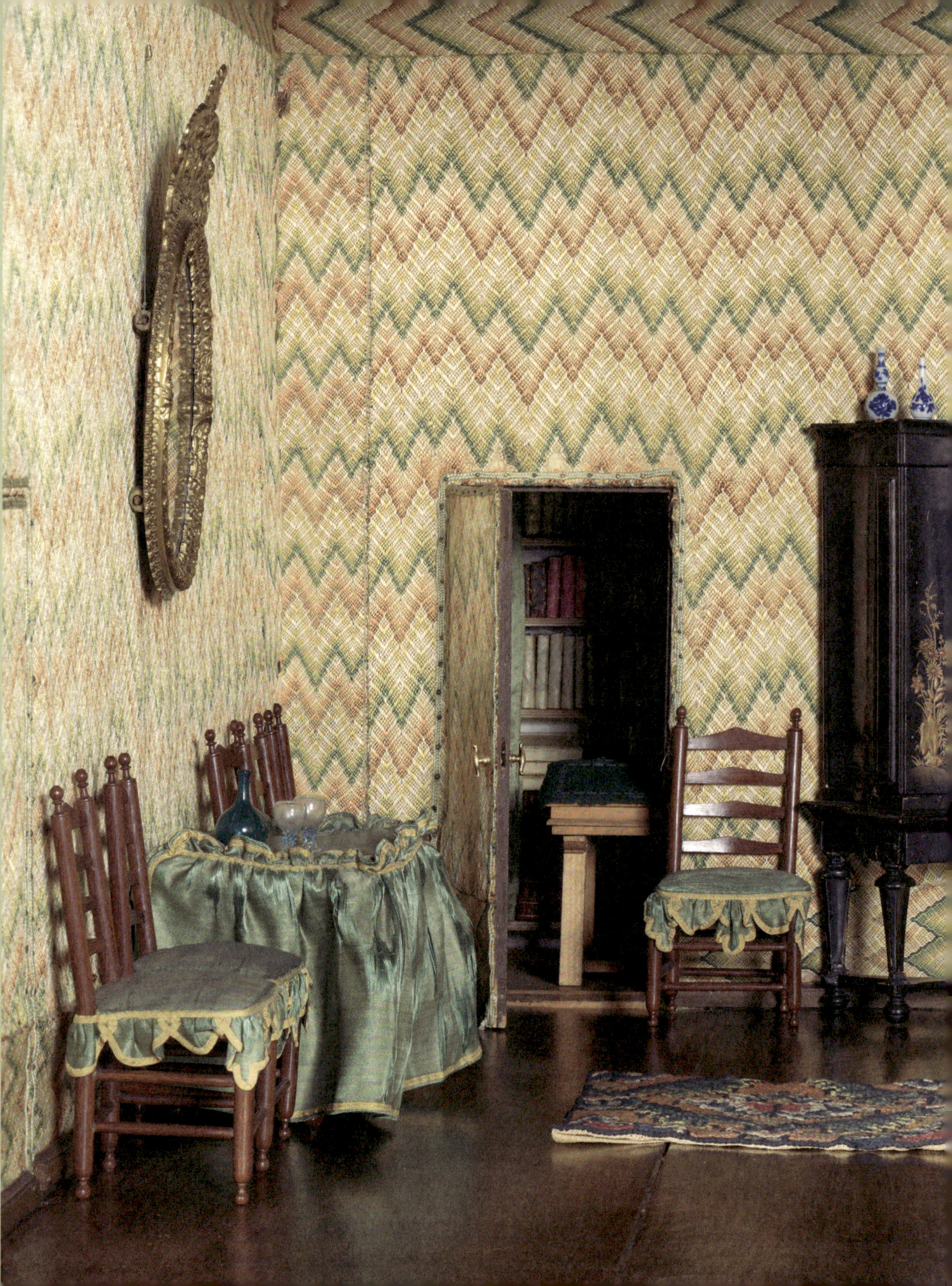

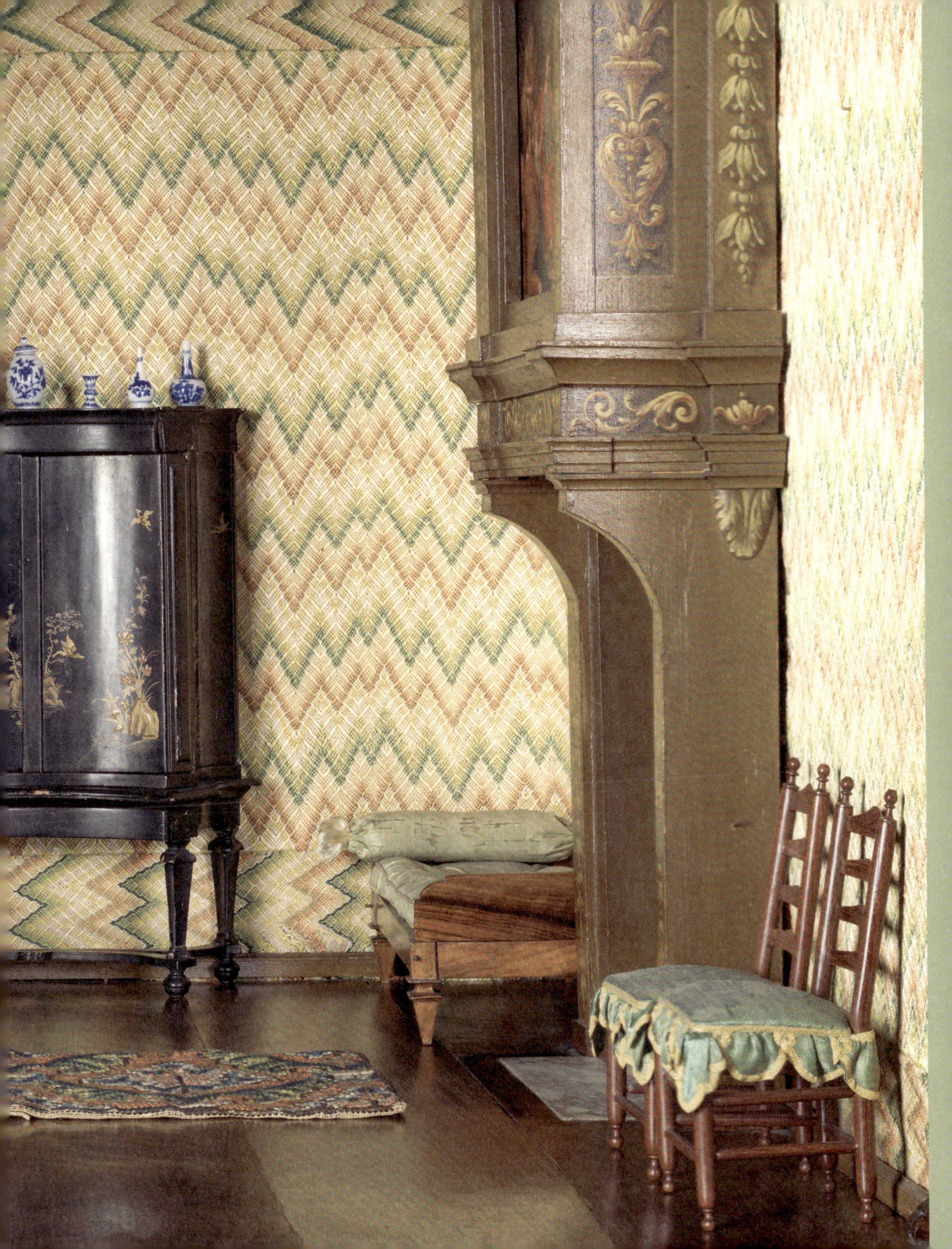

TAPESTRY ROOM AND LIBRARY

The lying-in chamber and the *zaal* were not the only reception areas. The tapestry room on the ground floor, named after the hanging with zigzag embroidery that covers the wall from floor to ceiling, was somewhat less formal yet still distinguished [PP. 36–37]. Tapestries with flame-stitch embroidery, as this design was called in the seventeenth century, were not as expensive as the velvet wall covering on the floor above; in real homes, the pattern was used in rooms with a slightly simpler decorative scheme. Glauburg describes this as a 'side room'. Nonetheless, the furnishings are quite elegant. Opposite the fireplace hangs a large mirror – one of the costliest items in a real seventeenth-century Dutch interior. This helped to illuminate the room by reflecting the fire in the hearth and other light sources. All the furniture is upholstered in green silk, including the daybed in the corner. The ladderback chairs have green silk cushions with yellow trim, and the table beneath the mirror has a matching cloth [FIG. 23]. Just as in the *zaal*, the chairs along the walls could be moved to the middle of the room when it was used for gatherings.

The most prominent piece of furniture in this room is a collector's cabinet with imitation lacquerwork [FIG. 24]. Asian and particularly Japanese lacquerware was prized for its unique sheen and hardness, produced by the sap of the native lacquer tree, but it was expensive and difficult to come by. This created a market for good imitations of lacquered furniture. Although this kind of work was certainly done in the Dutch Republic, this is one of just a few known examples. It is particularly well executed: against a deep black background, we see flowers and birds in the gold relief typical of Japanese lacquerware. The cabinet contains imitation red-lacquered drawers sprinkled with gold flakes.

The collector's cabinet holds a treasure befitting its Asian decoration: a collection of miniature shells, which Glauburg states was amassed by someone who spent forty years in Southeast Asia. Most do indeed originate from that region, although a few are from the coasts of Africa. Around 1700, these varieties were all relatively easy to obtain in Amsterdam. The majority of the shells are small by nature, but a few are juvenile specimens of larger shells, which are particularly rare and thus had even greater value to collectors than their fully grown counterparts. When guests viewed the doll's house, the

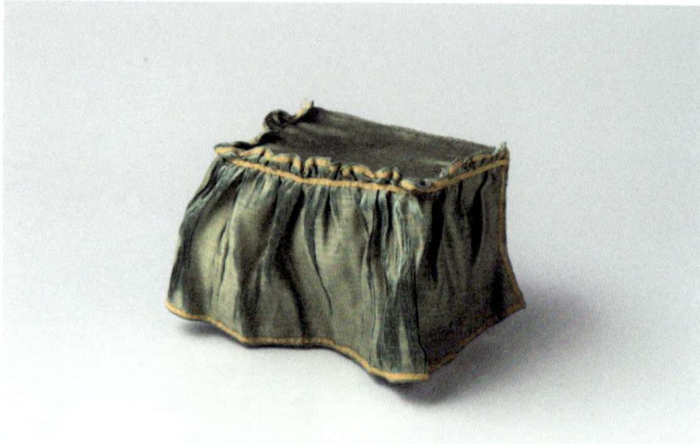

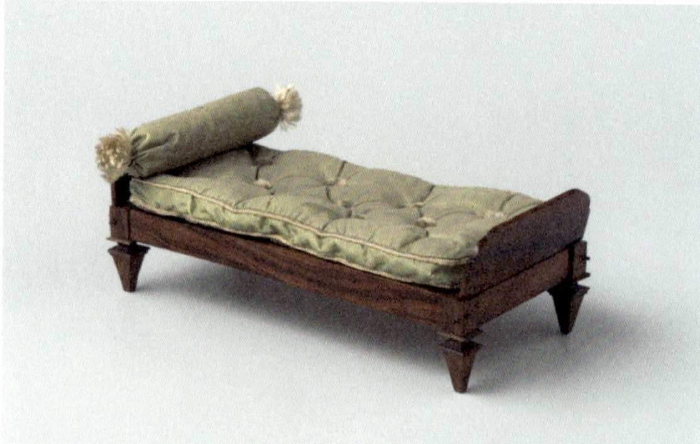

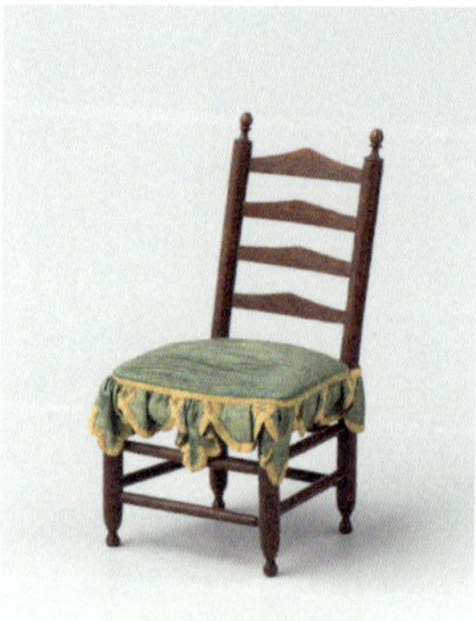

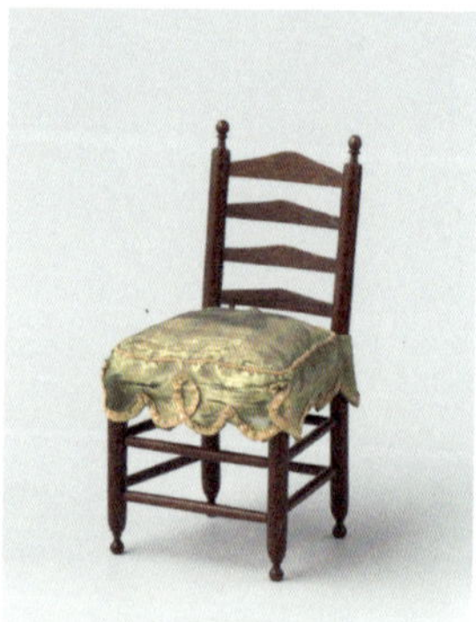

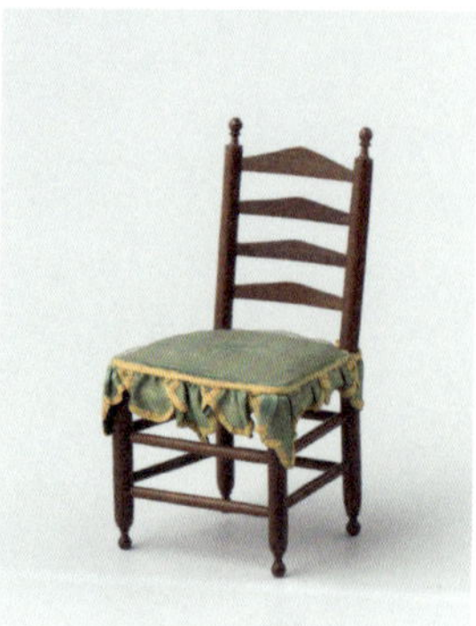

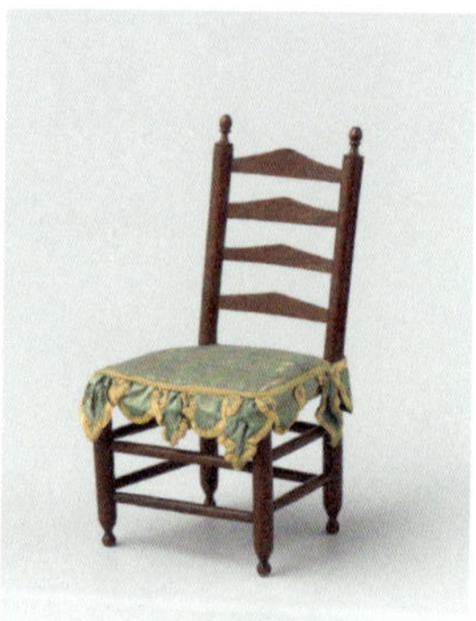

presentation of this remarkable, deep black glossy cabinet, followed by the disclosure of its contents drawer by drawer, must have been an especially impressive moment [P. 96].

The door in the rear wall of the tapestry room leads to yet another surprise: the library, which, like the garden, was in a separate compartment attached to the back of the doll's house [FIG. 25]. In Oortman's time, there was only one printed book among all the miniature volumes: the *Gebede Boeck* (Prayer Book) of 1683. As that was the book shown to the German visitors, they believed all the miniature books had been specially printed. Nothing could have been further from the truth: all the others had cut-out prints pasted in or were handwritten or left blank. Over time, three other miniature printed books have been added, including a *Kern des Bijbels* (Essence of the Bible) from 1750, which now rests prominently on the bookstand [FIG. 27]. Other miniature books have disappeared or been given away. For instance, one of the two Uffenbach brothers received a miniature dummy book as a gift for his own library.

In addition to the shell and book collections – which must have greatly appealed to the Uffenbachs, as serious collectors in their own right – Glauburg also writes at length about the dolls in the tapestry room. This was the setting of a poignant scene. On a dark carpet in the middle of the room, a small child was laid out in a coffin [PP. 40–41]. A governess, or 'French madame' as Glauburg calls her, supervised five children who had come to say farewell. Although Petronella Oortman lost her one-year-old daughter Hendrika in 1684, during her first marriage, this scene was probably not a personal expression of grief, but part of the larger story of the cycle of life told by the doll's house. Just as in the lying-in chamber, there is a painting by Johannes Voorhout (I) over the mantelpiece with a fitting subject: Christ welcoming the children. This biblical story emphasizes the innocence of children, for whom the gates of the heavenly kingdom are said to be wide open. The painting by Jacob Appel shows that family portraits originally hung here as well. Together with the deceased child, they stand for the importance of lineage and of preserving the memory of those no longer present, as well as for life after death.

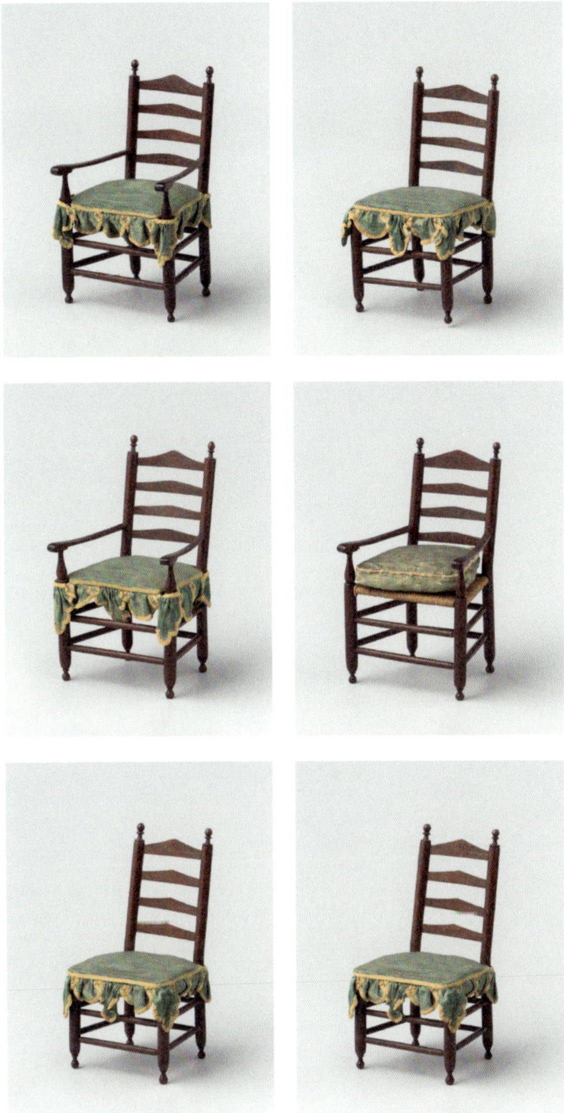

23
All the furniture in the tapestry room, from the settee and table to the chairs, is upholstered *en suite* in green silk with yellow and white trim, creating visual unity in the interior

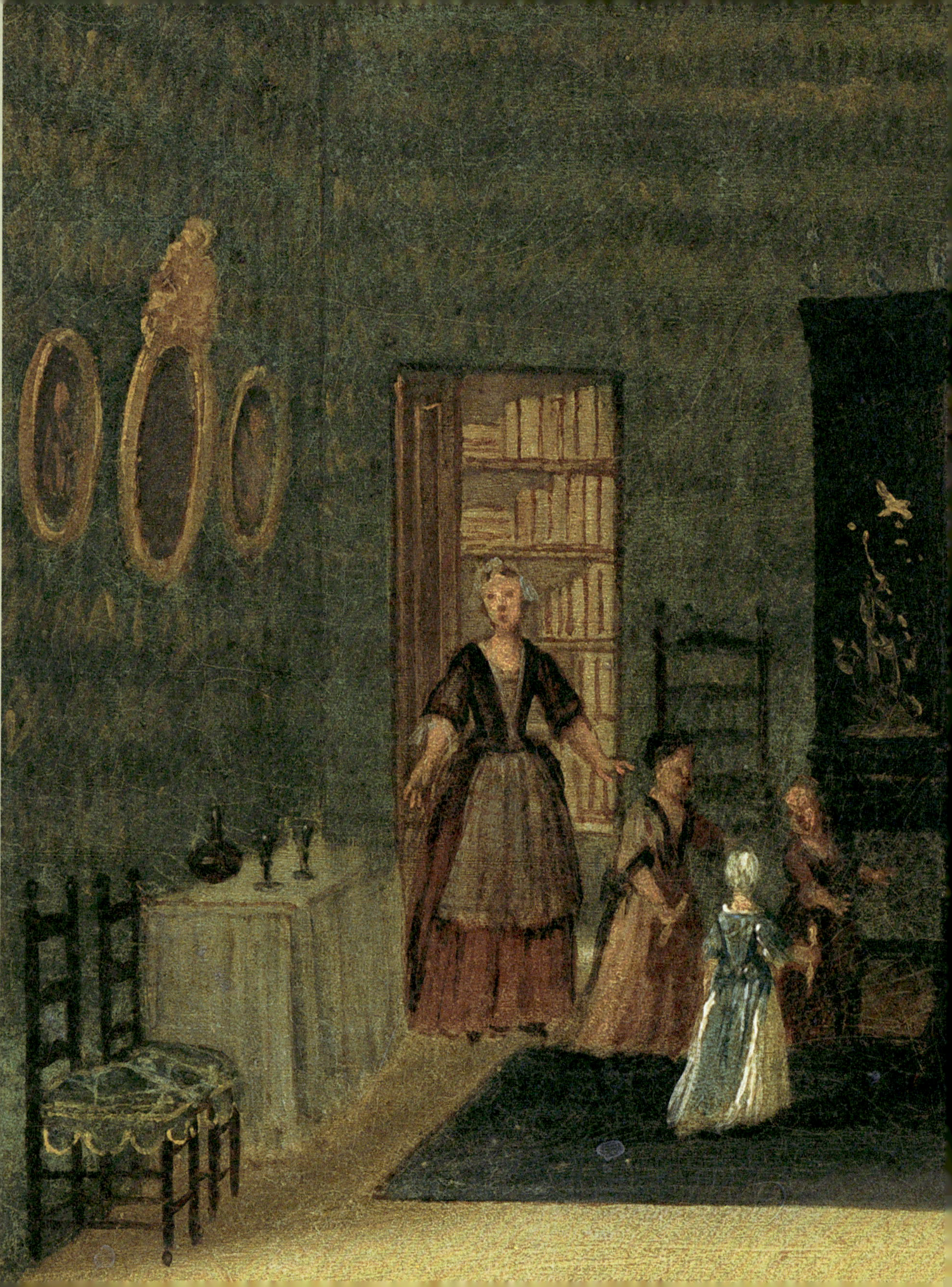

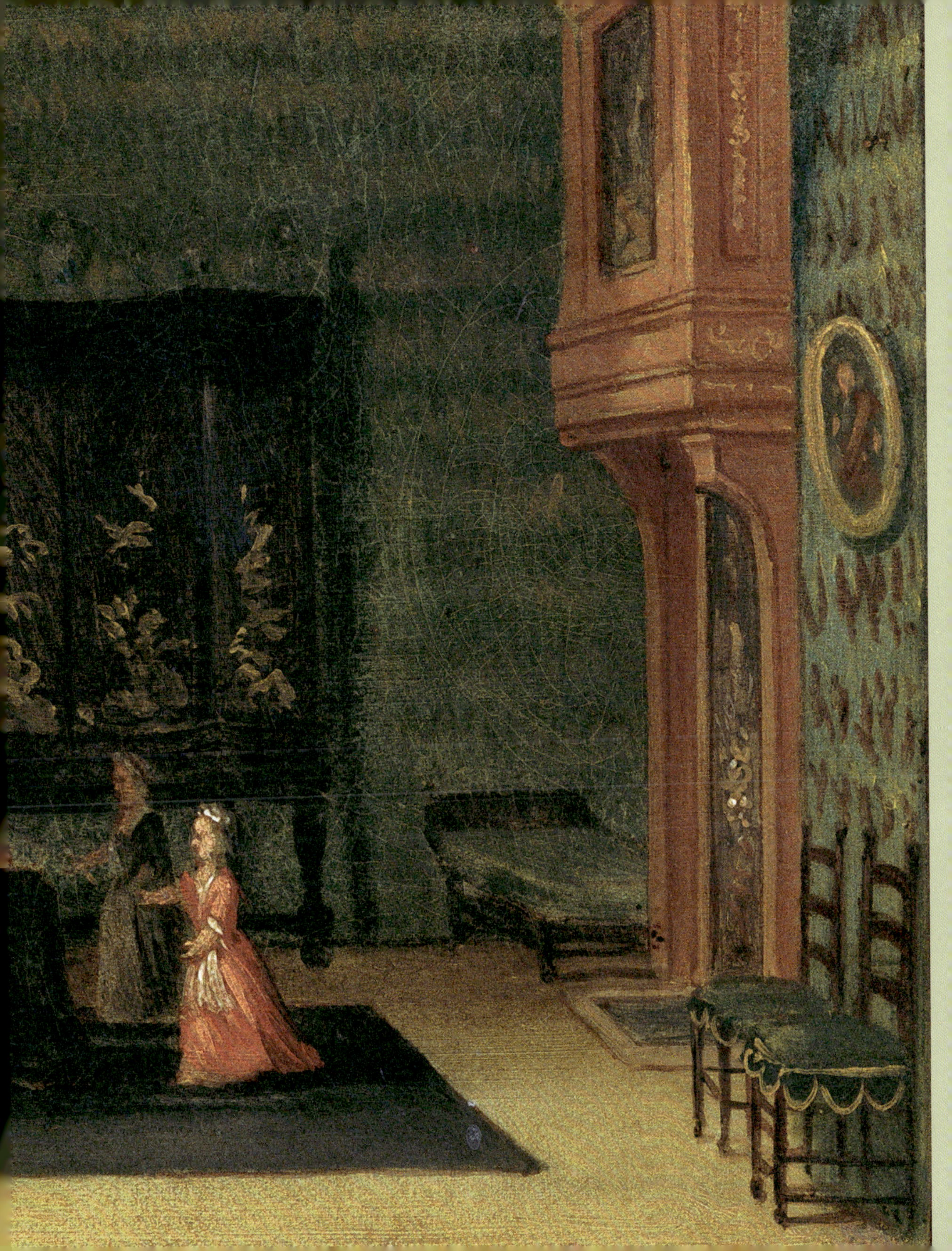

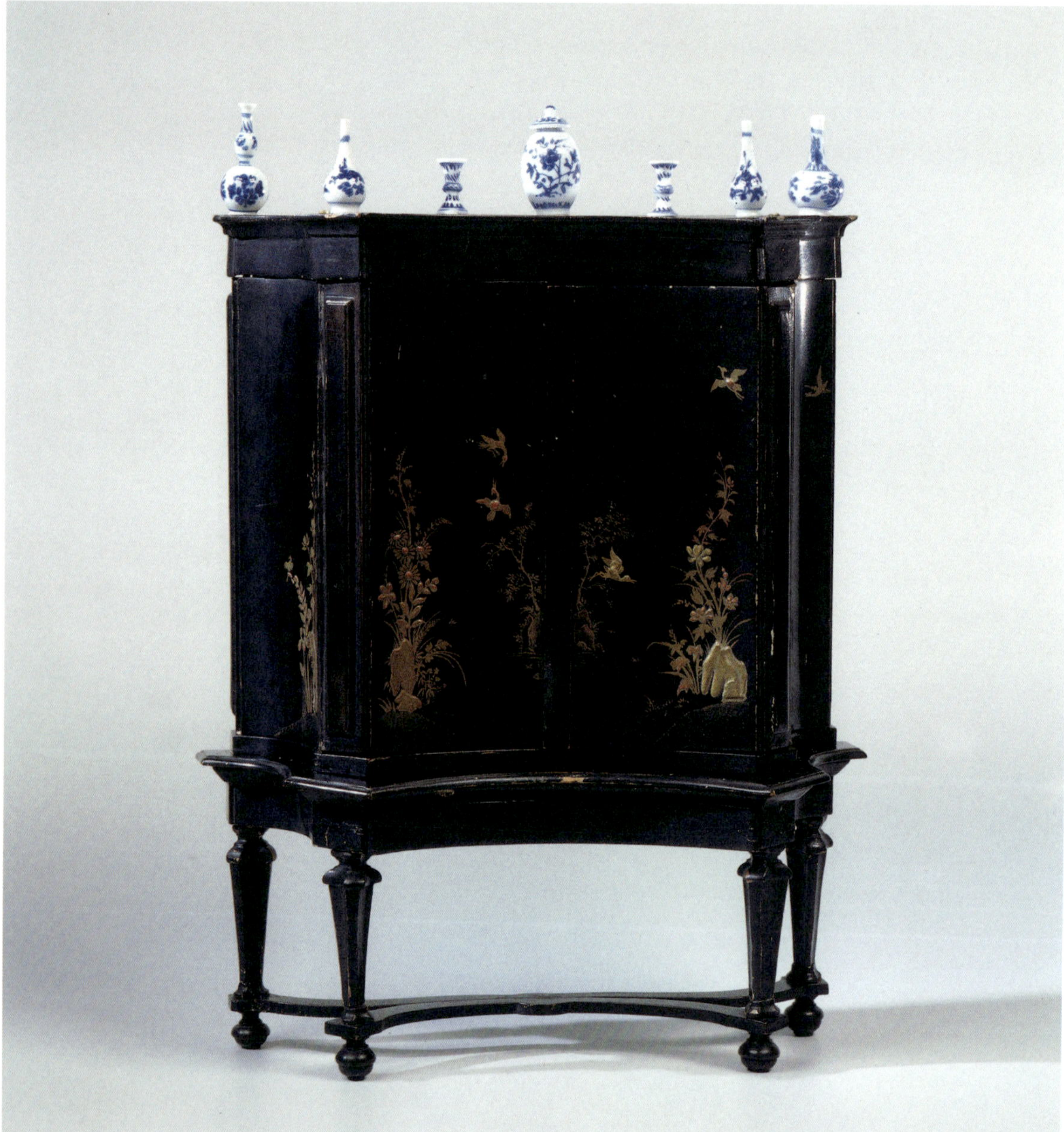

24
The collector's cabinet is one of the most valuable pieces of furniture in the doll's house, because of its precious lacquer finish and its contents. The shelves and drawers are filled with tropical shells in decorative arrangements

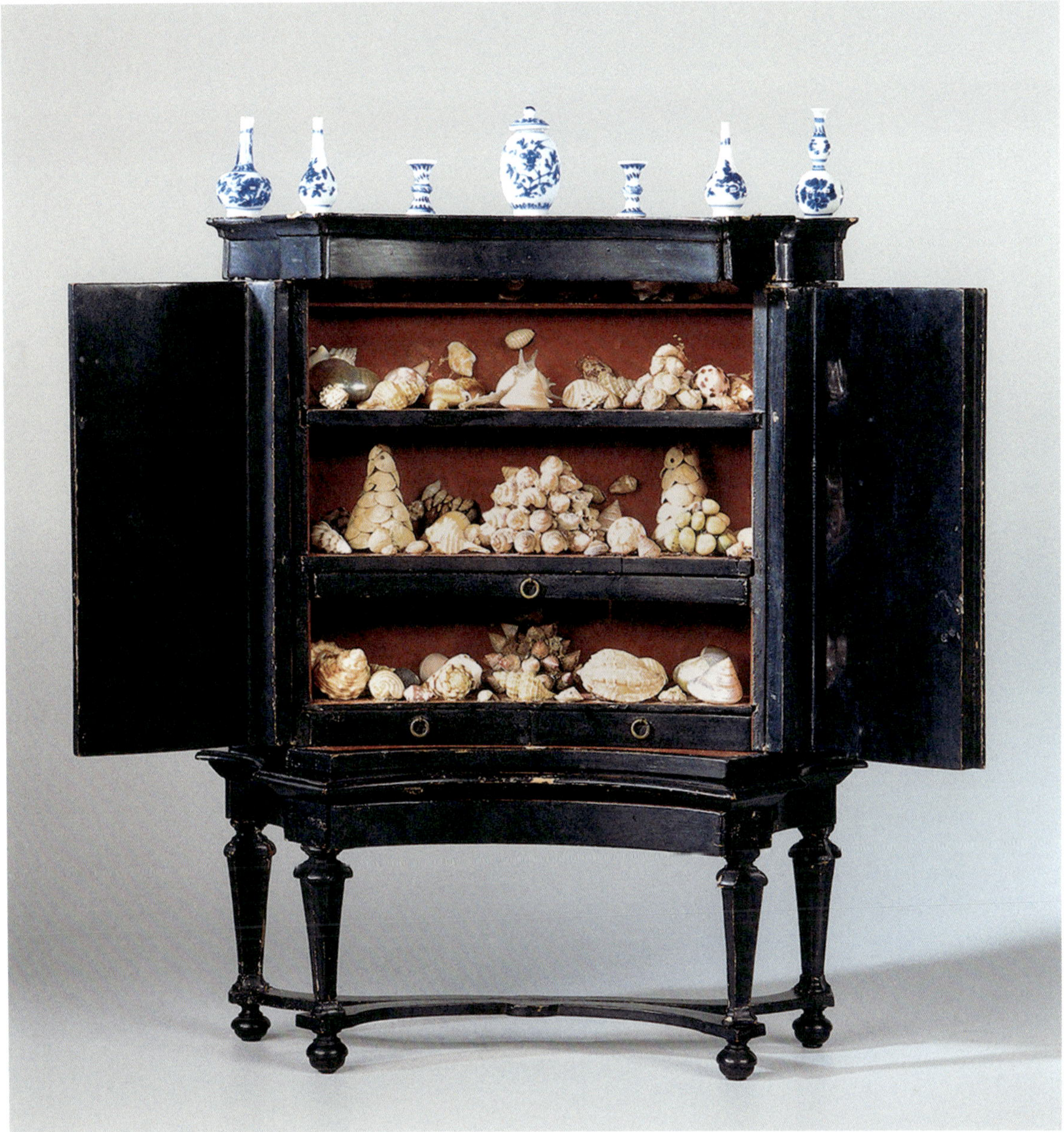

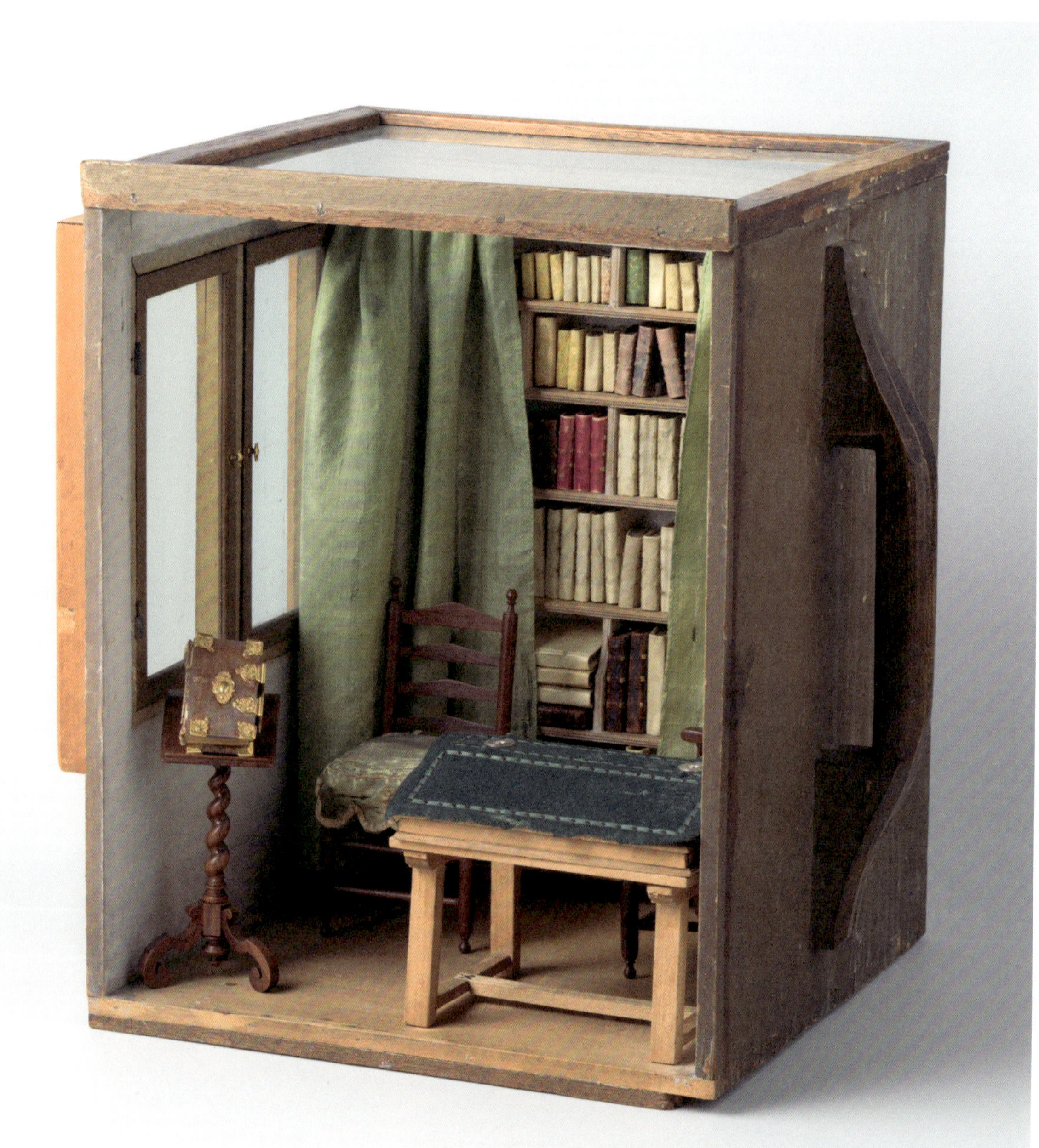

25
The library is a removable compartment furnished with two chairs and a desk for reading and writing, with two silver candle holders set into it for additional light. The shelves hold eighty-five books

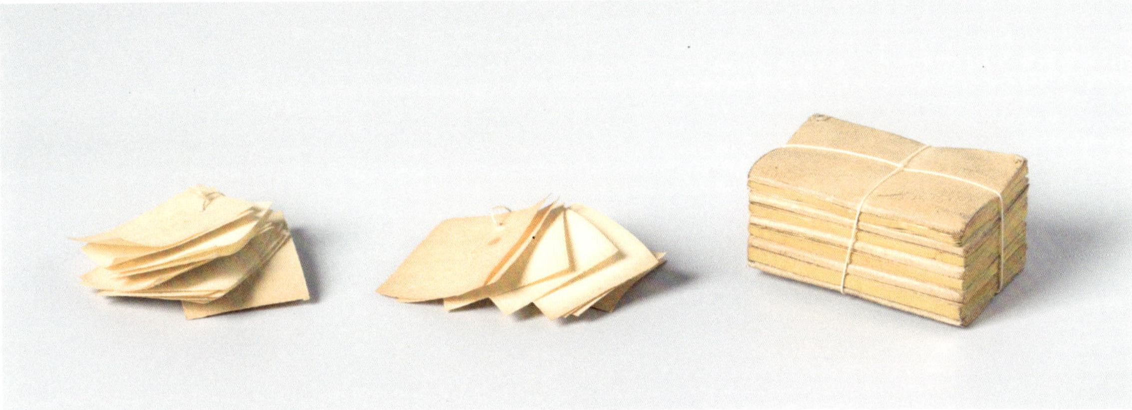

26
Under the lid of the writing desk are sheaves of paper and a stack of bound quires for a book that does not yet have a cover

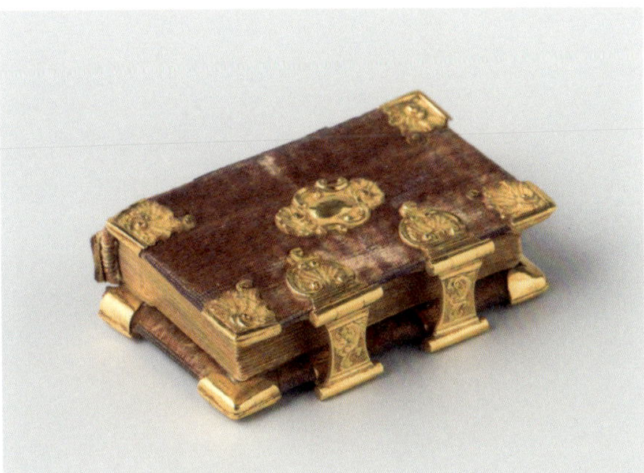

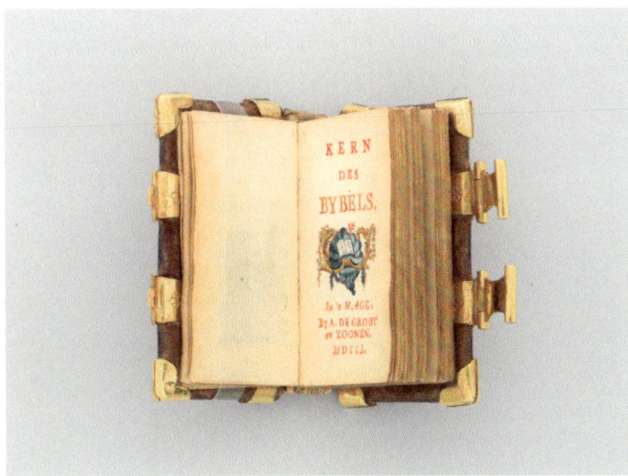

27
This beautifully bound *Kern des Bijbels* (Essence of the Bible) is among the few eighteenth-century additions to the doll's house

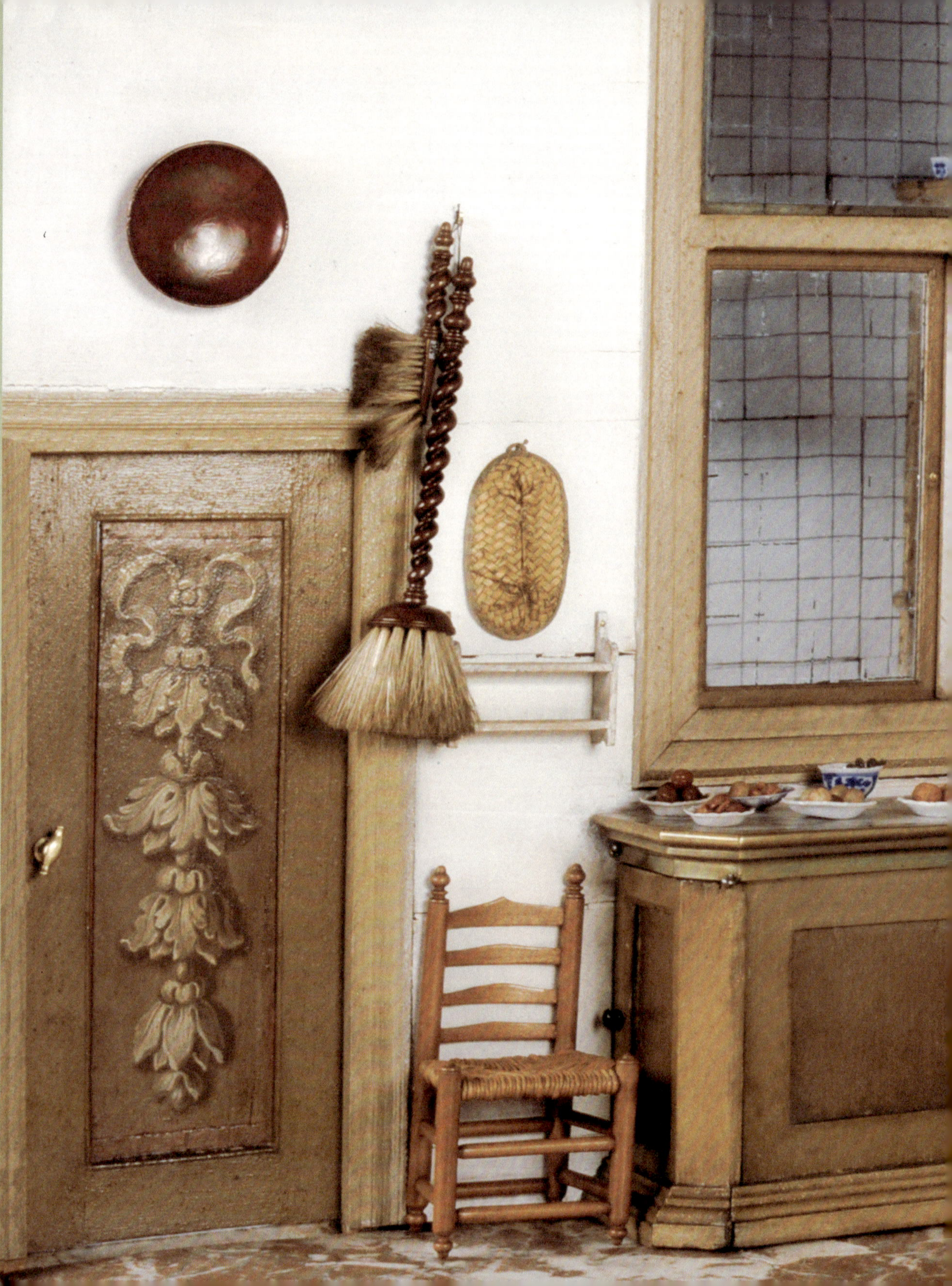

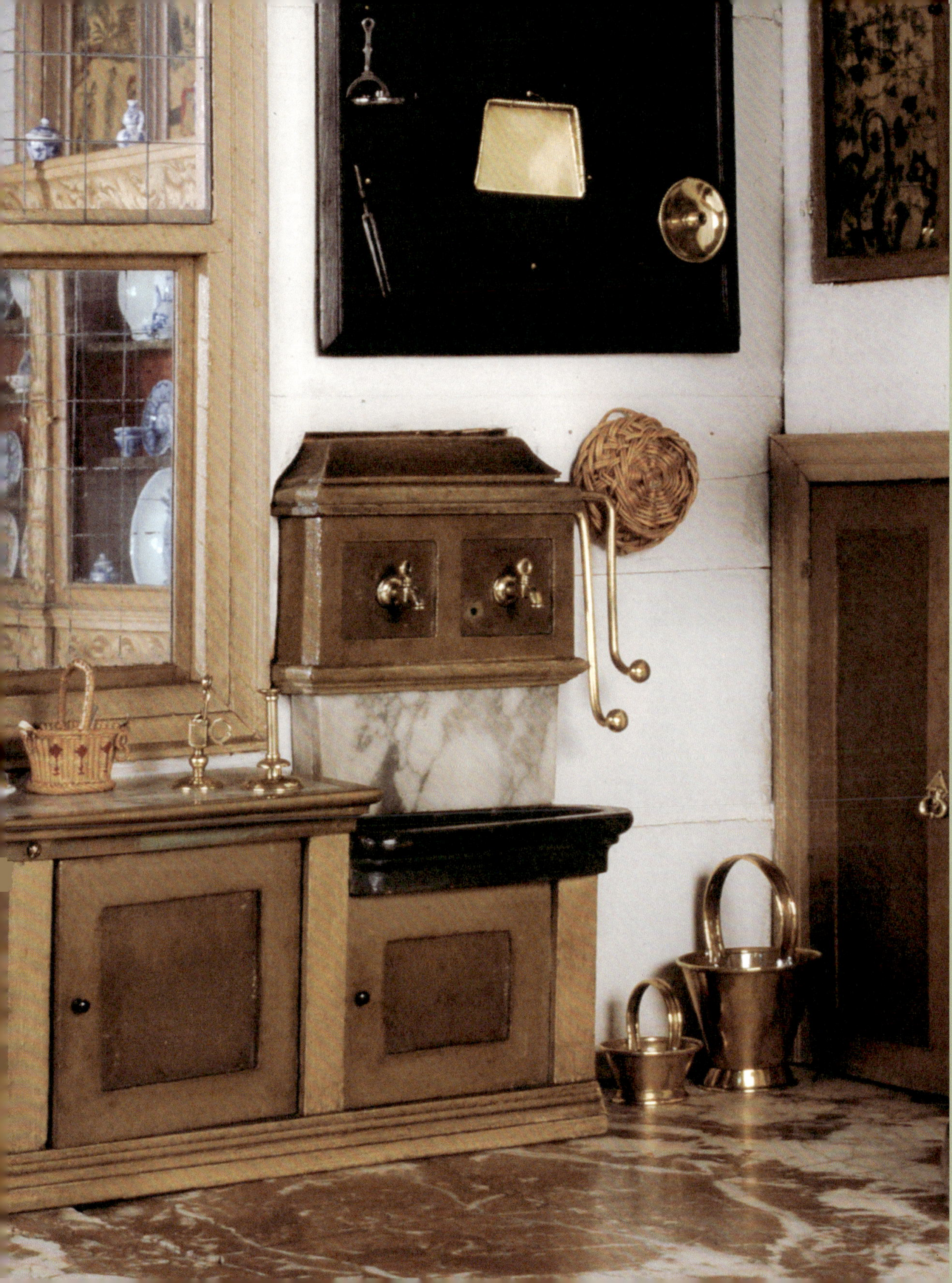

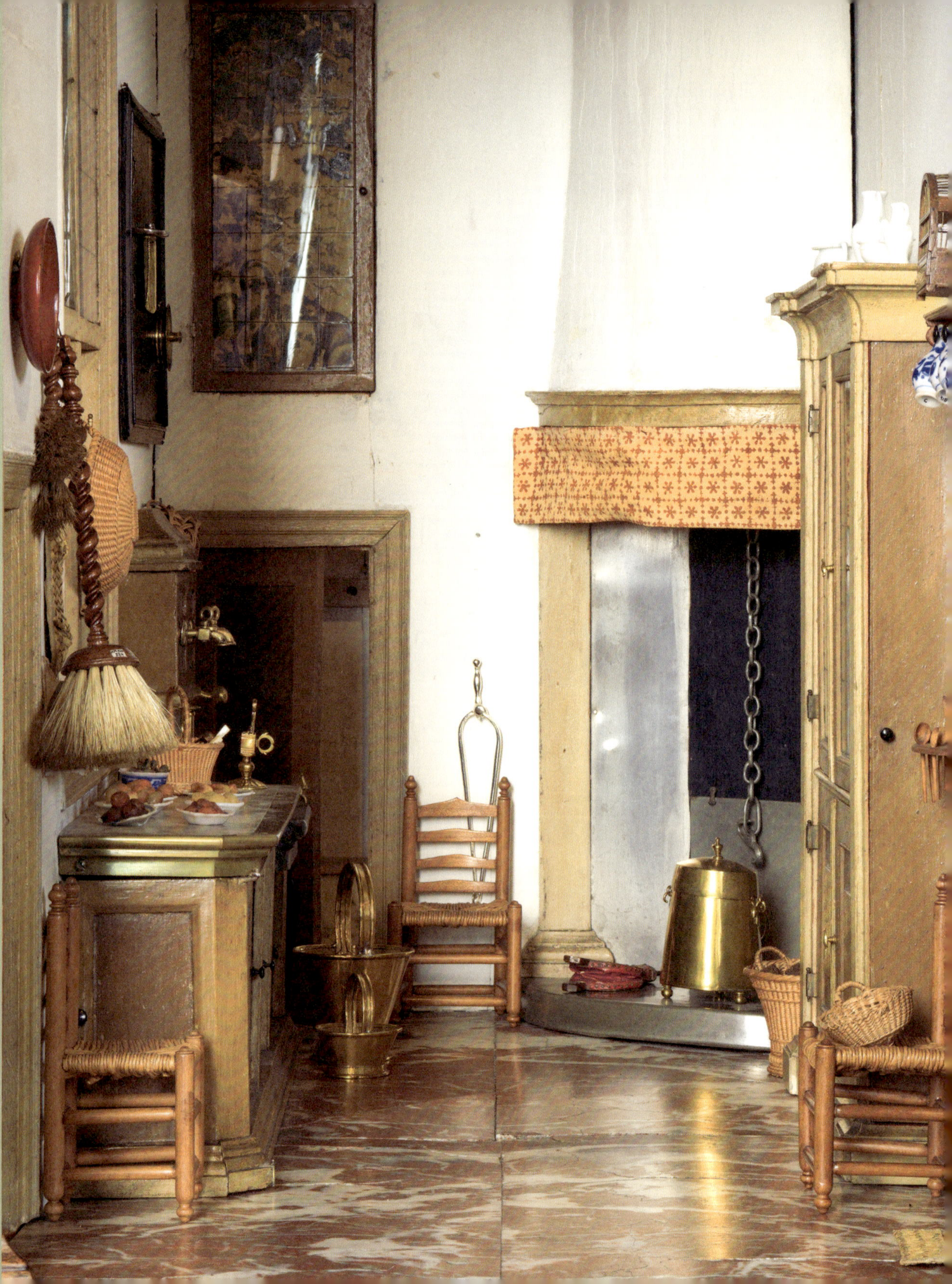

KITCHEN, PRIVY AND CELLAR

In the other rooms, the focus is not on major life events, but rather on the daily life of the household. To the left of the tapestry room is the kitchen [P. 48]. This room is small and therefore furnished very efficiently. The floor, made of red marble with white veining, is not only beautiful but also easy to clean. In the rear right corner is the hearth. The fire has been put out, and the last of the peat smoulders gently in the brass extinguishing pot. With the bellows to the left, the fire can be rekindled easily. There are also numerous practical options for storage: mounted on the left wall, to the left of the window, is an egg rack with space for twenty-eight eggs, and to the right of the window is a large ebony wall board with nails for hanging various kitchen utensils (of which only a dustpan, two chamber-sticks and a meat fork have survived) [PP. 46–47]. The advantage of a black hanging board such as this one was that kitchen items which were sooty or still slightly greasy did not touch the white wall. Next to the door in the right wall, we can see a spoon rack, above which are a jug rack and a finch cage [P. 51]. The baskets and brass buckets were intended for shopping at the market.

The large pewter cupboard against the right wall served as the main storage space. Ingeniously integrated into its side is a broom cupboard: inside the door on the right, a brush is tucked away [SEE P. 51]. The large stock of pewter dishes is safely yet prominently displayed inside the glass doors. The shelves are fitted with grooves so that the dishes can be attractively presented, upright against the red background. In a seventeenth-century household, pewter was polished until it shone like silver. In all Dutch dolls' houses, however, the 'pewter' dishes were made of silver, which is harder and allows for more realistic miniatures [FIG. 29]. Alongside the plates, imitation porcelain dishes are on display. These are actually made of opaque white glass with blue decoration; glass, similarly, was easier to work with on this small scale than real porcelain. The maid, still visible in Appel's painting, has taken some of the 'porcelain' out of the cupboard and filled the dishes with fresh and candied fruits, modelled in wax. Laid out on the countertop, they are ready to be served as the final, sweet course of a banquet [FIG. 28].

In this room, the German visitors were, once again, most struck by the high degree of realism. For instance, a basket on the countertop holds tiny

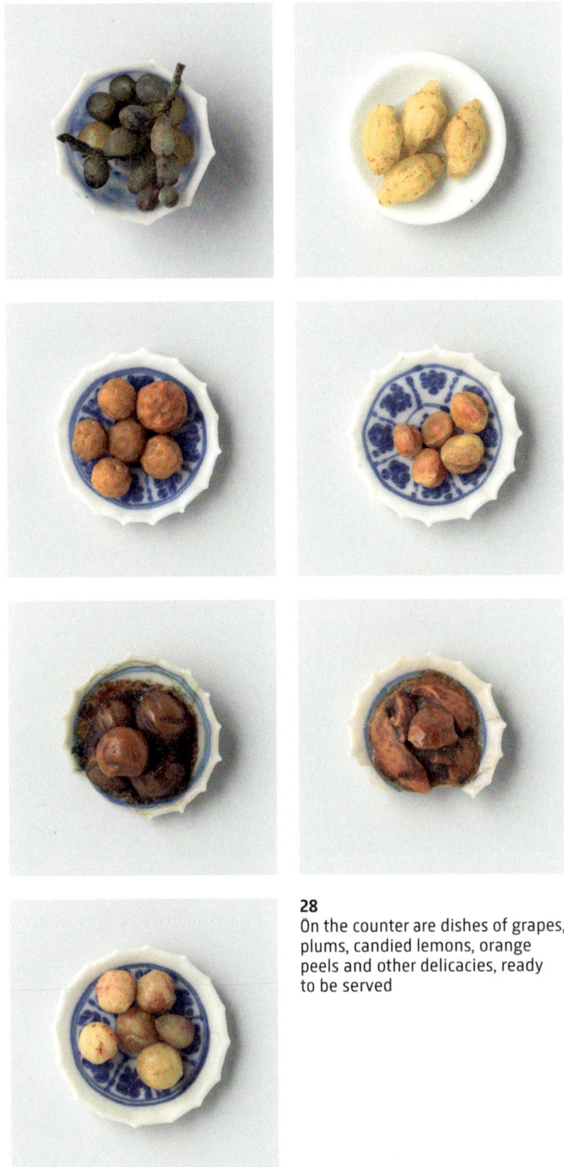

28
On the counter are dishes of grapes, plums, candied lemons, orange peels and other delicacies, ready to be served

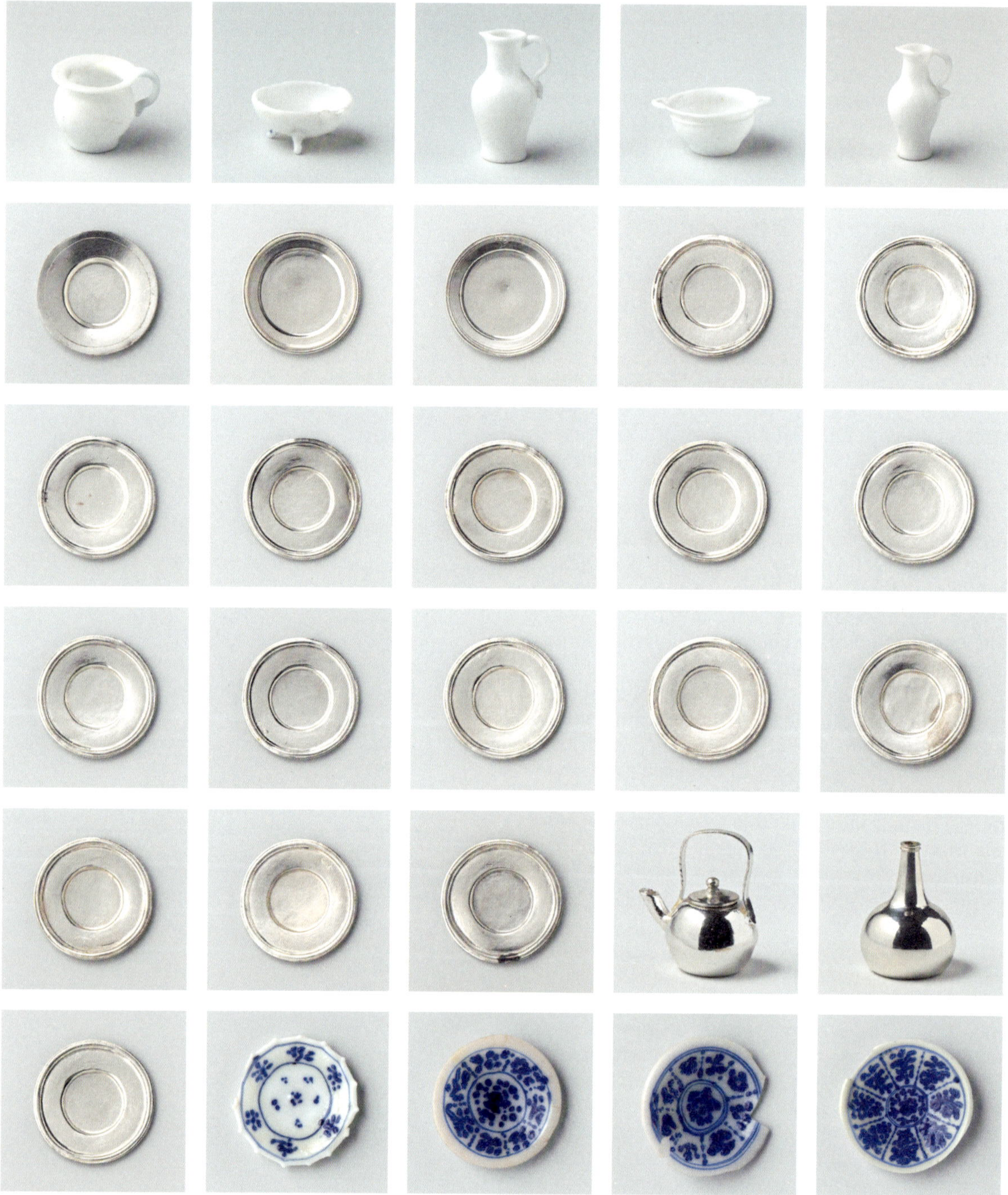

29
The pewter cupboard is full from top to bottom. The silver plates and dishes represent the lustrous polished pewter that was actually used

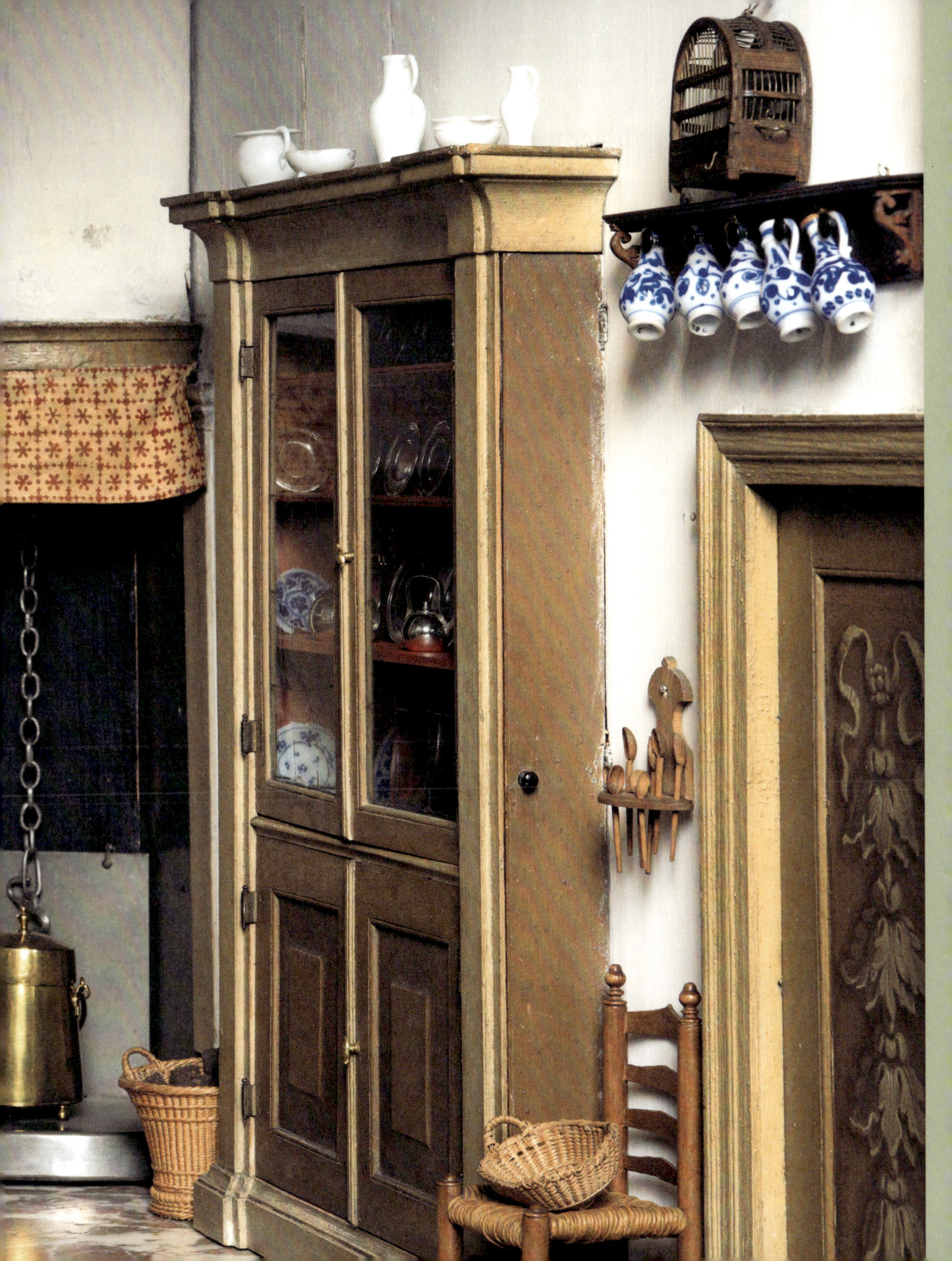

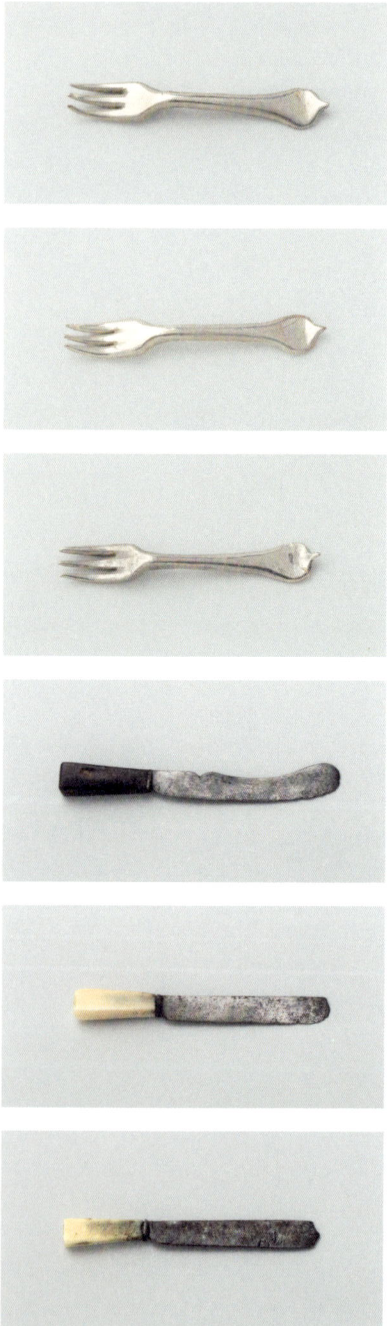

30
Cutlery sets with knives, forks and spoons were a novelty in the late seventeenth century. The spoons have been lost but are mentioned by Glauburg

forks and knives [FIG. 30]. There is also a brass candlestick which, like a real one, consists of four separate parts that can be seamlessly screwed together [FIG. 31]. The snuffers, a special pair of scissors for snuffing and trimming the candle wicks, can be opened and shut, and they fit perfectly into the holder of the corresponding stand [FIG. 32]. Still more astonishment greeted the pump, which actually worked. Water could be pumped from a tank through lead pipes, a system that remains intact to this day.

The door next to the pump provided access to the privy [FIG. 33]. Like the garden and the library, this is a separate compartment attached to the back of the doll's house. Its handle made it easy to remove for a better view. Again, great care went into making every detail lifelike. There are grey marble tiles on the floor, a coat rack for hanging loose clothing while heeding nature's call, and even a recess in the wall that serves as a paper holder. The privy could be covered with a wooden lid to reduce the stench from the cesspit below.

Along with the working pump and the privy, the kitchen holds a third, much bigger surprise. When the left door of the cupboard under the counter is opened, it offers a glimpse of a stairwell. The front part of the red marble floor can be removed to expose the cellar beneath the kitchen, concealed in a wooden compartment that is suspended in a drawer in the middle of the cabinet's base [FIG. 34]. When this room was suddenly revealed, it must have caused quite a stir.

The cellar is divided in two by a barred gate with a lock, behind which the supply of drink is securely stored. On the wall is a shelf with holes for storing wine bottles: upside down, if they were empty, or right side up if they were full and corked. In the absence of a standard bottle size, this was more practical than a rack. The beer and wine barrels are on a platform below, which raises them from the damp cellar floor [FIG. 37]. One noteworthy detail is that the beer kegs are marked with a swan, in reference to the brewery De Zwaan, which was run by Petronella de la Court, the widow of brewer Adam Oortmans and owner of the doll's house now in the Centraal Museum [FIG. 72]. It is quite possible that the two Petronella's knew each other and even exchanged miniatures. In the *comptoir* of De la Court's doll's house, a gentleman sits in a chair identical to the set in the children's room of Oortman's house [SEE FIG. 9 AND PP. 68–69].

Like the kitchen, the cellar is quite full. Not only drinks and food were stored there, but also cooking

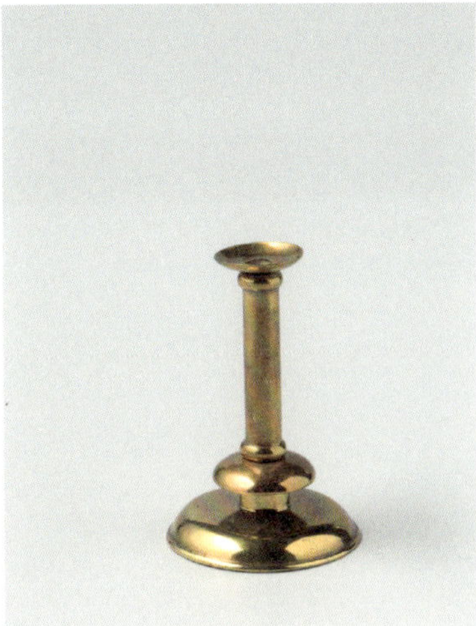
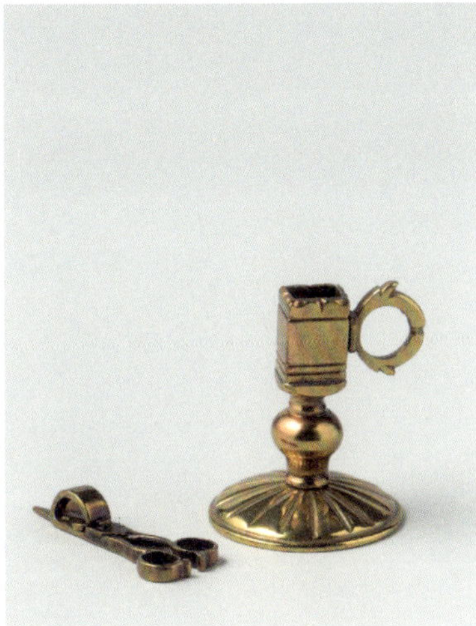
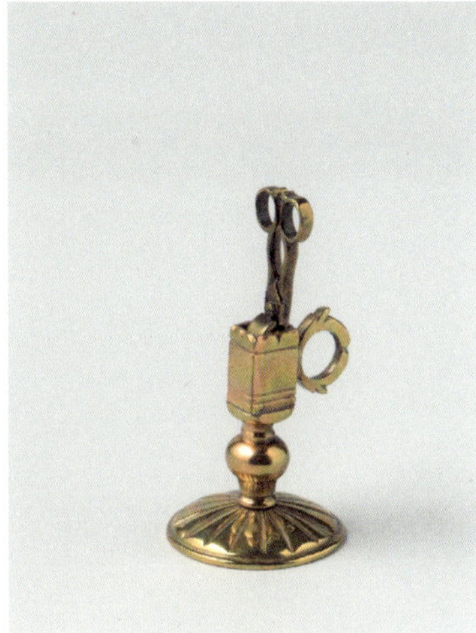

31, 32
Unlike an oil lamp, a candle in a brass candlestick was an expensive source of light. The trimmer was used to shorten the wick so that the candle would burn more evenly and last longer

utensils and cleaning supplies. We find a variety of pots and pans there, made of yellow or green glass, in imitation of red-firing or green-glazed earthenware [FIG. 35]. In addition to jugs for serving, there are others for heating liquids, identifiable by the three legs on which they stood in the hearth, as well as cauldrons, also with legs. The cellar also contains a tin-plated copper cauldron [FIG. 36], a wall-mounted container of sand to use for scouring, a whisk broom without a handle, made of bundled twigs, a long-handled scrubbing brush for cleaning the floor, and besoms, one of which is somewhat worn [FIG. 38]. Did Petronella Oortman actually sweep the floor of her doll's house? It could certainly have done with a good cleaning now and then. All the dust sometimes made the German visitors sneeze so hard that they almost blew the furniture out of place.

Glauburg was especially intrigued by the tap fittings for the kegs, the hinges and locks of the gate, and the 'Dutch earthenware cooking utensils'. Even today, the precision of the cellar's execution is fascinating. We have hardly any sources of information on utilitarian rooms, such as this one, in seventeenth-century Dutch houses. They are rarely found in paintings, and estate inventories provide an incomplete picture, as they do not mention inexpensive earthenware, wooden kitchen utensils or furnishings nailed in place, such as a gate. It is precisely these very ordinary, everyday elements that make this miniature cellar so special – not only now but even in its own time.

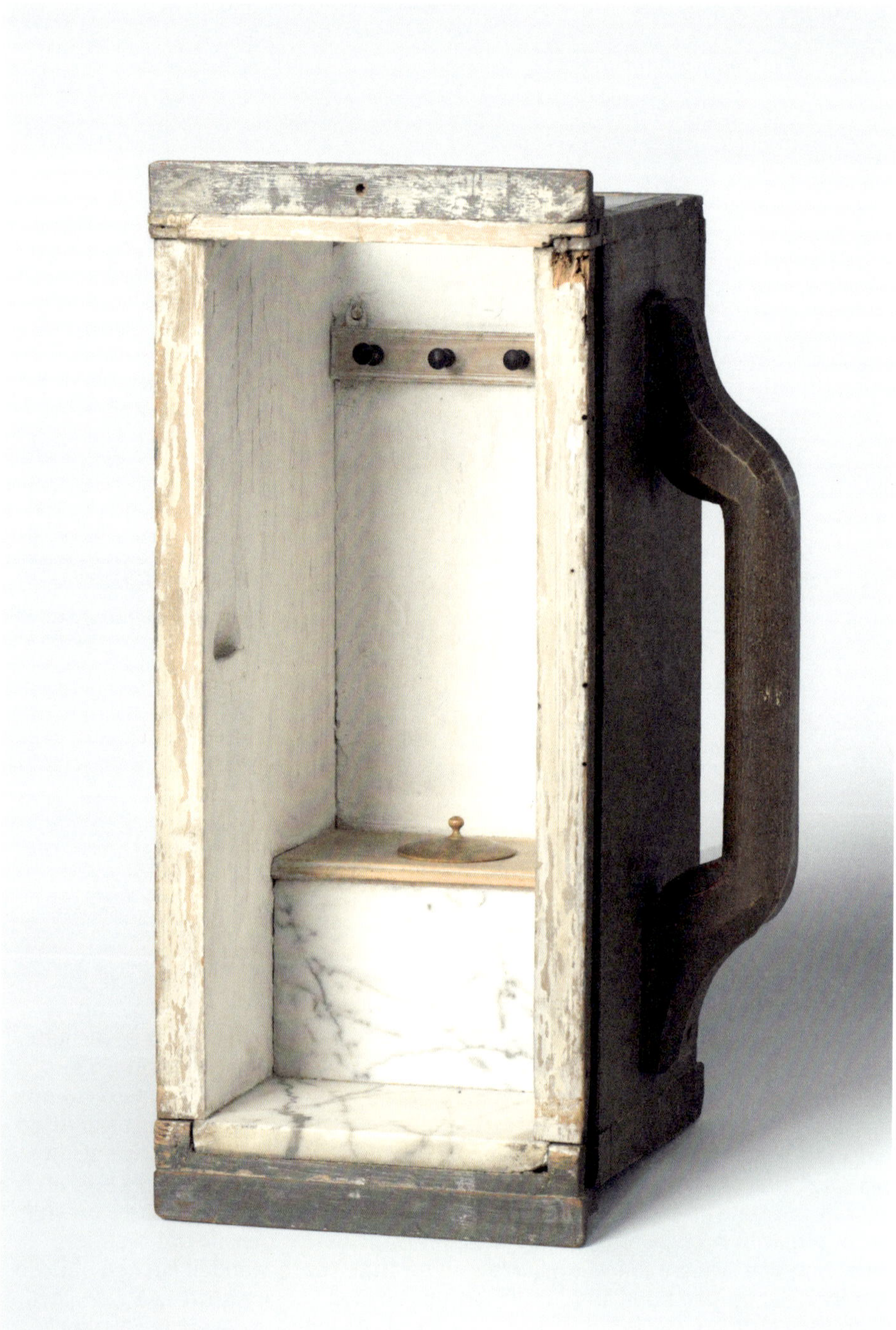

33
The privy, in a compartment attached to the kitchen, is equipped with every convenience, from a coat rack to a paper holder

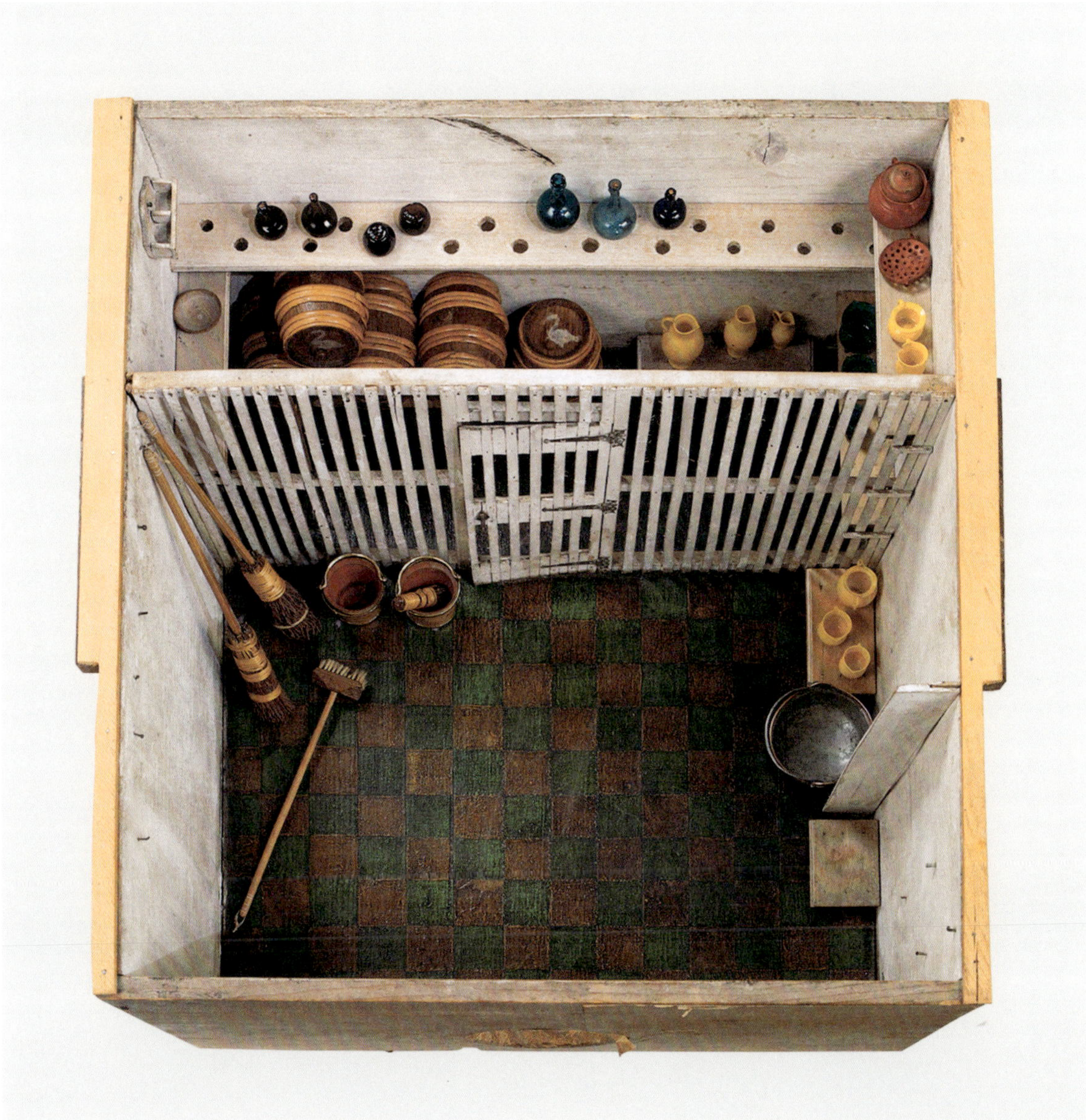

34
The cellar is ingeniously hidden in a drawer of the cabinet. This is where beer and wine are stored, along with unused cooking and cleaning utensils

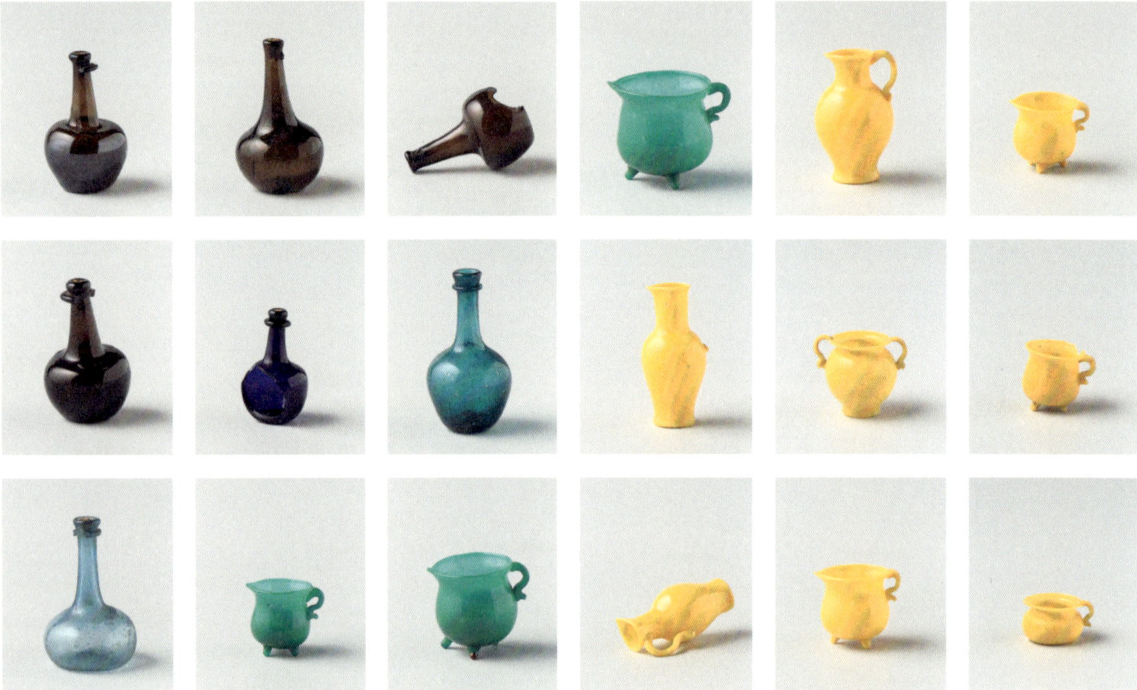

35, 36
In the cellar, we find glass wine decanters and a wide range of cooking utensils. The copper cauldron is tin-plated to prevent a toxic relation between acidic foods and the copper

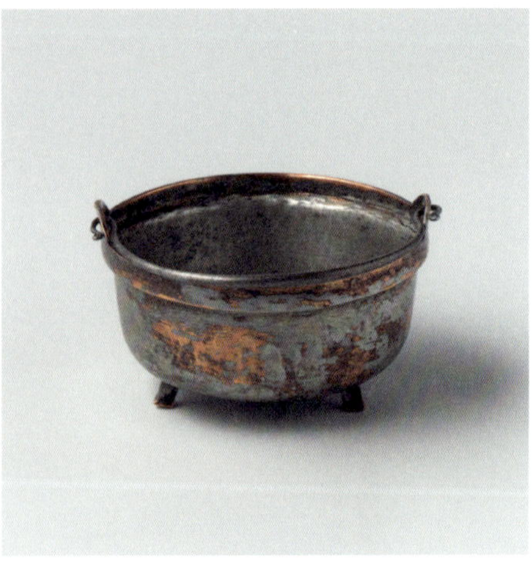

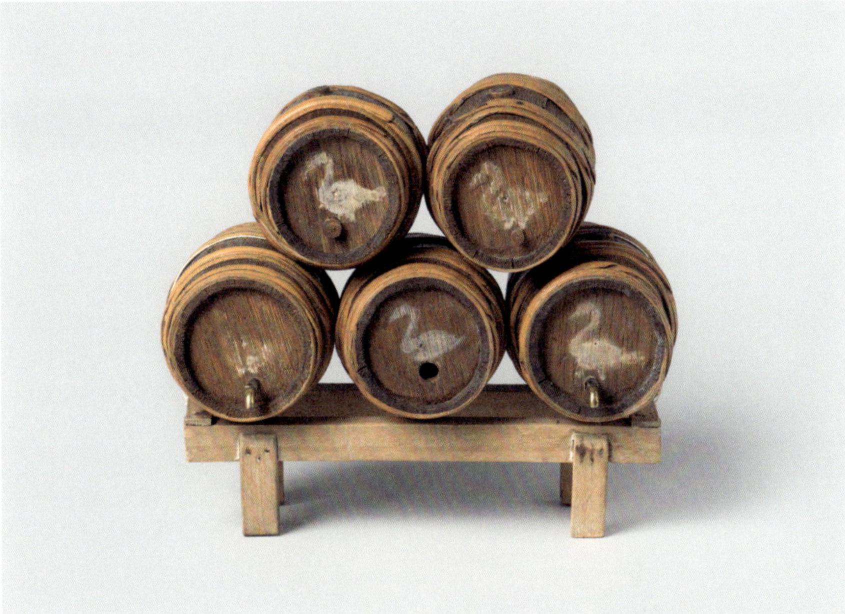

37
Just like real beer barrels, these have marks identifying the brewery. The brass taps, which were hammered into the barrels at home, are executed in great detail

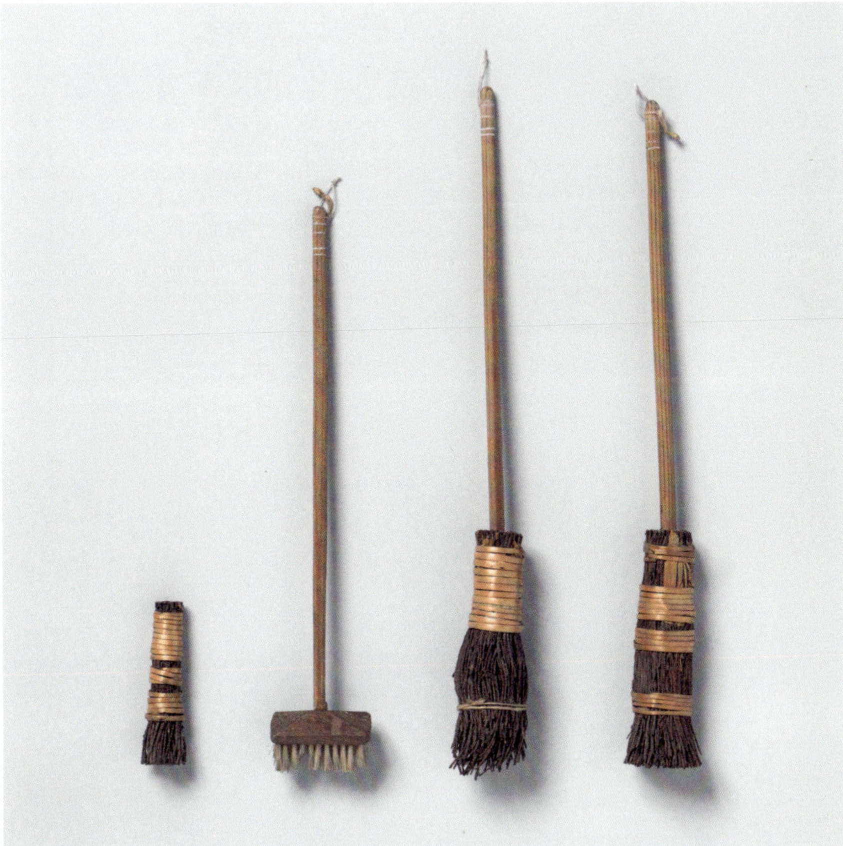

38
Keeping the house clean required a whole arsenal of brooms and brushes. There was a special variety for every type of surface or tricky corner, from a broom without a handle to a scrubbing brush

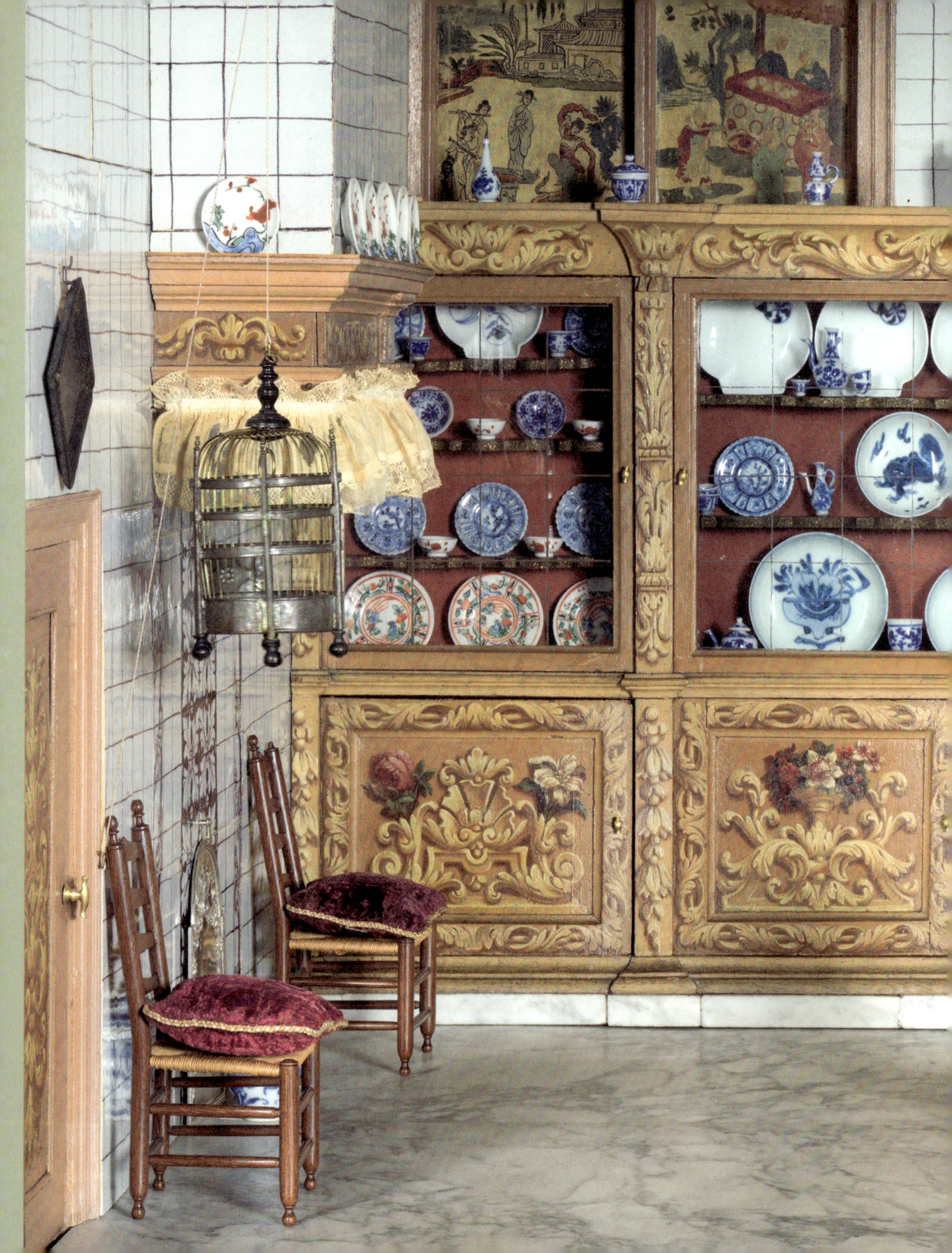

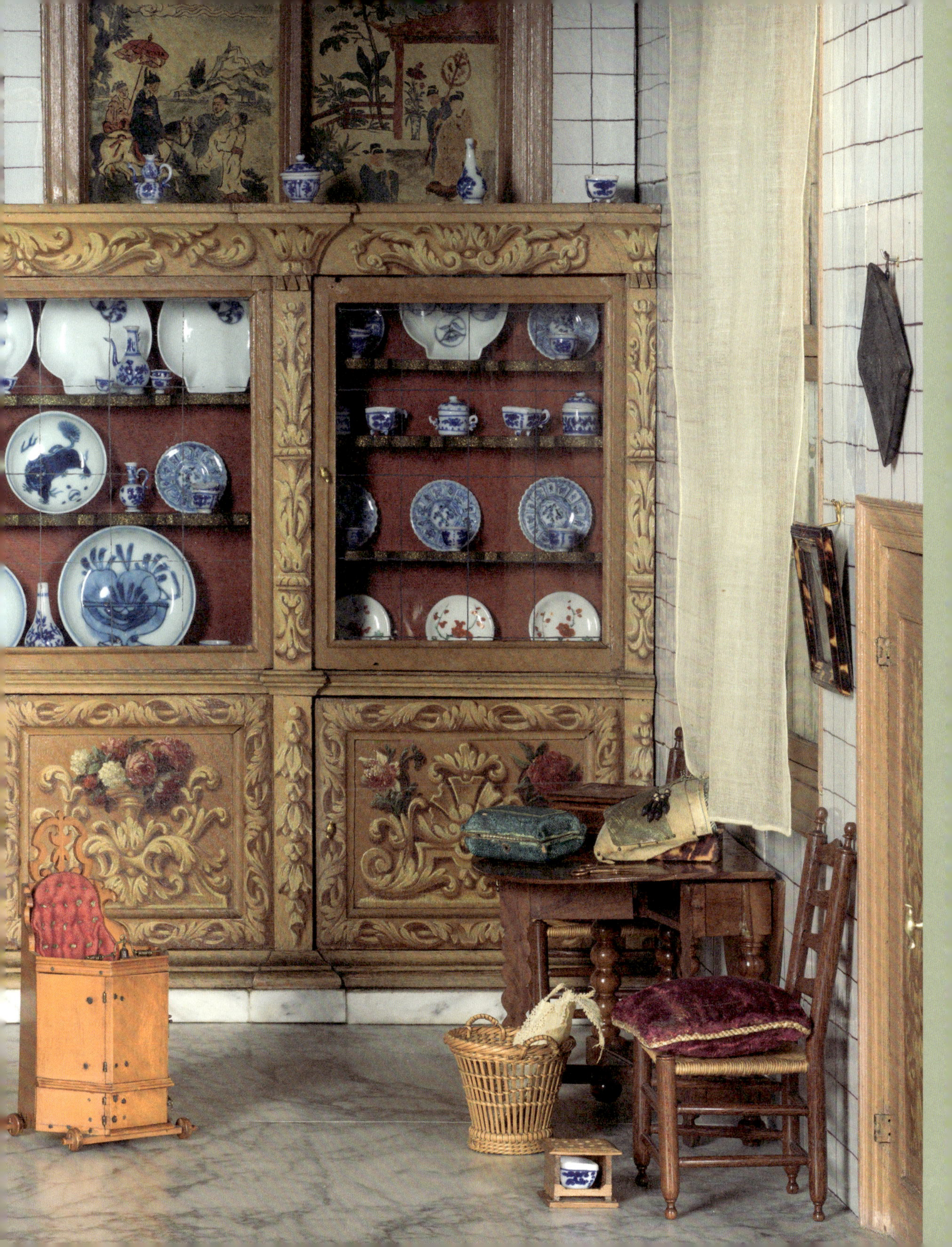

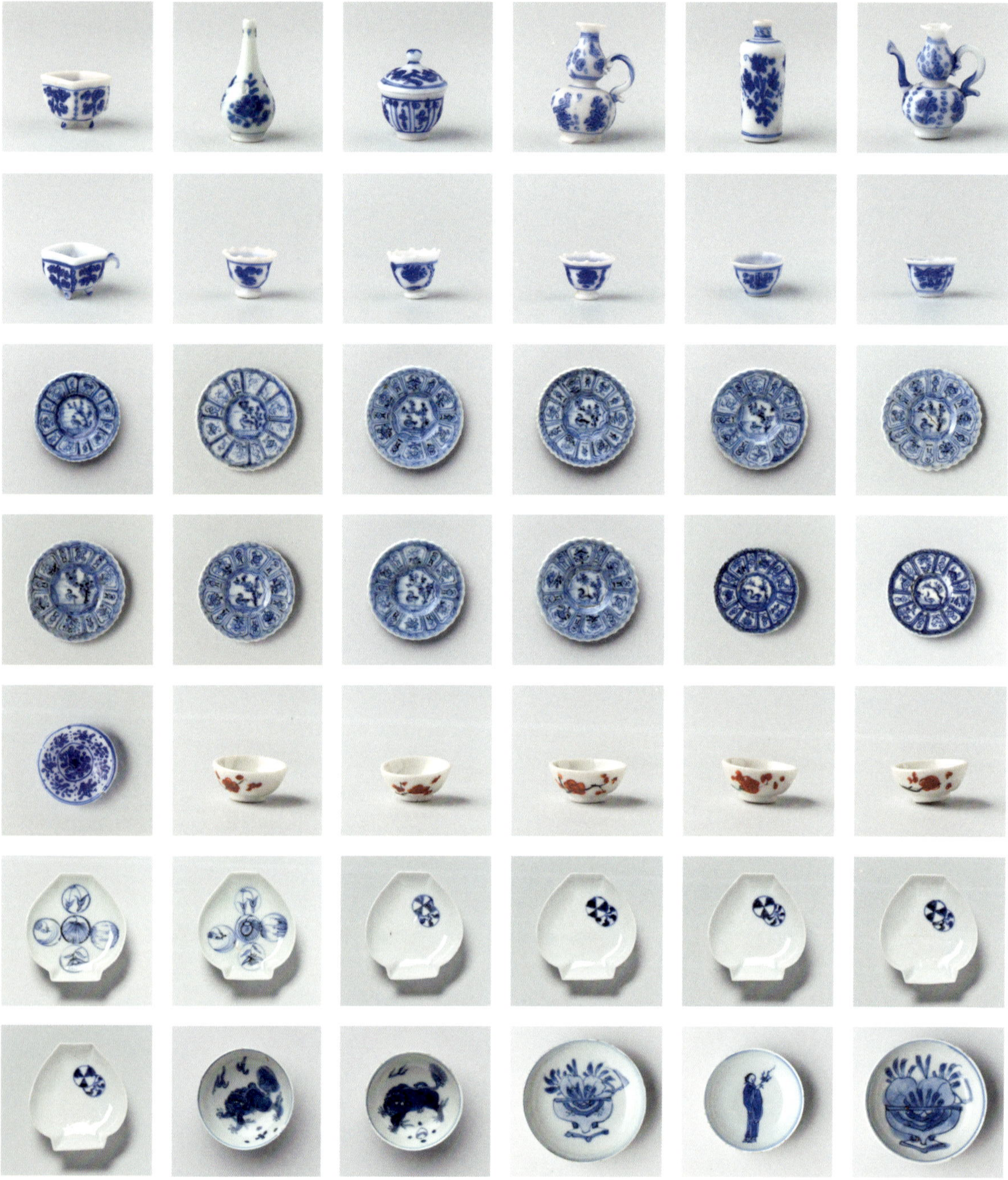

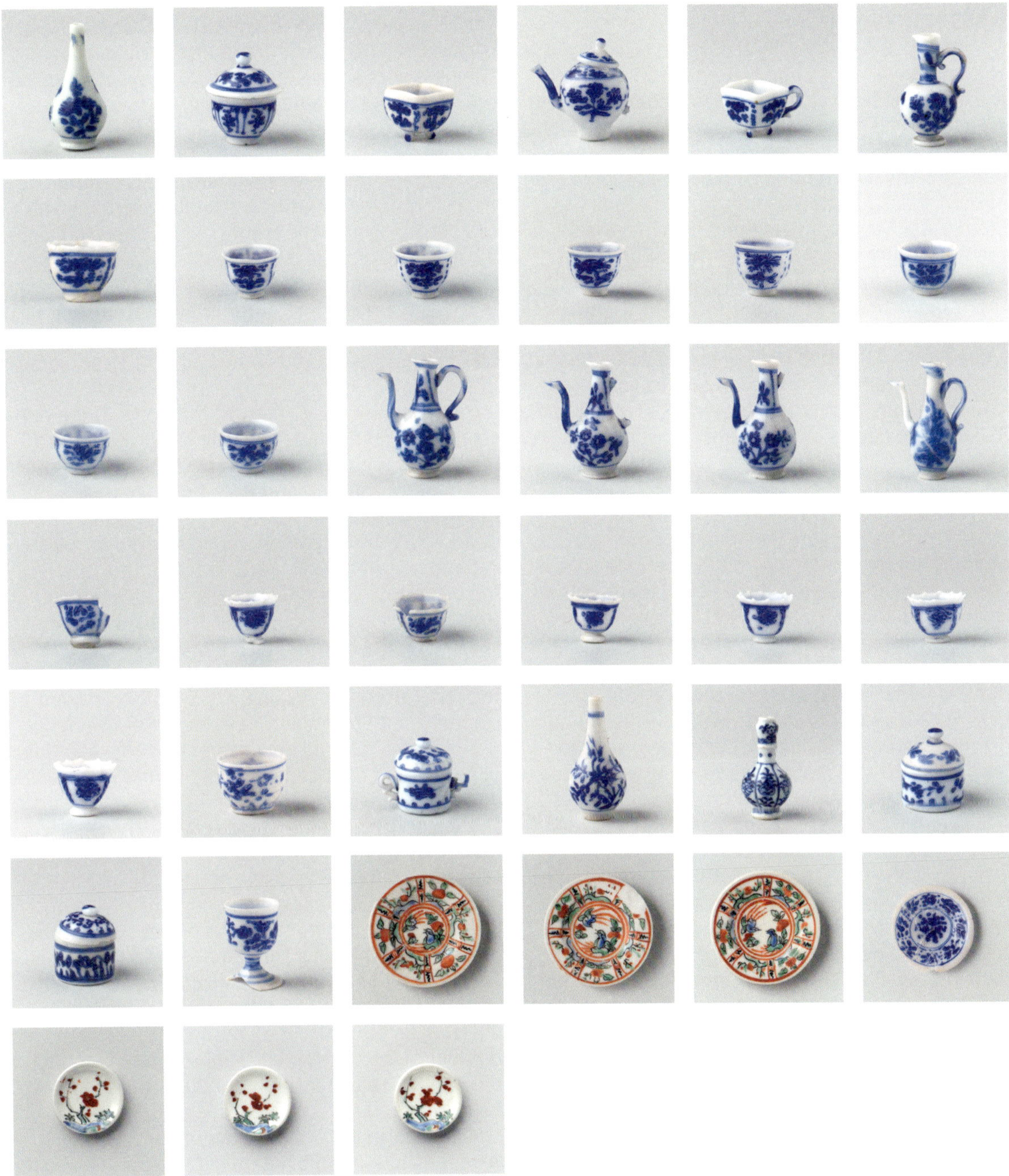

39
The porcelain cabinet is filled with Chinese and Japanese porcelain, as well as glass imitations. Because of trade with East Asia, porcelain was ubiquitous in Dutch interiors

BEST KITCHEN

The humblest homes had just one room, which was used for every kind of activity. Cooking, eating, mending, reading and sleeping all took place around the hearth. In contrast, more distinguished residences came over time to have separate rooms for each of these functions. For example, a separate dining and living room emerged, which in the seventeenth century was often still referred to as the kitchen, even though the cooking was no longer done there. In Oortman's doll's house this 'best kitchen' (*pronkkeuken*), on the far left of the ground floor, is a beautifully decorated living space for daily use that was also suitable for small dinner parties [PP. 58–59].

In this room, aesthetics and practicality go hand in hand. The floor is composed of four slabs of white-and-grey marble. The walls are covered with small white tiles in the standard size of approximately thirteen by thirteen centimetres, but with lines painted on them that make them appear to consist of many miniature tiles. Against the rear wall of the hearth, they are decorated with an elegant foliate motif. When the doll's house was restored in the 1990s, an inscription was discovered beneath the tiles on the wall: 'this is not painted, stones [= tiles] needed here'. The eighteenth-century catalogue describes it as 'adorned with white stones in an astonishingly neat fashion'. What made it so astonishing was the fact that most dolls' houses imitated tiles with mere wallpaper, and it was called neat because it was attractive and genuinely easy to keep clean.

An even more spectacular feature is the trompe-l'oeil painting on the ceiling, which depicts a domed skylight [PP. 64–65]. It is unclear whether Oortman had this installed because illusionistic ceiling paintings were on the rise in bourgeois interiors, or whether she wished to suggest that it was a genuine skylight (a type of feature mentioned regularly in inventories and floor plans from the period, particularly in or near the kitchen). Regardless, great attention was devoted to the daylight in the best kitchen. On the back wall, just below the dome, are four windows with *sassinetten*, wooden secondary windows with painted silk panels instead of glass panes. The scenes are derived from prints by the Amsterdam engraver and bookseller Petrus Schenk, who worked from Chinese models. The rays of the sun bring the scenes to life, even as the silk panels filter the light.

The Chinese influence in the decorative scheme is consistent with one of the room's main purposes. The best kitchen was the place to show off Chinese porcelain in wall cabinets with glass doors [FIG. 39]. Just like the pewter cupboard in the kitchen, the porcelain cabinet has a dark-red back wall against which the blue-and-white tableware is symmetrically arranged, creating a stunning contrast. The cabinet, along with the room's ceiling, doors and door frames, is painted in a European style with acanthus vines and bouquets, a choice that heightens the unity of the room. The outer edges of the shelves, however, are inspired mainly by Asian aesthetics: black paint, glazed and varnished, and a sprinkling of gold flakes make them resemble lacquerware.

In this doll's house, many of the items in the porcelain cabinet are indeed made of porcelain. Such miniatures were imported from China by the early seventeenth century and later from Japan as well, but they were often somewhat oversized for a doll's house. Instead, they were displayed in special cabinets or alongside larger pieces of porcelain. Nevertheless, Oortman chose to include some of these pieces in the cabinet, such as a set of five sharply tapered bowls for the Japanese tea ceremony. They look somewhat out of proportion to the other items on the shelves. She also ordered custom-made porcelain, including a set of twelve dishes from China. All are decorated with a painting of a duck in a landscape, bordered with flowers and stylized figures in panels on the rim of the dish. The decoration is characteristic of early seventeenth-century Kraak ware, which was made specifically for export and was still abundantly present in households in the Republic during Oortman's time. Cracks in the bottoms of several dishes suggest the difficulty of producing such small items. Once again we see to what lengths the collector went to create a convincing interior to scale, from deliberately ordering an outdated style because it was found in the typical Dutch porcelain cabinet, to demanding the utmost craftsmanship from the potter to achieve such small sizes.

Multi-coloured porcelain in the Japanese Kakiemon style reached the Dutch Republic around 1680, after blue-and-white Kraak ware. Oortman also had this made to order: three plates with phoenixes, a set of nine smaller plates with blossoming branches and five matching bowls. They brought her porcelain cabinet completely up to date and made it extraordinarily valuable. Six of the nine Kakiemon plates

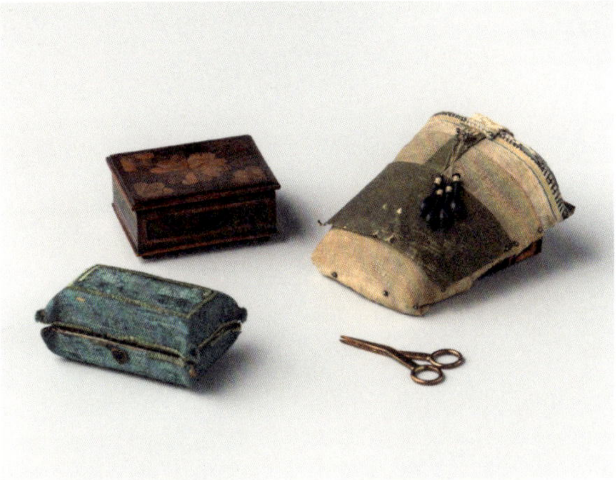

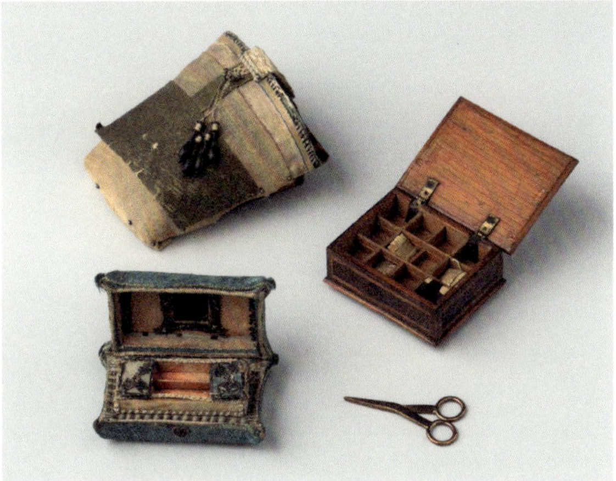

40
Sewing and mending were skills that every woman had to master. Both the sewing pillow (trimmed with silver galloon) and the lacemaking pillow (lined with tortoiseshell) are executed in an exquisite and costly fashion

41
The hole in the seat and cushion of the potty chair allows young children to relieve themselves into the pot on the shelf below. Playing with the rings and the bell on the tray would keep them entertained for a while

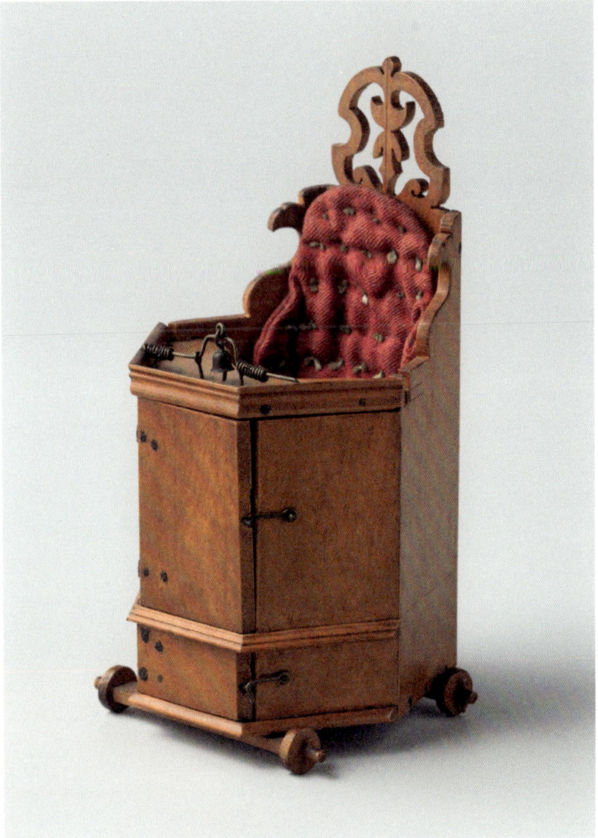

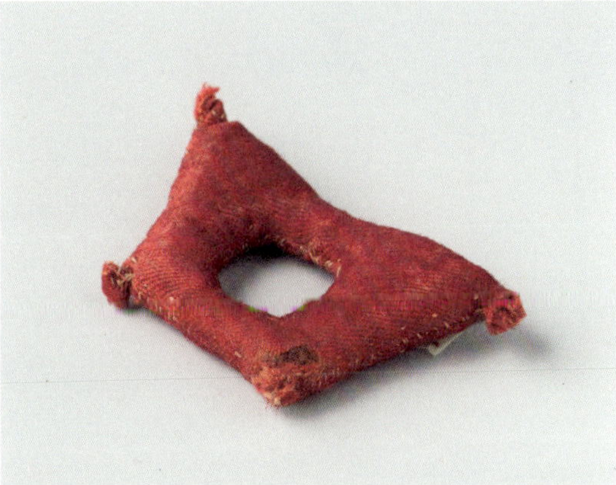

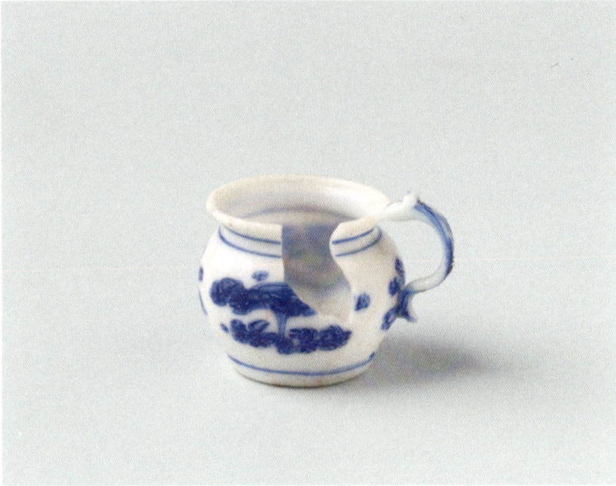

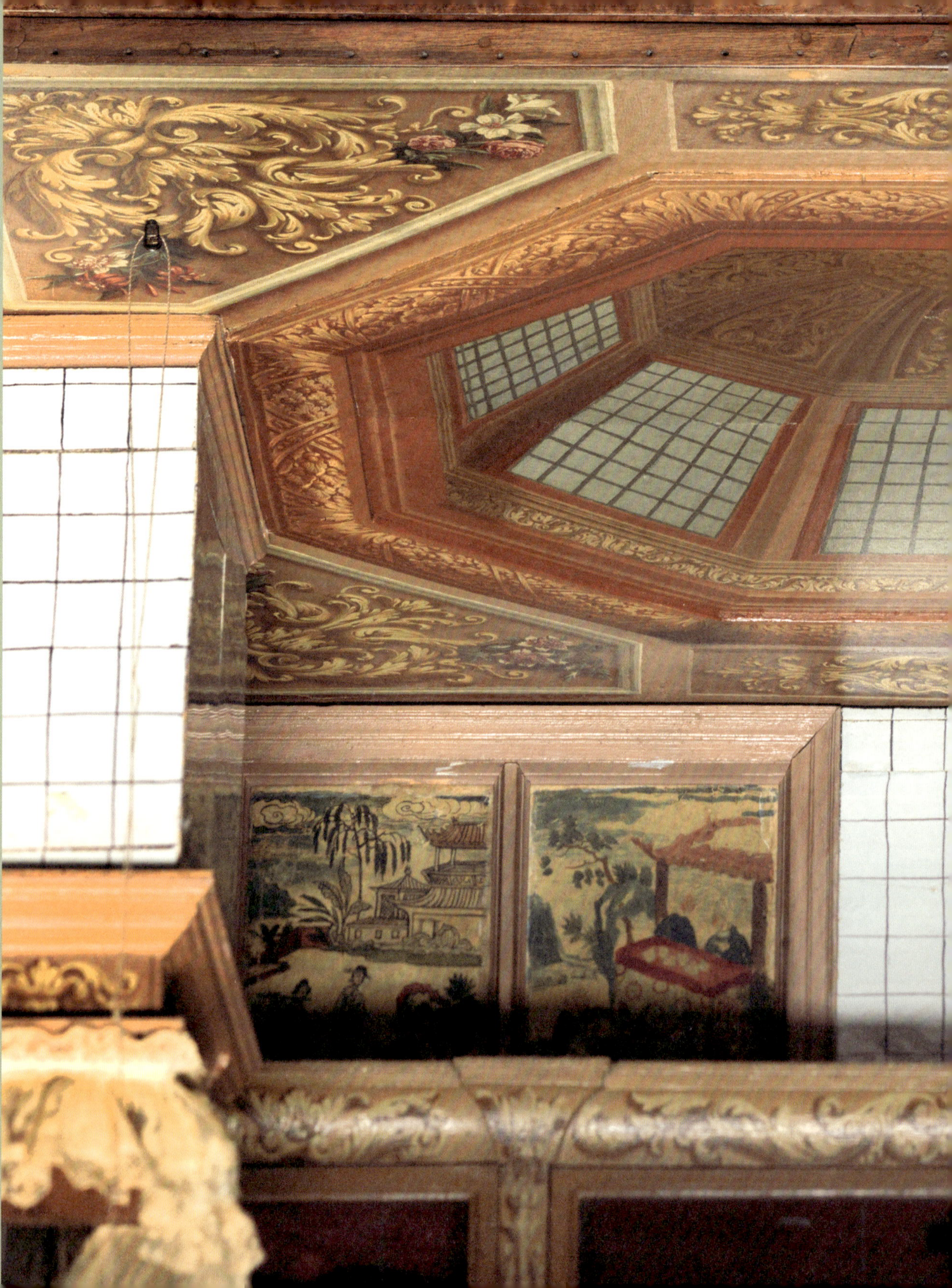

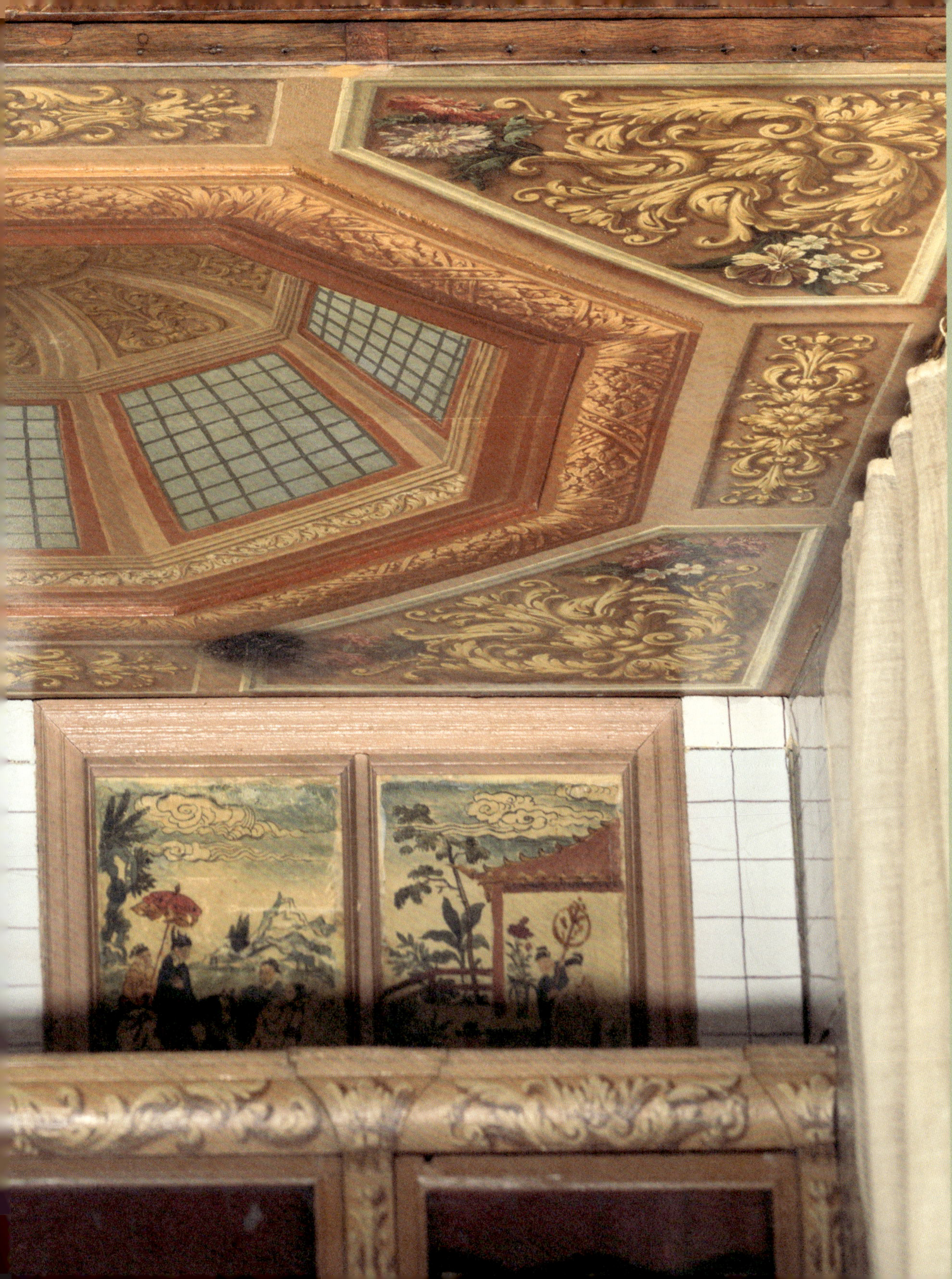

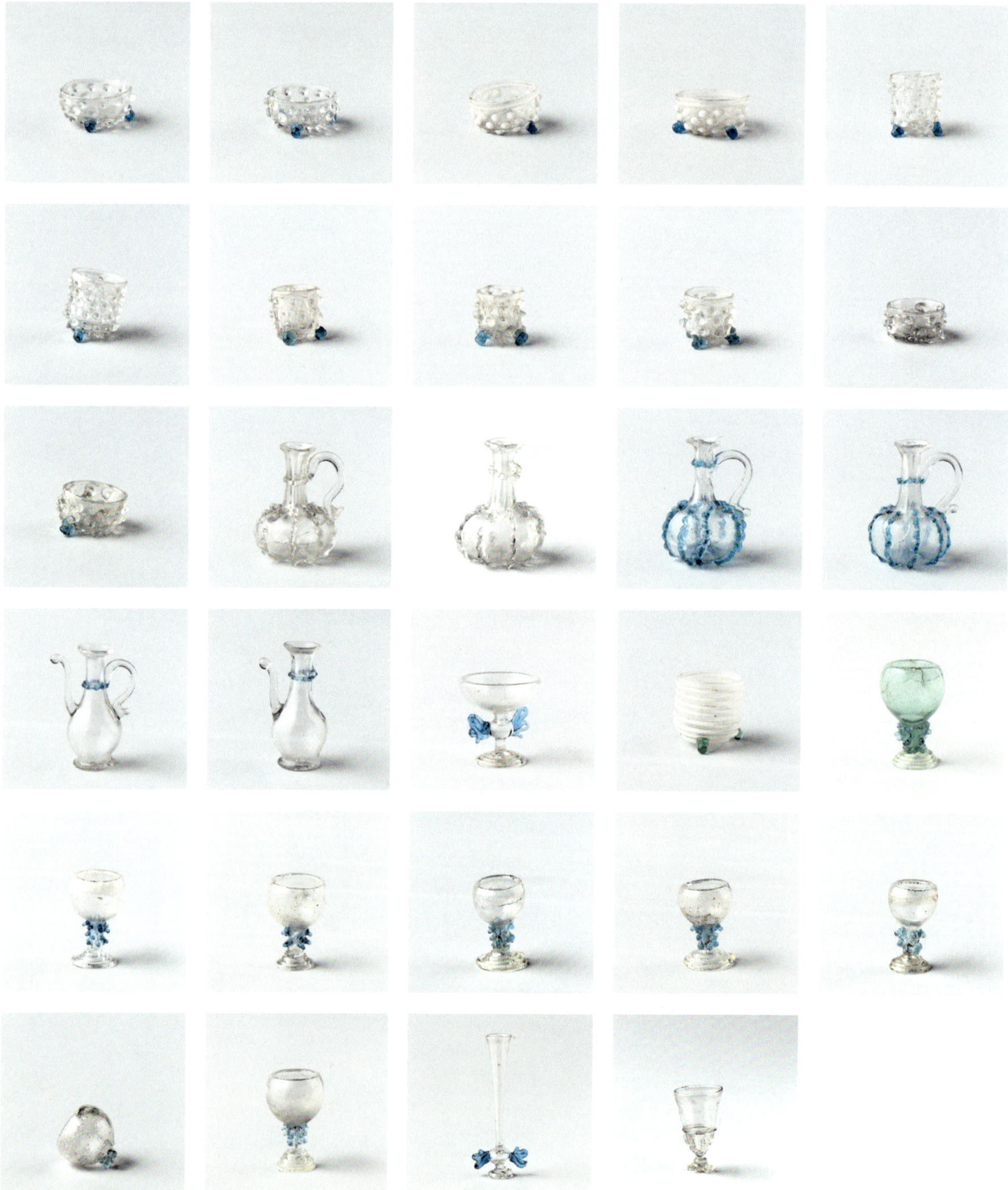

42
Inside the lower doors of the porcelain cabinet are various carafes and glasses for beer and for red and white wine

even received a place of honour on the mantelpiece. More complex forms such as teapots, cups and covered jars simply could not be made of porcelain, so instead she opted for glass. The collection as a whole took her visitors' breath away. Glauburg noted that the porcelain was this room's most remarkable feature and that it was crafted with the greatest delicacy after models sent to Asia for that purpose.

The cabinet's lower doors were also opened for the German guests. There the glassware was kept [FIG. 42]. Some of it has in all likelihood been lost over time; the shelves were originally full. Six decanters remain, as well as eight rummers for white wine and twelve small transparent glass cups and beakers with blue feet for beer. This is a typical collection of glassware for daily use in a wealthy household. Four other glasses, for red wine, are in a more luxurious Venetian style.

The practical storage space for the glassware indicates that the best kitchen was not merely designed to impress; it was also a functional space. That explains why it is directly connected to the kitchen. A window makes it easy to look into each room from the other, and the door between the two rooms can actually be opened and shut. Furthermore, Appel's painting shows that a maid was at work here. She sat comfortably with her feet on a foot-warmer or stove and a sewing pillow on her lap, doing her mending. Her sewing kit and lace-making pillow are within easy reach on the folding table beside her [FIG. 40]. Meanwhile, she keeps an eye on two young children. The youngest is still seated in the potty chair, a child's chair on wheels with a hole in the seat beneath which a chamber pot was placed [FIG. 41]. The cushion has a neat opening in the middle. We also see evidence of a house pet: a cage for a parrot, which, like the Asian porcelain, brought distant parts of the world into this Dutch home [FIG. 43].

Notably absent from the room is a large dining table; like the furniture in the *zaal*, it was cleared away when not in use. The oval drop-leaf table against the wall, beside which the maid is seated, could be moved to the middle of the room and unfolded [FIG. 44]. For larger groups, one or more trestle or folding tables could be set up, depending on the number of diners. One is stored in the attic [FIG. 54]. Once the table was laid with attractive linen tablecloths, porcelain and silver, its simple mechanism was concealed from view and it became the temporary focal point of the dining room.

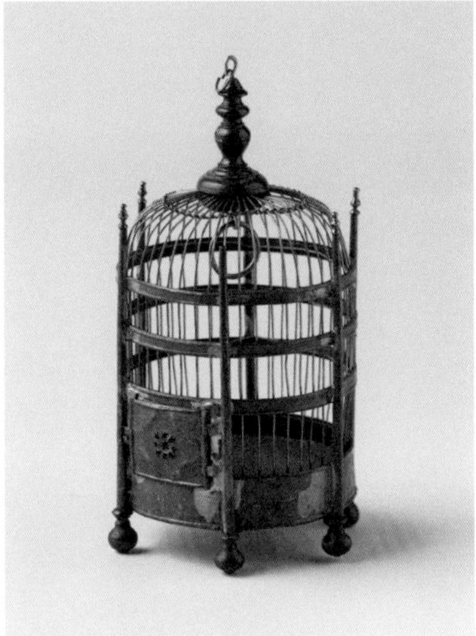

43
Parrots were kept as pets. This parrot cage has a removable drinking bowl and a door that can actually open and close

44
The drop-leaf table with turned legs is a practical piece of furniture: when partly folded, it can be placed against the wall, and when fully extended, it can serve as a full-sized dining table

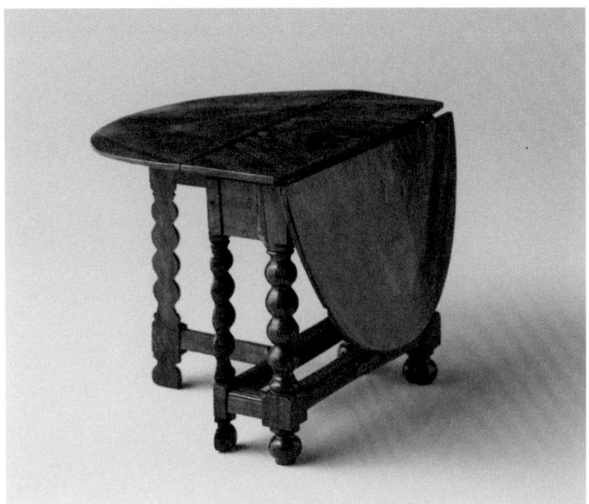

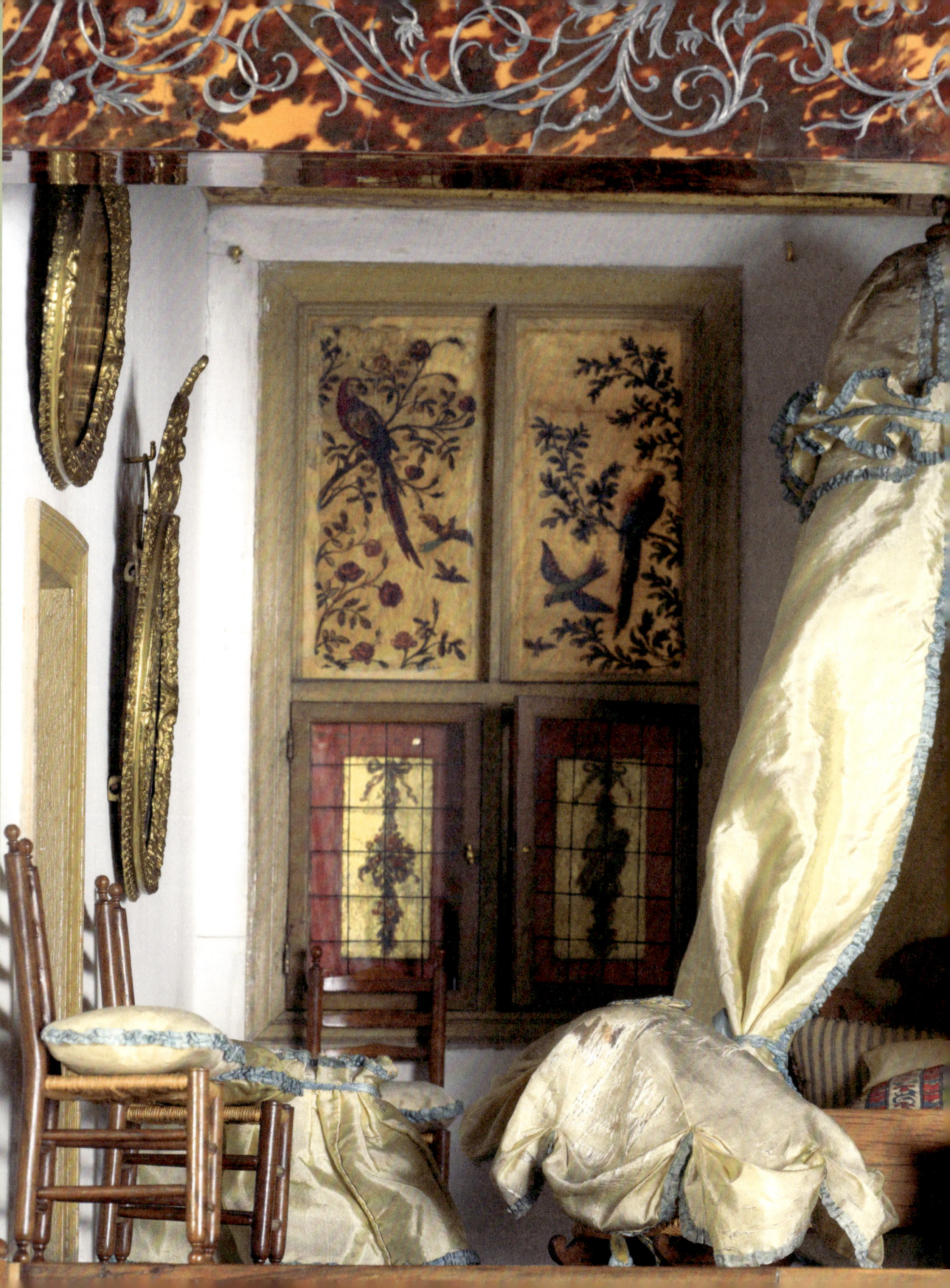

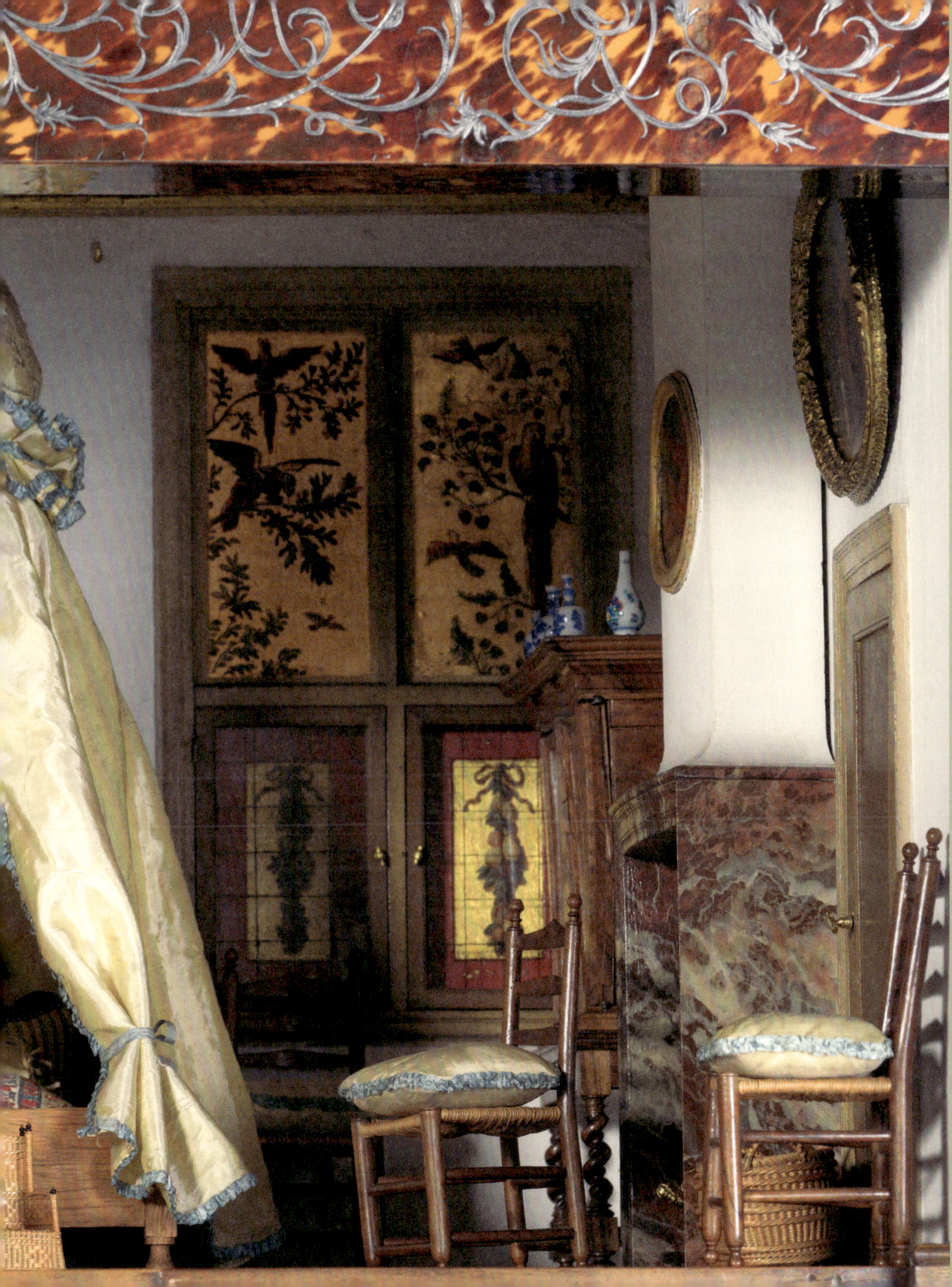

CHILDREN'S ROOM

The children's room, located on the right of the top floor, was once as lively as the best kitchen [PP. 68–69]. Here, too, Appel painted children: a standing girl and a younger child sitting on the lap of a man wearing the regional dress of farmers and fishermen from Waterland. His exact role in the doll's house remains unclear. He may have been a visitor or a servant.

The children's room is not immediately recognizable as such, especially now that the dolls are gone. Only the cradle and the small wicker chair still suggests the room's purpose [FIGS. 47, 48]; toys and other traces of youthful presence are absent. Rooms used for sleeping in Oortman's time did not yet possess the intimate character we associate with the bedroom today. Just like the reception room with a bed, which was temporarily transformed into a lying-in chamber after a birth, the children's room combines public and private functions. It is richly furnished, with a marble fireplace and luxurious furniture. The large canopy bed dominates the room; its canopy, attached to the ceiling, gives it the form of a tent. Its colours are coordinated with the cradle's light-yellow silk upholstery with blue ruffles, the cushions on the chairs, and the tablecloth.

A great deal of effort went into making the children's bed comfortable [FIG. 49]. The base of the bed is not a wooden platform, as was still very common, but a woven structure of taut webbing that is slightly springy. At first glance, the mattress looks rather small for the bedstead, but the yellow and blue silk braid with which it is trimmed tells us it was made to accompany the canopy. It is stuffed with down – a filling that is very comfortable to sink into and considerably more expensive than straw, horsehair or sea grass. The chintz blanket has a fine pattern that was undoubtedly specially selected for the doll's house. Meanwhile, the youngest family member was not forgotten. The osier cradle (made of woven willow) has a wooden base with rocking legs, which the mother or a maid would keep in motion with a cord [FIG. 48]. Under the elegantly draped cradle cover are another down mattress and pillow. This cover completely protected the baby from draughts and cold; in those days, there was less concern about oxygen and ventilation.

The decorative bed curtains and crib cover were insufficient on their own to retain warmth. In winter, the fire often had to be stoked all through

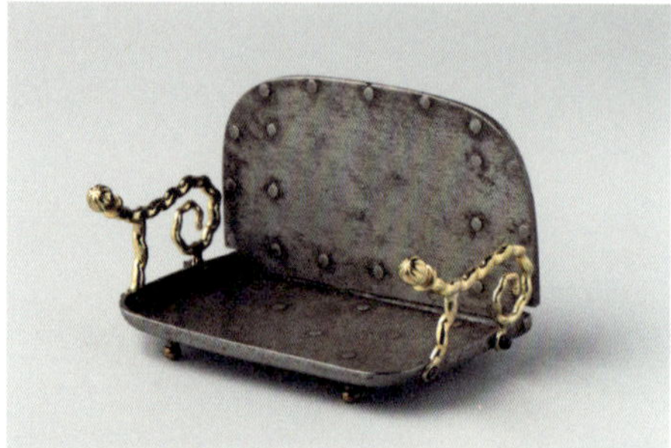

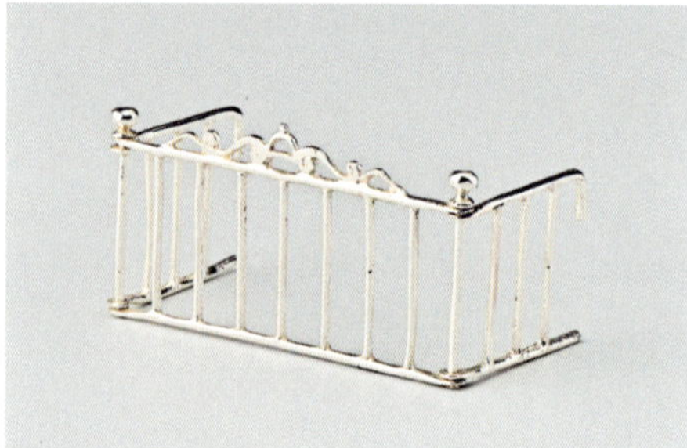

45, 46
The fire basket keeps the ashes in the hearth neatly contained. In Petronella Dunois's doll's house, there is also a fireguard in the children's room to protect the younger ones

47
The wicker chair is very small and suitable for young children

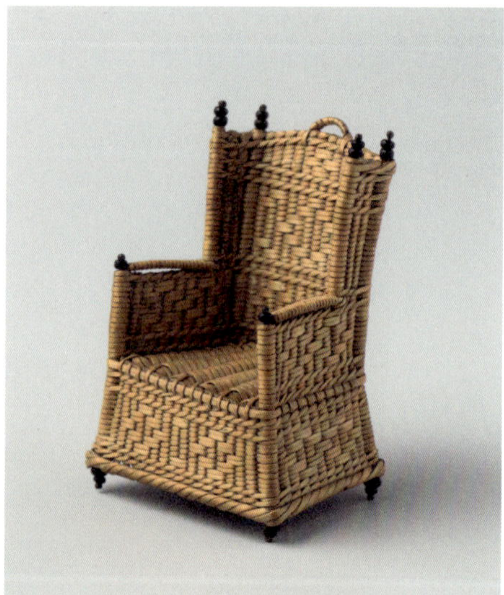

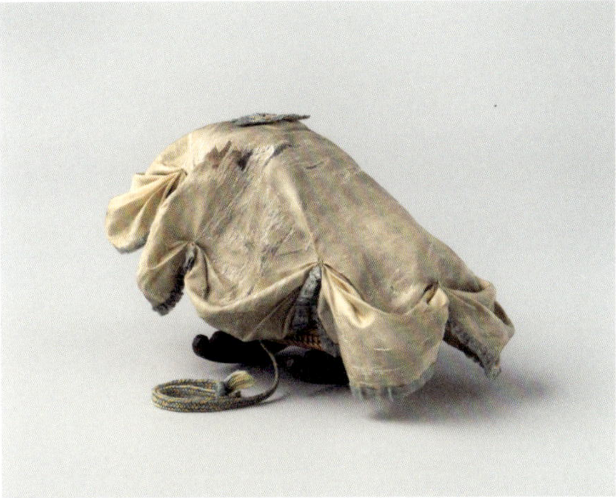

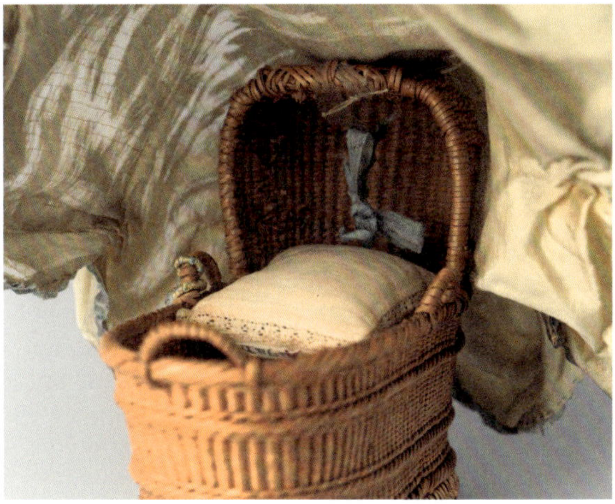

48
This cradle illustrates how the care of small children is influenced by views on comfort and status. The cover holds in warmth and is coordinated with the other textiles in the interior

49
This bed for a child has a down mattress and a chintz coverlet. The colour of the canopy sets the tone for the rest of the room's decor; not only the cradle cover but also the pillows are executed in light yellow silk

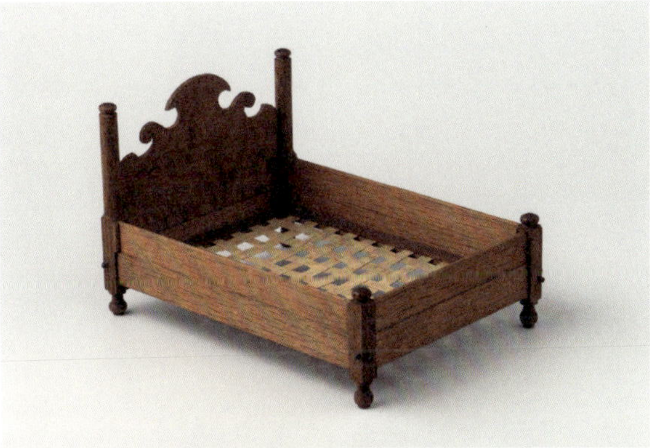

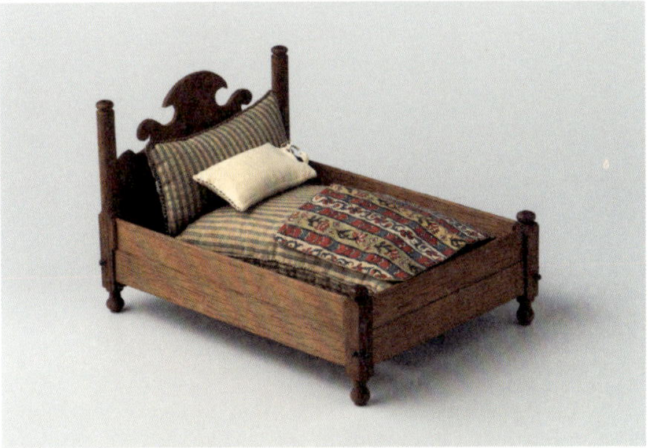

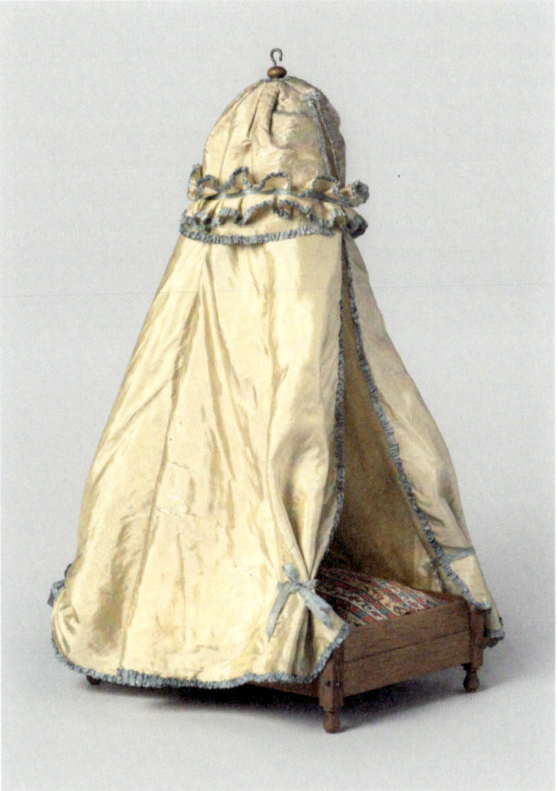

the night. On the top floor, the children's room is the only space with a fireplace to provide heat and light. The iron fire basket in the hearth, meticulously crafted to resemble real examples, complete with riveted iron reinforcing bands, was essential for effective heat distribution and for keeping the floor clean [FIG. 45]. Notably absent is a fireguard – present in the children's room of Petronella Dunois's doll's house [FIG. 46] – to protect young children from burns.

Glauburg wrote little about this room, finding only the set of imitation porcelain vases on the cabinet worthy of mention [FIG. 53]. It was evidently striking to the Germans that in Amsterdam, porcelain could be displayed on a cabinet even in a room meant for children. The rest of the decoration is equally distinguished. The paintings on the walls are not surprising; they were omnipresent in the homes of the Republic's burgher class. However, the fact that the frames match that of the large oval mirror (which sports an additional crest) demonstrates a high degree of refinement [FIGS. 50–52]. The impressive decoration of the windows also contributes to the room's allure. The upper windows, like those in the best kitchen, are fitted with *sassinetten*; these depict parrots either flying around or perched on flowering branches. The leaded-glass windows below have external shutters that can be opened and closed. When they are closed, we see a decorative painting with garlands alluding to the four seasons: flowers for spring; sheaves of corn for summer; grapes and apples for autumn; and citrus fruits for winter. This was not only pleasing to the eye but also served as a subtle reference to the stages of human life.

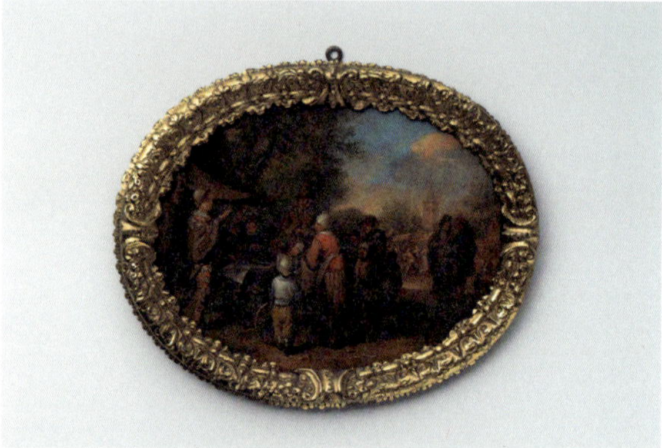

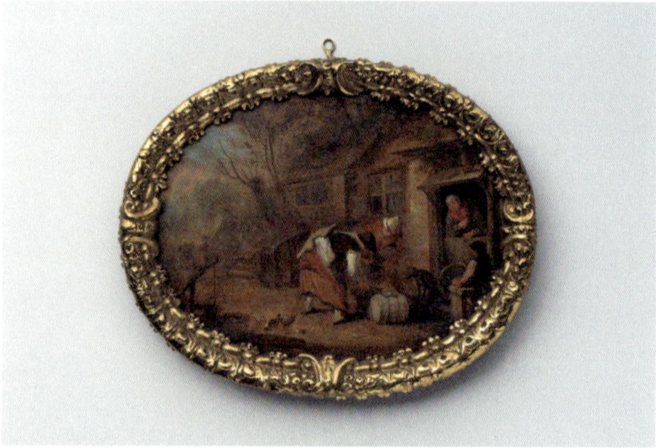

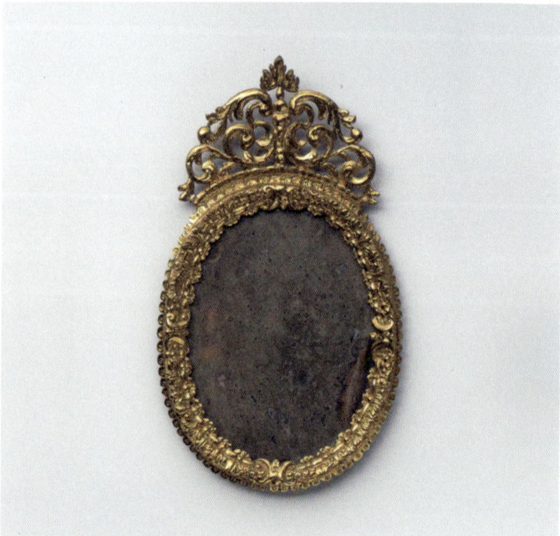

50–52
The paintings depict scenes with a quack doctor and a woman street vendor. The maker of the gilt frames also supplied the frame for the mirror

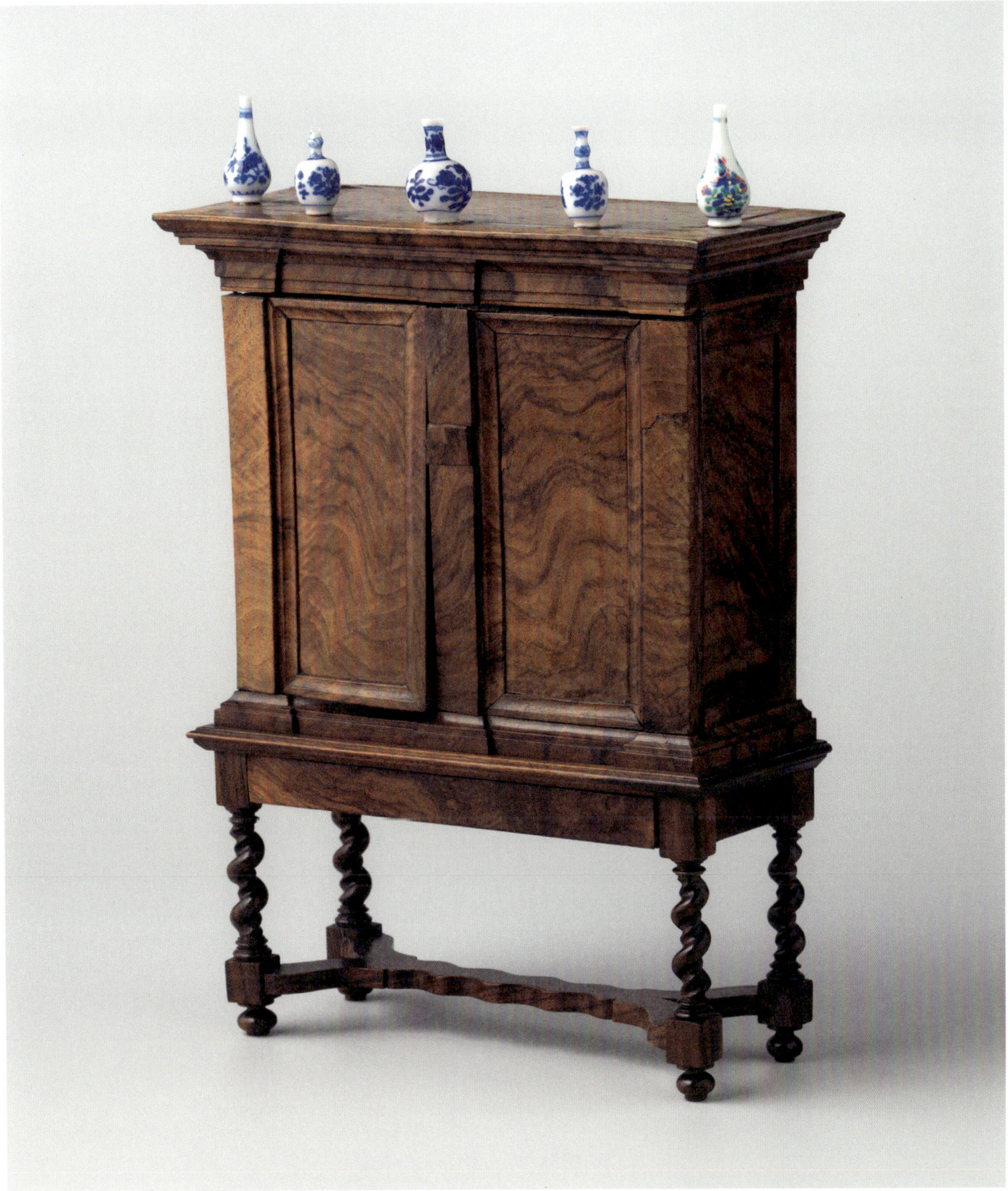

53
This fashionable cabinet on a stand is in use as a wardrobe. Inside its double doors are a pair of stockings and a pair of trousers

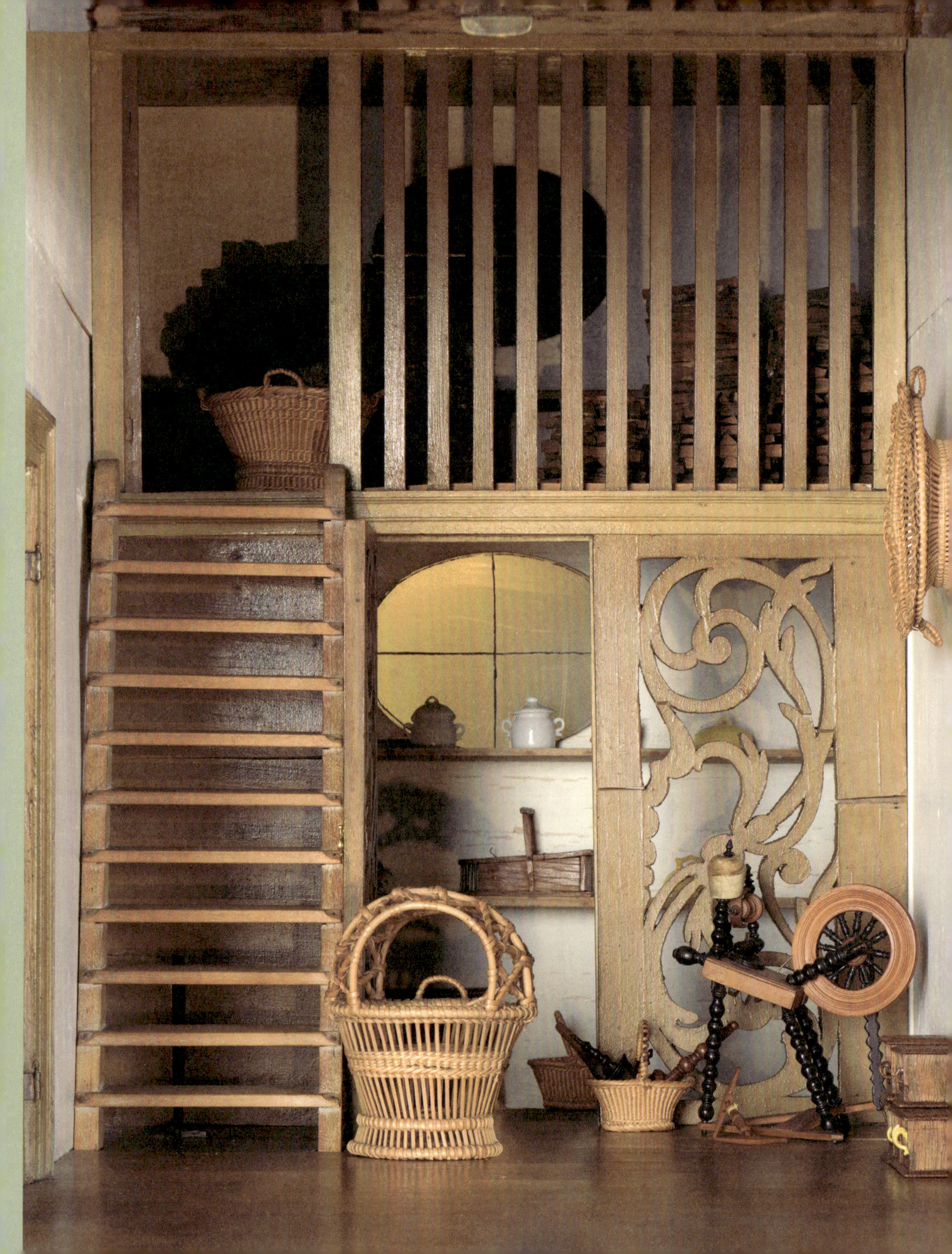

STORAGE ATTIC

The top floor of a seventeenth-century Dutch doll's house always includes areas for storage and household chores such as laundry, as well as rooms for the staff. This was often the case in real houses too. These are the simplest rooms, with whitewashed walls and wooden ceilings, where no guests were received and the family did not go either – except for the lady of the house. She was responsible not only for the decoration of the elegant rooms where guests were received, but also for general household management, in which the attic played an indispensable role.

Oortman divided the attic of her doll's house into several sections. The middle room on the top floor has areas for peat, provisions and general storage [P. 74]. These are the only parts of the doll's house where no dolls were present. The stored supplies stand as silent witnesses to the work of maintaining the household. The sections are separated by a partition, with ornately carved doors that close off the provision area. To the left, a staircase leads to the peat loft. In front of it is storage space for all the items not used daily: a folding table [FIG. 54], a mirror, baskets, a waffle iron for winter treats (now lost), and a spinning wheel, in which Glauburg took a special interest. Made of 'artfully turned' ebony and maple wood, it is fully functional [FIG. 60]. The treadle that sets the wheel in motion is hinged with small pieces of leather. The bobbin with thread makes it complete. This high level of detail and verisimilitude at such a small scale understandably excited great admiration.

The same is true of the rat-and-mouse trap behind the wooden doors in the storage area for provisions [FIG. 62]. Part of the mechanism has been lost, but originally the hinged trapdoor would snap shut when the bait hook in the cage was disturbed. This type of trap was essential in a place where food was kept. Three storage jars, two with lids and another covered with a piece of chamois leather, are on the shelf above the trap [FIG. 56]. On the floor, there is also a basket for groceries or for taking food from the attic to the kitchen.

The supplies of peat and firewood are stored high and dry in the loft [FIGS. 57, 58]. Although peat produced considerable smoke – necessitating thorough cleaning and regular whitewashing – it burned more steadily than wood and was the primary fuel in the cities of the Republic. In large houses, the stock was

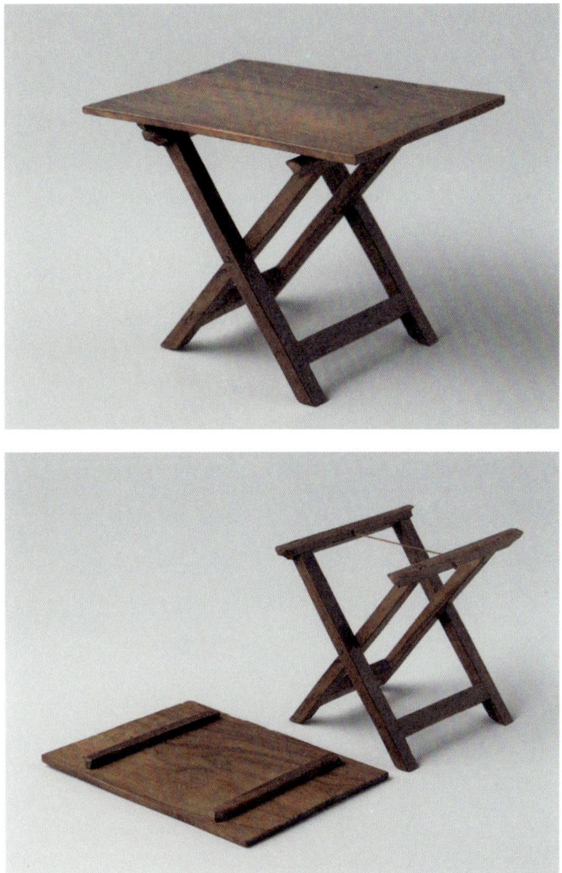

54
The items stored in the attic include a trestle table, which can be set up quickly for visitors

55
Foot stoves that were not in use in the summer were stored in the attic

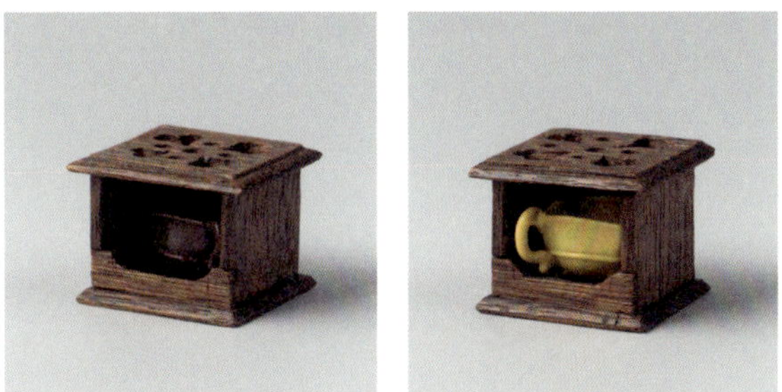

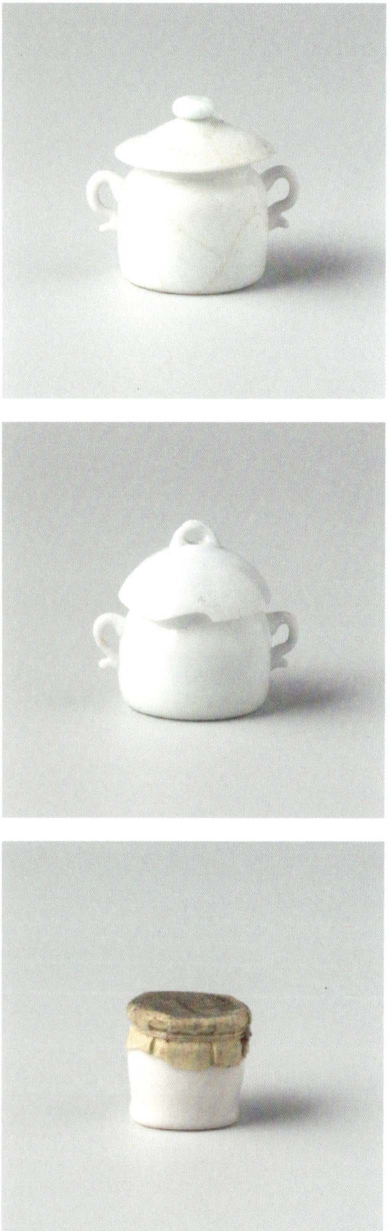

56
In the storage attic are jars
of preserved foodstuffs

replenished monthly, and many households purchased a large additional supply twice a year, in early autumn and again in winter. While this was regarded as a man's job, in practice the task was often undertaken by women. In the doll's house, everything is neatly organized: the miniature briquettes (made of real peat) are stacked against the wall. They could be carried from the attic to the house's hearths in large baskets. In the working kitchen, a full basket can be found between the pewter cupboard and the fireplace. The loft was always well stocked with peat for heating the house, preparing food and boiling water for laundry and cleaning.

In addition to its permanent fireplaces, the house also had smaller, mobile heat sources, which were stored in the attic. Against the right wall is a whole stack of wooden foot stoves, all still equipped with their fire pans [FIG. 55]. These receptacles – normally earthenware, but in this case made of glass like the cooking utensils – were filled with glowing peat. The foot stoves themselves were inexpensive and simply designed. There is also a fire basket, into which a fire pot or a tin of hot coals could likewise be placed. Such fire baskets can be found in every lying-in chamber – including Oortman's, where one is placed in the middle of the room, covered with a red cloth [SEE FIG. 15]. The baby could be tended to beside the basket without catching a chill, and wet nappies were dried over the wicker hood.

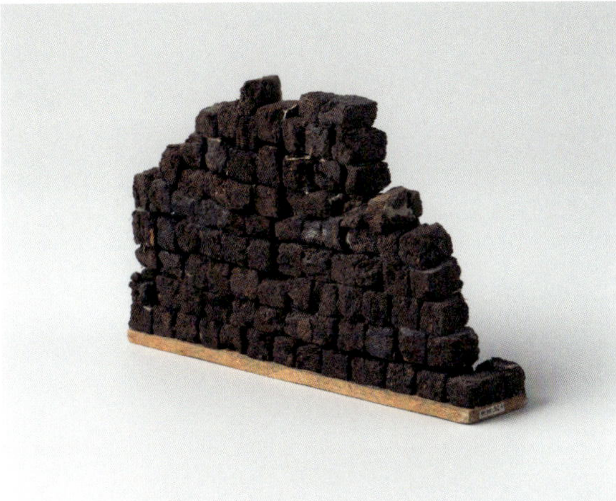

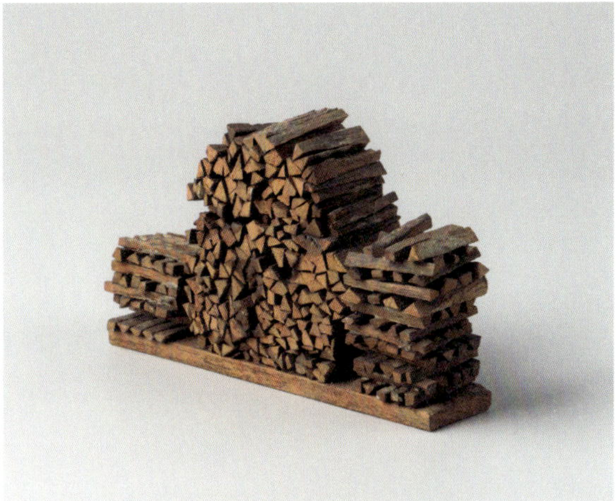

57, 58
Stacks of dry peat and firewood are stored under the roof. The briquettes are made of real peat

59–62
In many dolls' houses, including Petronella Dunois's, miniature objects such as mouse traps and spinning wheels were made of silver. Oortman, in contrast, had everything made from the appropriate materials. Both spinning wheels really work

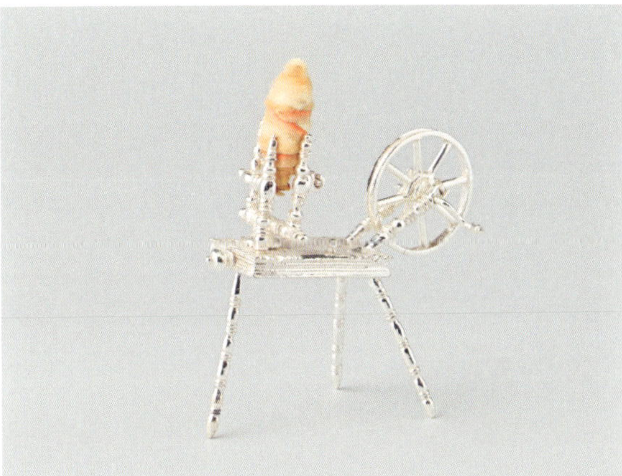

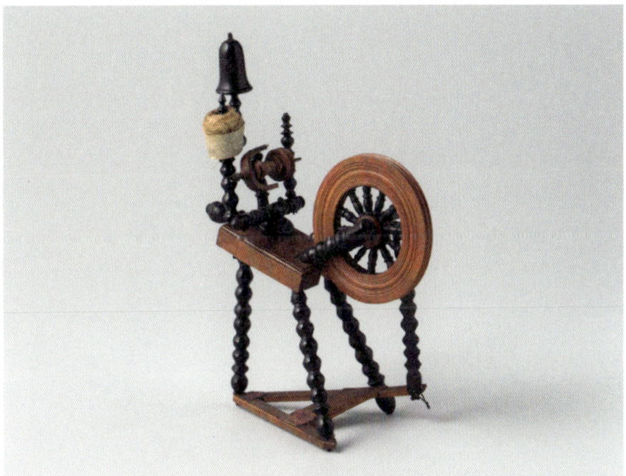

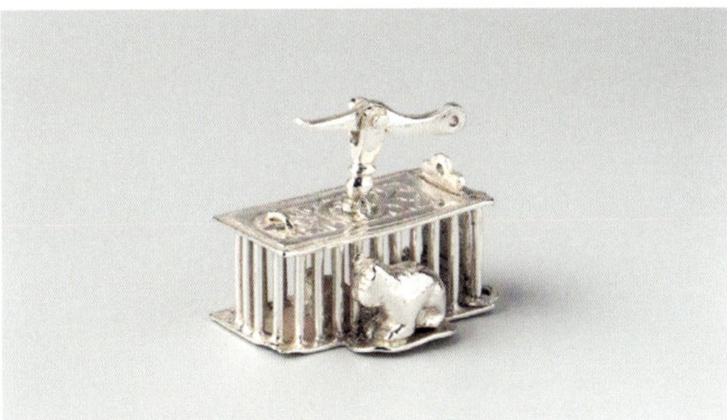

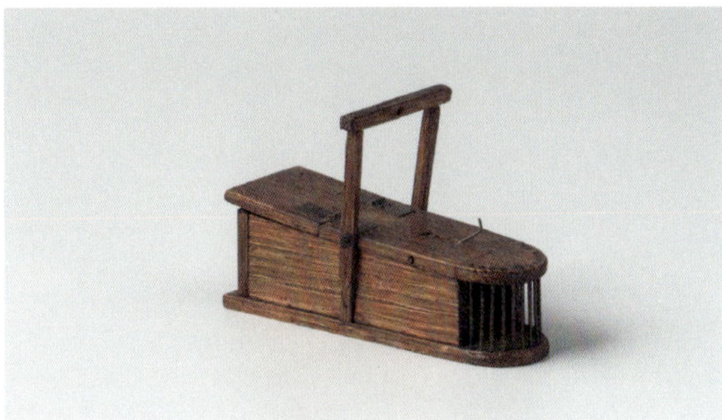

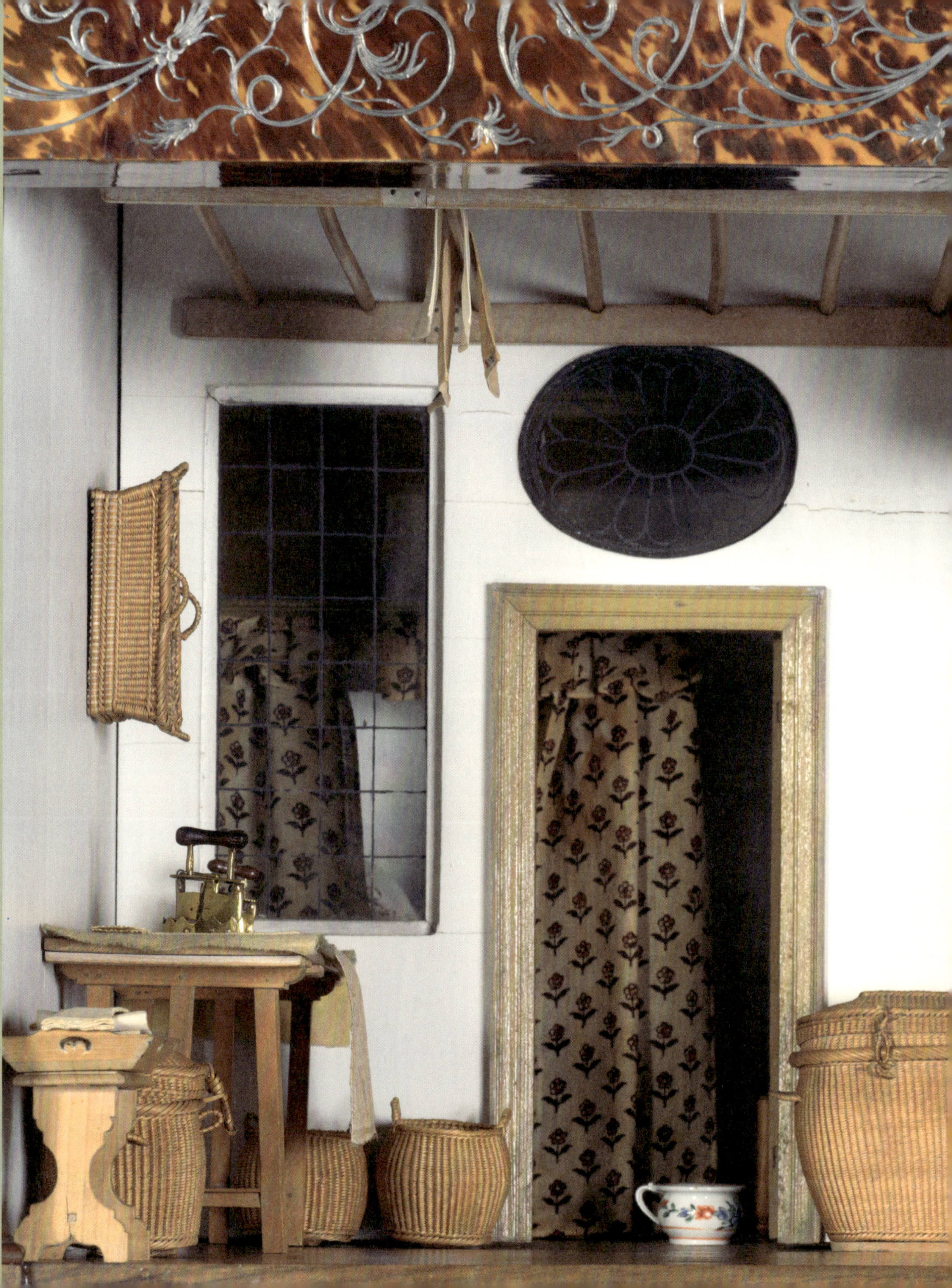

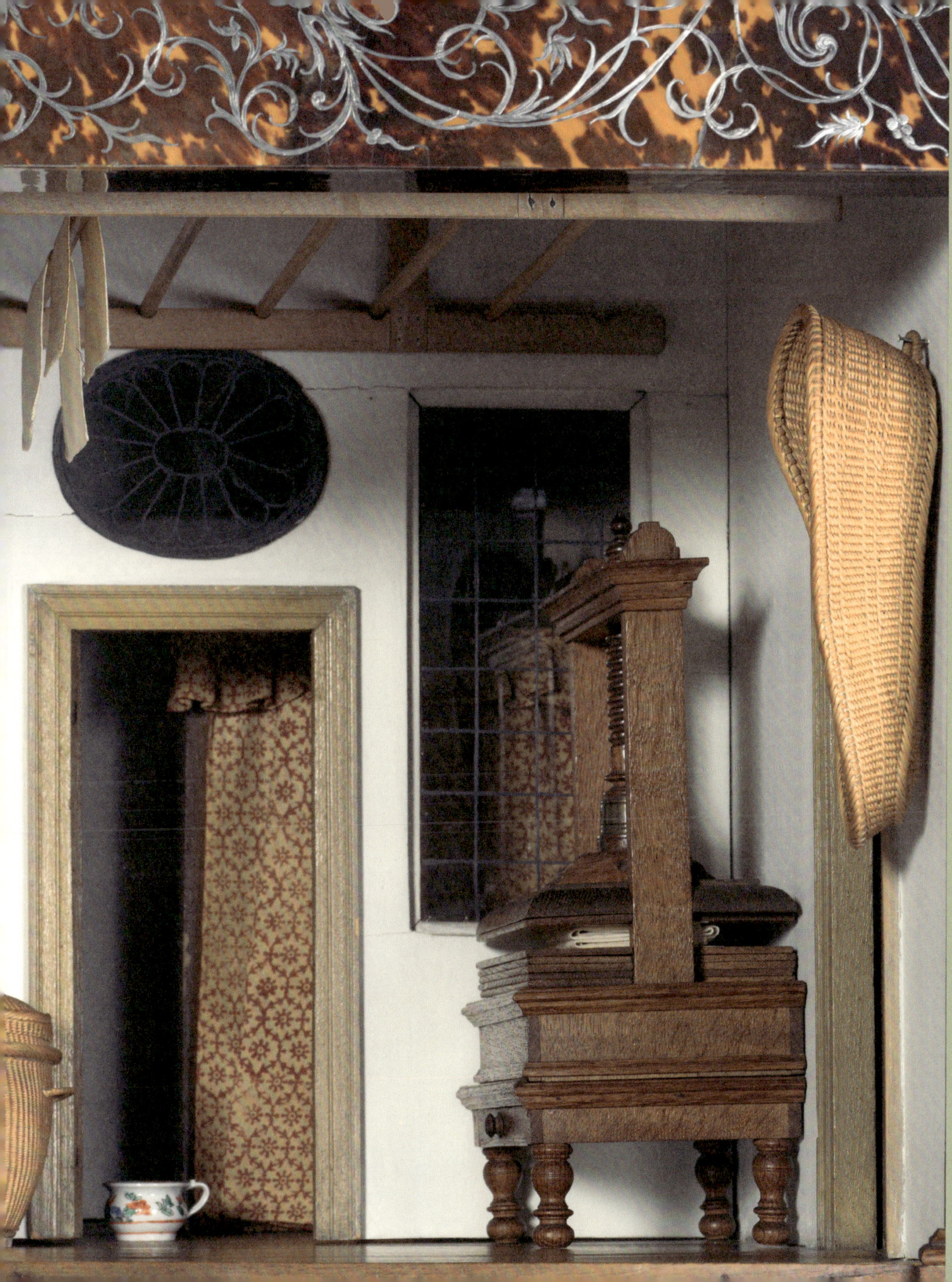

LAUNDRY ATTIC AND MAIDS' ROOMS

In the laundry attic, the laundress was originally hard at work [PP. 78–79 AND FIG. 2]. Here, everything revolved around the labour-intensive process of preparing the clean laundry: ironing, mangling, stiffening and pressing. Crisp, snow-white linen symbolized the house's cleanliness and, by extension, the family's respectability. The seventeenth-century term *zindelijkheid* encompassed both meanings: the effort to keep everything clean and hygienic, and the sense of beauty and propriety. The laundry was therefore one of the most important household tasks – and also the first to be entrusted to others when funds allowed, as it was demanding, time-consuming work.

In the doll's house, the laundry was sent out. The dirty shirts, bed linens, towels, tablecloths and napkins left the house in a large basket secured with a padlock to be washed elsewhere, where running water was close at hand [FIG. 63]. Only linen was soaked in soapy water; woollen or silk outer garments were merely brushed and aired. The wet linen was then bleached in the sun, rinsed again, and returned home still damp. It was all hung to dry in the attic, on the clothes rods attached to the beamed ceiling. There we find several of Oortman's precious napkins, with the mirror monogram 'BO' (Brandt–Oortman) and two birds woven into them [FIG. 67]. Personalized linen damask such as this was among a household's most valuable linen – no wonder the laundry basket was securely locked.

The linen was mangled and ironed to make it smooth and neat again. Against the left wall is a trestle table with a thick woollen ironing cloth [FIG. 68]. The irons, luxuriously crafted in brass, could be kept on the matching rack when full of hot coals. The napkin that the maid had begun to iron is still lying there. Once linen was wrinkle-free, it was folded and placed in the linen press [FIG. 69]. The crisp folds of a spotless white tablecloth or apron indicated that it was fresh from the cupboard. Next to the table is a wooden bench with a linen basket in which the pressed laundry is neatly stacked [FIG. 70]. In this type of basket or a large hamper (like the one hung on the left wall [FIG. 64]), the housewife or a maid could carry the pressed linen to the linen cupboard in the lying-in chamber – one of the main rooms for receiving guests, where fine linen was used and could be admired [SEE P. 23].

On the right wall of the laundry attic hangs an item for the children's room: a *bakermat* [FIG. 65].

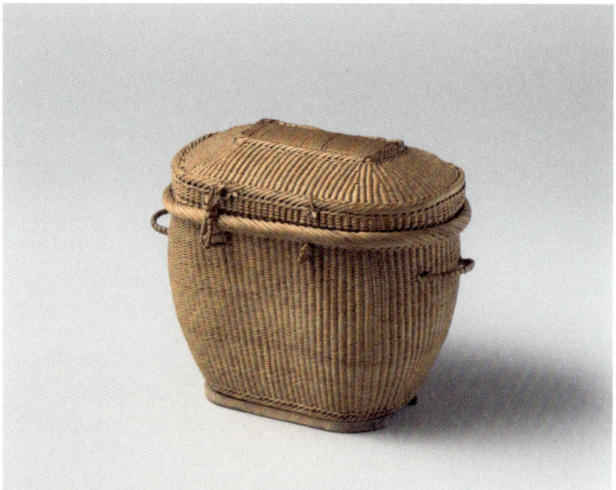

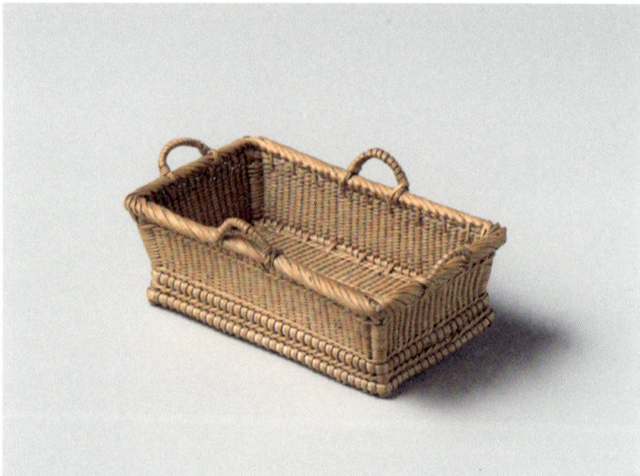

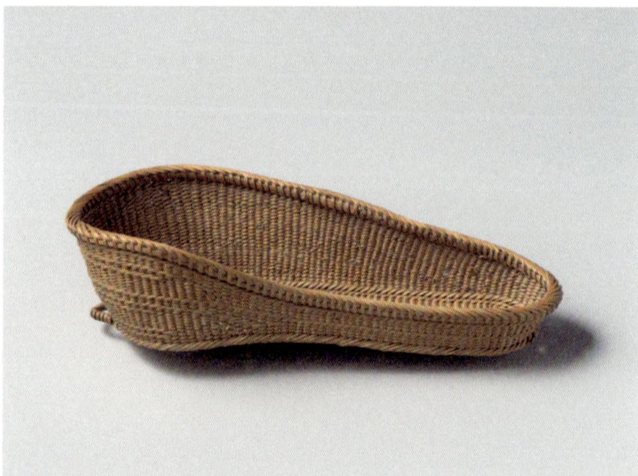

63–65
Dirty laundry was taken to a washing site outside the home in a closed basket. Open baskets were practical for sorting the laundry. An unused *bakermat* cradle hangs on the wall

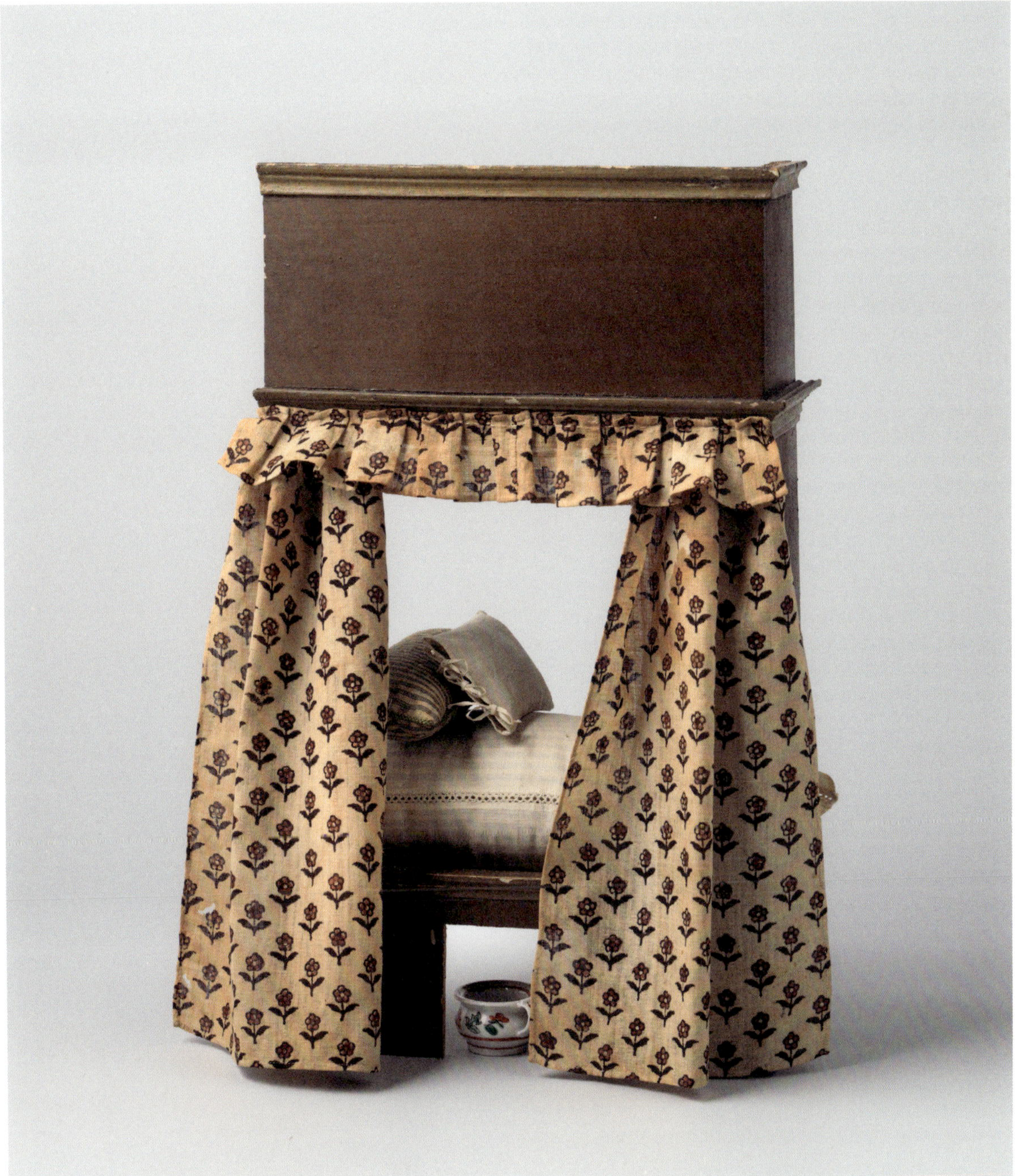

66
The box beds in the maids' quarters were cosy and warm; curtains and valances kept out draughts and retained heat. Thanks to the chamber pot, there was no need for nocturnal visits to the privy downstairs

This type of wicker cradle is found in all seventeenth-century dolls' houses. It is lightweight and therefore easy to move. The mother or the nurse (also referred to as the *baker*) would sit in it with her legs extended to change and feed the baby; the raised edge, used with a cushion, served as a backrest.

Behind the laundry attic are the servants' rooms, which are very sparsely furnished. Here we see box beds, rather than the kind of expensive bed found in the children's room [FIG. 66]. They are simple, but not uncomfortable. The mattresses are stuffed with down, and when the curtains were closed, a box bed retained more heat than the open canopy bed. That was important because, unlike the other rooms with beds, the maids' quarters have no fireplace. The box-bed curtains are made of printed cotton – almost a mass-produced fabric by the late seventeenth century. Yet precisely because it was so commonplace, very few examples have survived. The only other furnishings are a ladder-back chair and a chamber pot, although the latter is made of real Japanese porcelain [SEE FIG. 66]. The interior reflects a certain ambivalence towards domestic staff. On the one hand, it was important to take good care of the resident maids; on the other hand, the difference in social status had to be acknowledged. Their wages were relatively low, and their accommodations were modest. Nevertheless, we have learned from probate inventories that maids quite frequently owned porcelain objects, although more often tea cups than chamber pots.

The realistic irons are the only objects in the laundry attic that Glauburg mentions in his travel account. Did the German guests have no particular interest in the laundry and the living conditions of the staff, or were they so overwhelmed by all the rooms that followed that they could not clearly recall the laundry attic? After all, this was the room where Hendrina began the tour, perhaps because the room was such a vital part of the house. Starting in the attic may not have made for a grand entrance, but it did take visitors straight to the heart of matters, certainly from the perspective of the woman who managed the entire household.

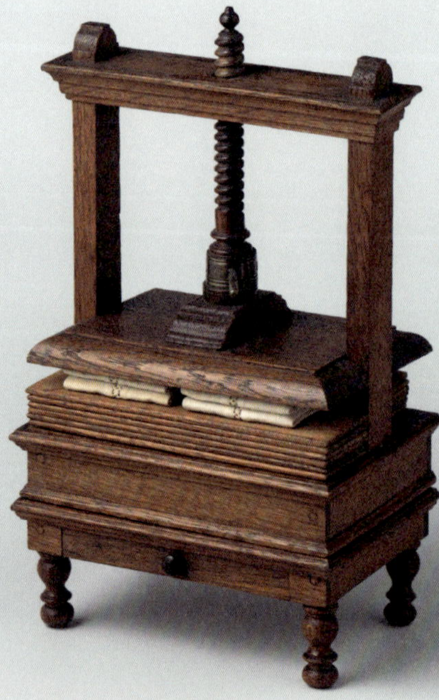

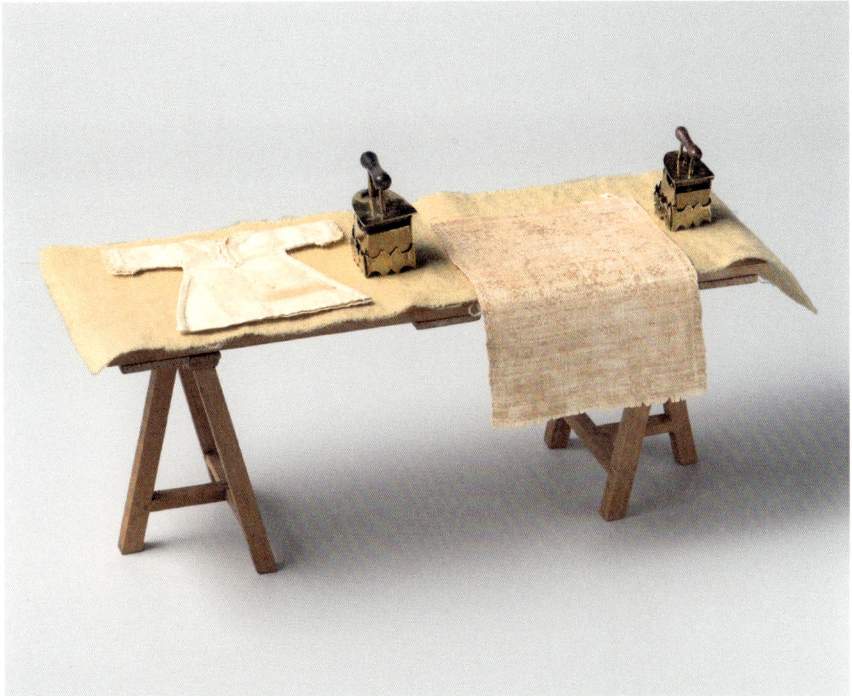

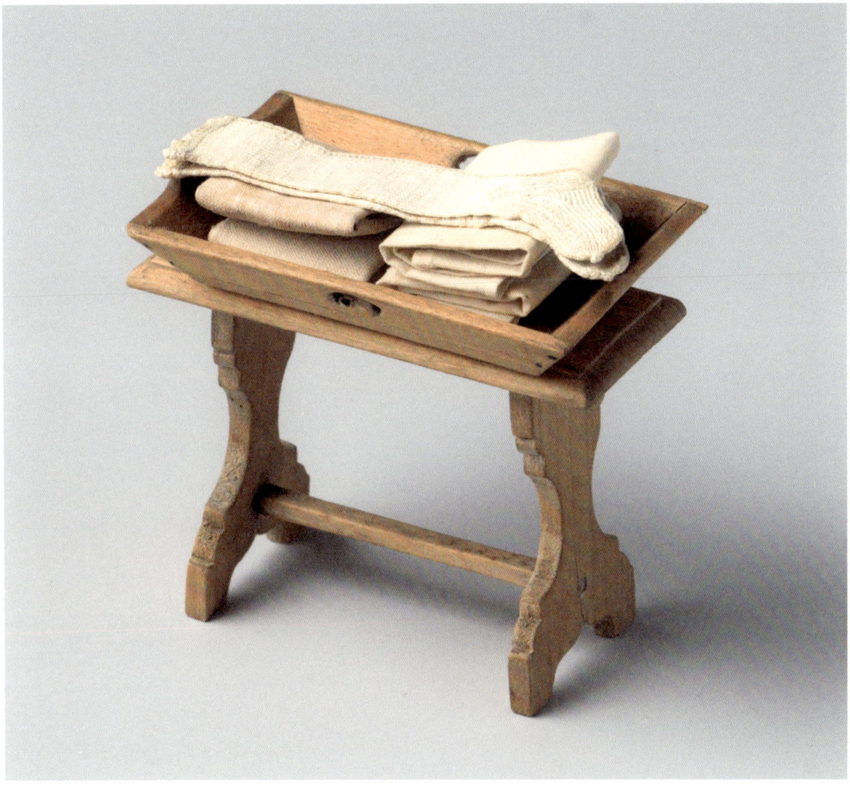

67–70
Clean linen – from tablecloths and napkins to bed linens and undergarments – was ironed, folded and pressed in the attic. The neatly stacked linen was then taken to the linen cupboard in a basket

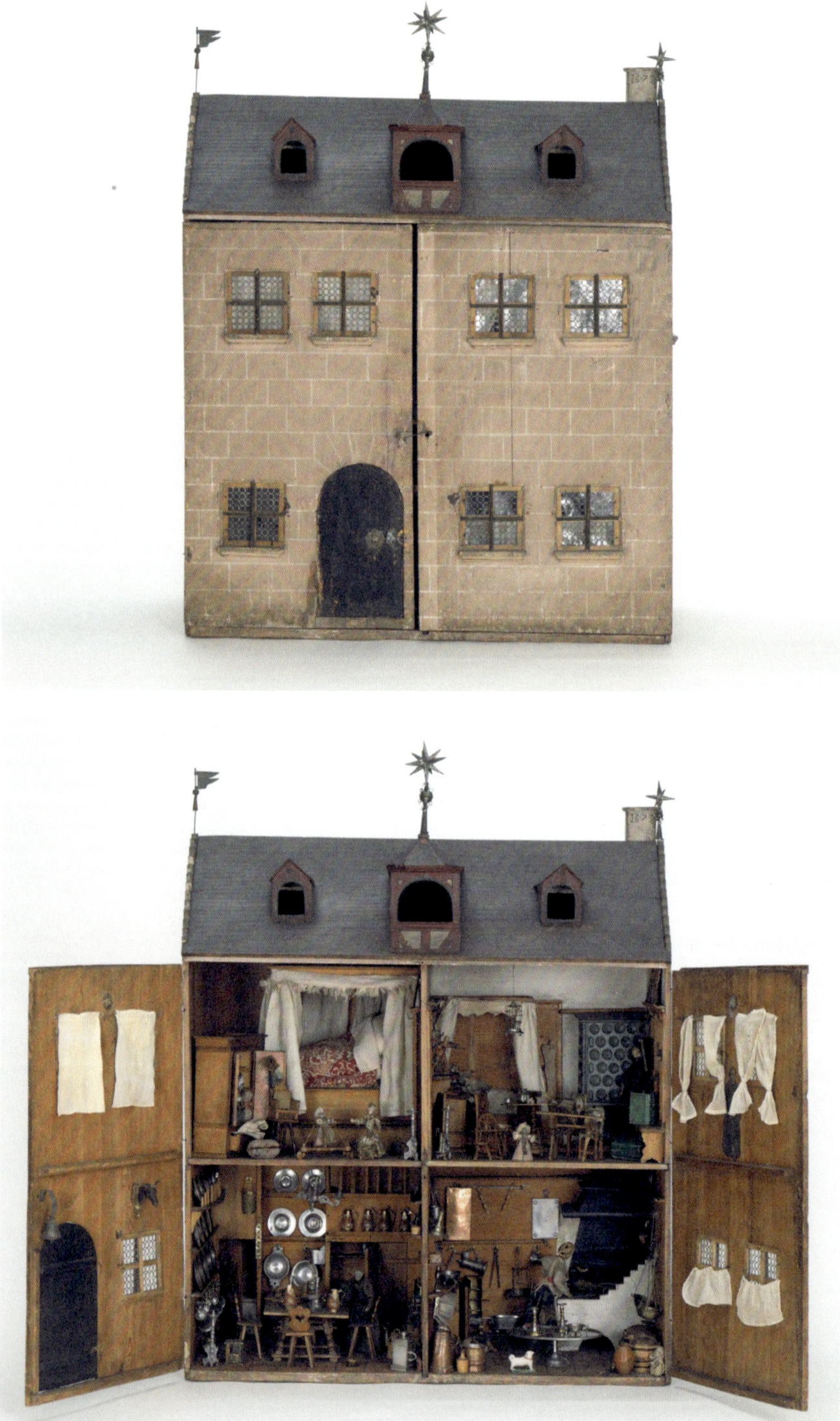

71
Seventeenth-century German dolls' houses, like later examples in England, resembled real houses, with roofs and façades

MINIATURE WORLDS

Petronella Oortman's doll's house was not an entirely unique phenomenon. Dolls' houses were made not only in the Republic, but also in Germany and, from the eighteenth century onwards, in England. There are two substantial differences, however, between the Amsterdam dolls' houses and their foreign counterparts. While Oortman and others in Amsterdam had access to precious materials from the world's farthest corners (such as porcelain, tropical hardwoods, ivory and silver), the main materials we find in German dolls' houses are earthenware, local woods and pewter. Less was spent on crafting the houses, and both in Germany and in England, the work shows less precision. Furthermore, the exteriors of these dolls' houses are like those of actual homes: the closed doors form a façade, as illustrated by a Nuremberg example from 1673 [FIG. 71]. In contrast, Oortman's doll's house takes the usual form of a two-door cabinet on a base, as do those of Petronella de la Court and Petronella Dunois [FIGS. 72, 73]. This is characteristic of late seventeenth-century Dutch storage cabinets; a wardrobe in Oortman's doll's house looks quite similar [SEE FIG. 53].

Because Dutch dolls' houses are designed as cabinets, with compartments full of precious miniatures, they are often compared to collector's cabinets of curiosities. These pieces of furniture, which originated in the early sixteenth century, housed collections of treasures from nature (*naturalia*) and man-made objects (*artificialia*). The combination showcased both the beauty of the natural world and the creative capacity of humankind, thus reflecting the grandeur of God's Creation. It was the entire world encapsulated in a cabinet, to be revealed and admired drawer by drawer. We know that alongside her doll's house De la Court also owned rarities and works of art.

Oortman's familiarity with this culture of collecting is evident from the imitation lacquer cabinet in the tapestry room, with its remarkable collection of shells [SEE FIG. 24]. In fact, creating the interior of her doll's house was a form of collecting in itself; she worked on it for twenty-five years. Just like the objects in a cabinet of curiosities, her miniatures originate from or allude to all four known continents, with Asian objects ranging from Chinese and Japanese porcelain to Indian chintz, a servant and shells from Africa, a parrot cage for a bird from South America, and European items varying from Haarlem linen to Venetian mirrors.

But the similarities extend still further. In the seventeenth century, the household was seen as a reflection of the divine order: God rules over his Creation, the king over his realm and the father over his household. In this scheme, the household was not only the basic building block of society but also a miniature version of Creation. A doll's house therefore offered a glimpse of the world as a whole, much like an art cabinet. The connection between the large and the small seems to be depicted literally on the doors of Petronella Dunois's doll's cabinet [FIG. 73]. The inlay work – with rosettes and stars on a cloudy walnut background – suggests maps of the celestial firmament. By opening the doors, you go from the great whole to the smallest detail and back again.

It was not only the Reformed authors in the Republic who propagated these ideas. In the sixteenth century, the German theologian Martin Luther was the first to treat the family as the cornerstone of society. Opposing the Catholic idea that a secluded, celibate life in a monastery was the best way to honour God, Luther instead emphasized the importance of bearing and raising children. This led to a reassessment of the institution of marriage and the role of women as managers of the entire household. Lutherans saw a well-run home – scrubbed clean, filled to the rafters with food and fuel, and occupied by a Christian family with well-brought-up children – as fundamental to the social order and another way of praising God. Oortman, as a Lutheran, had internalized this attitude just as much as her Protestant compatriots had. The theme of good upbringing and caring for the entire household runs like a common thread through all the rooms of her doll's house, from the drying attic where her daughter began the tour, with its laundry baskets and linen press, to the cellar with its brooms and supply of drinks, culminating in the entrance hall where the tour ended, with its grisaille paintings on childrearing.

Glauburg's account of this visit is reminiscent of descriptions of the exceptional cabinets of curiosities made for the great European courts. These were, above all, designed to impress; crafted from precious materials by leading artists, they were meant to be viewed and admired. Glauburg and the Uffenbach brothers had already seen quite a few cabinets of curiosities in collectors' homes, but Oortman's doll's house was a unique specimen. They delighted in the luxury items, such as the dolls' jewellery and the porcelain in the best kitchen. But the everyday objects attracted just as much attention. To make his description as accurate as possible, Glauburg was even permitted to take a doll from the cabinet and peek under her skirts to see that she wore underpants 'in the Dutch manner'. The hidden rooms, such as the *comptoir* and the cellar, along with ingenious details like the moving figures in the garden and the working pump in the kitchen, astonished the German guests. Oortman may also have made use of a light source hidden behind the doll's house. The windows in the rear wall at the level of the children's room, the best kitchen, and the library allowed light to stream in [FIG. 74]. It was a theatrical spectacle, laced with humour, but conveying a serious message.

MYTHICAL PROPORTIONS

The visit to Warmoesstraat made a profound impression on the German travellers. Upon returning to Frankfurt, Zacharias von Uffenbach commissioned a doll's house for himself. In 1732, it was viewed at length in his home by the admiring members of a society for natural science and art founded by his brother Friedrich, who was also captivated by it and had personally crafted various pieces of furniture and other miniatures for Zacharias.

Oortman's doll's house remained in the family for two generations after her death; through her husband, it passed to their eldest son Jan Brandt, then to his younger brother Jacob, and finally to Jacob's daughter Alida. By the time of Alida Brandt's death in 1809, it is unclear whether she still owned the doll's house. It had probably already been sold to the Amsterdam art dealer Cornelis Sebille Roos, who was then a key figure in the cultural realm. In his home, the Trippenhuis on Amsterdam's Kloveniersburgwal, he established an art gallery for his own exhibitions and auctions. It is highly likely that he exhibited the doll's house there and was the author of the late eighteenth-century catalogue which so vividly describes it as an artwork without equal.

In 1814, Jacobus Scheltema, author of a book on Peter the Great, made even more grandiose claims about the doll's house. He spread the story that Tsar Peter, during his visit to the Republic, had asked the Amsterdam consul Christoffel Brants to have the doll's house made after the model of a 'Dutch patrician house' as a gift for the tsarina. Scheltema claimed that because of the exorbitant cost, 30,000 guilders, the Russian monarch did not go through with the purchase, and the doll's house remained in Amsterdam. In his description, Scheltema also mentioned several renowned artists who had supposedly contributed to the doll's house, such as 'Vianen', referring to either Adam or Paulus van Vianen, both celebrated silversmiths.

After Roos's death in 1820, his estate was auctioned off. The sale catalogue reveals that the dolls were still present, albeit in poor condition. A Rotterdam dealer bought the doll's house for 2,135 guilders and, just six months later, offered it to the director of the Royal Cabinet of Curiosities, Reinier Pieter van de Kasteele, who managed to persuade King William I to pay 2,800 guilders for 'the art cabinet of Peter the Great'. In 1875, the collection of the Cabinet of Curiosities was transferred to the Nederlandsch Museum, which in turn merged into the Rijksmuseum. Somewhere in the process, the wax dolls and their clothing must have been lost. Not until 1942 was the myth about Peter the Great debunked in a museum catalogue, and it took another eleven years after that before Petronella Oortman was acknowledged as the rightful patron of the famous doll's house.

Clearly, the Uffenbachs were not the only ones fascinated by this doll's house. Even today, it remains a major attraction. Nowhere else does daily life in a seventeenth-century household feel so tangible. In the twenty-first century, it continues to captivate the imagination. It inspired British author and actress Jessie Burton to write the novel *The Miniaturist*, which was published in 2014 and adapted into a BBC miniseries. The protagonist Nella, however, has little in common with the historical Petronella Oortman. The largest, most beautiful, and most impressive doll's house of the seventeenth century still gives rise to new myths.

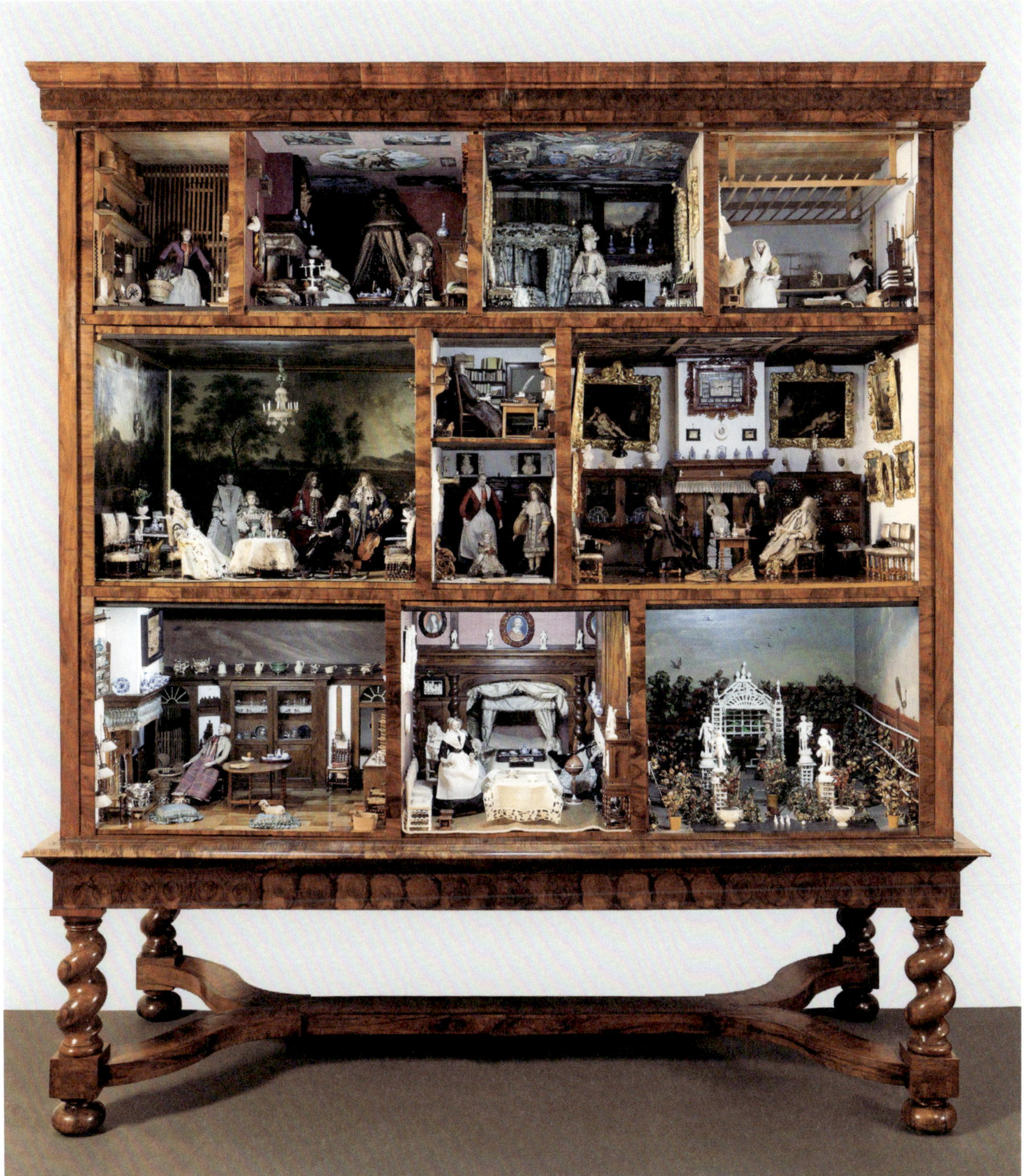

72
The earliest extant Dutch doll's house is Petronella de la Court's. She began collecting miniatures in 1668 and finished decorating the cabinet around 1690

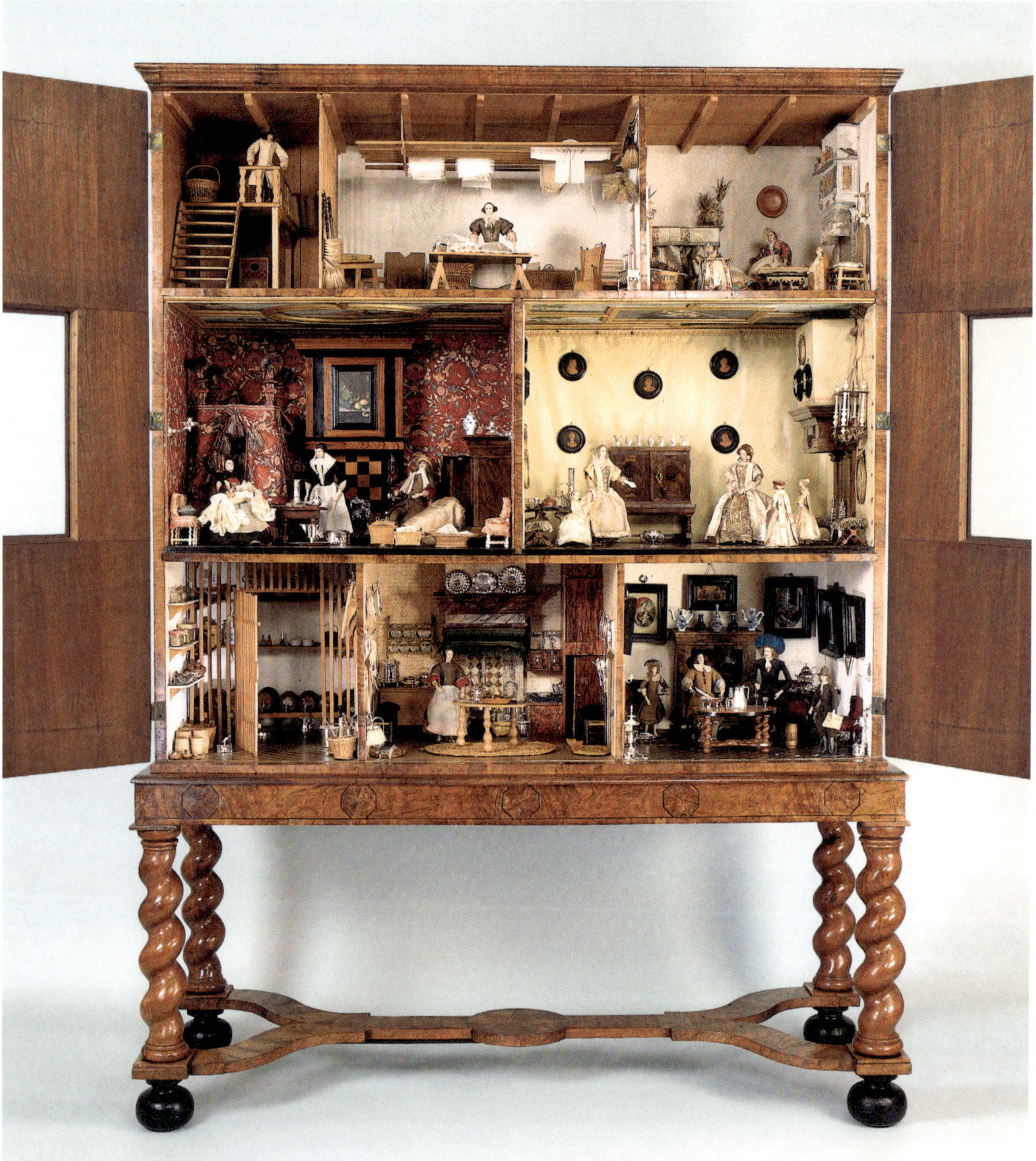

73
Petronella Dunois's doll's house was completed around 1676 and still contains the original dolls and a large quantity of miniature silver. The doors have windows that give a view of the most lavish rooms: the lying-in chamber and the *zaal* (reception room)

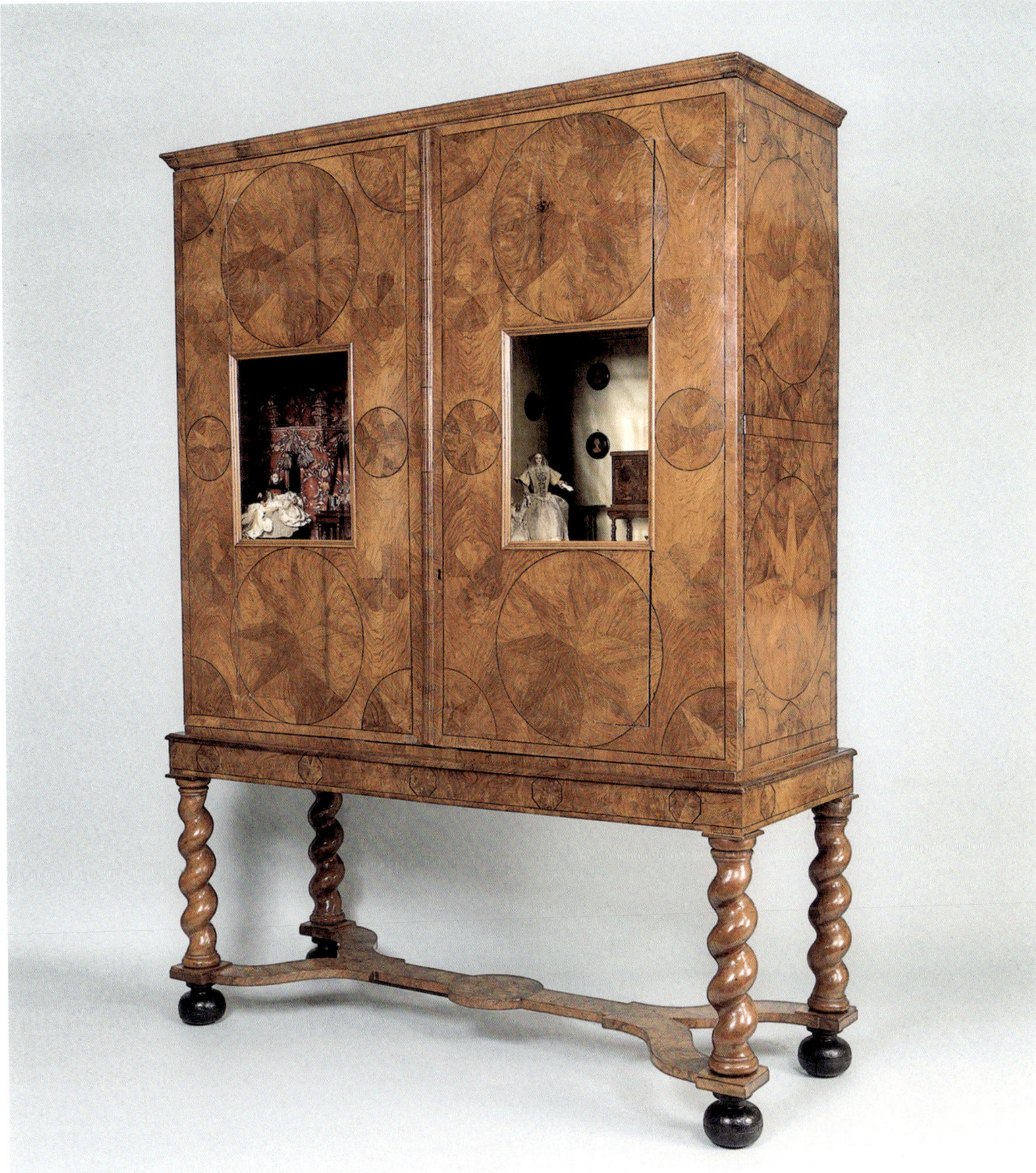

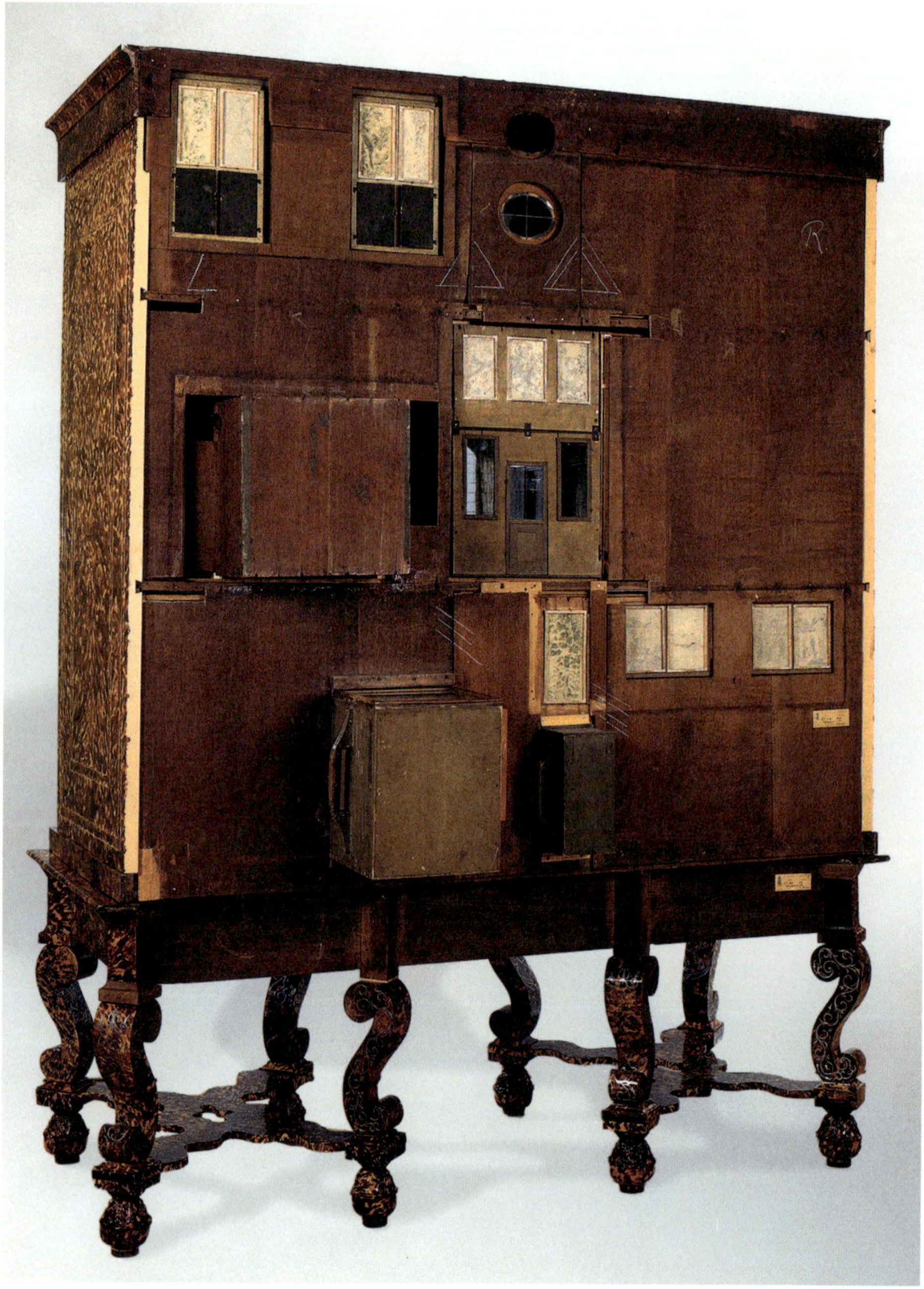

74
The rear view of Petronella Oortman's doll's house reveals the compartments for the library, the privy and the alcove in the lying-in chamber. Oortman may have placed candles or oil lamps here, so that light would enter the house through the windows

BIBLIOGRAPHY

R.J. Baarsen, *Furniture in Holland's Golden Age*, Amsterdam 2007

E. Bergvelt and R.E. Kistemaker (eds.), *De wereld binnen handbereik. Nederlandse kunst- en rariteiten-verzamelingen, 1585–1735*, exh. cat. Amsterdam (Amsterdam Historisch Museum) 1992

S. Broomhall and J. Spinks, *Early Modern Women in the Low Countries: Feminizing Sources and Interpretations of the Past*, Ashgate 2011

S.J. van Dijk (ed.), *At Home in the 17th Century*, exh. cat. Amsterdam (Rijksmuseum) 2025

I.H. van Eeghen, 'Het poppenhuis van Petronella Oortman, huisvrouw van Jacob Brandt', *Amstelodamum: Maandblad voor de kennis van Amsterdam* 40 (1953), pp. 113–117

C.W. Fock (ed.), *Het Nederlandse interieur in beeld, 1600–1900*, Zwolle 2001

J.R. ter Molen, 'Een bezichtiging van het poppenhuis van Petronella Brandt-Oortman in de zomer van 1718', *Bulletin van het Rijksmuseum* 42 (1994), no. 2, pp. 120–136

J.R. ter Molen, *Een plezierreis in de zomer van 1718. De familie Von Uffenbach in de Nederlanden*, Zwolle 2017

M. Moseley-Christian, 'Seventeenth-Century *Pronk Poppenhuisen*: Domestic Space and the Ritual Function of Dutch Dollhouses for Women', *Home Cultures: The Journal of Architecture, Design and Domestic Space* 7 (2010), no. 3, pp. 341–363

H.H. Pijzel-Dommisse, *'t Is poppe goet en anders niet. Het poppenhuis in het Frans Halsmuseum*, Haarlem 1980

H.H. Pijzel-Dommisse, *Het poppenhuis van het Haags Gemeentemuseum*, The Hague 1988

H.H. Pijzel-Dommisse, *Het poppenhuis van Petronella de la Court*, Utrecht 1987

H.H. Pijzel-Dommisse, *Het Hollandse pronkpoppenhuis. Interieur en huishouden in de 17de en 18de eeuw*, Amsterdam/Zwolle 2000

L. von Wilckens, *Das Puppenhaus. Vom Spiegelbild des bügerlichen Hausstandes zum Spielzeug für Kinder*, Munich 1978

LIST OF IMAGES

Detail pages
p. 1: entrance hall; p. 2: *zaal*; p. 3: lying-in chamber; p. 4: tapestry room; p. 6: best kitchen; p. 14: entrance hall; p. 17: entrance hall (Jacob Appel, fig. 2); pp. 20–21: lying-in chamber; p. 23: linen cupboard, lying-in chamber; p. 26: lying-in chamber; pp. 28–29: *zaal*; pp. 32–33: *zaal* (Jacob Appel, fig. 2); pp. 36–37: tapestry room; pp. 40–41: tapestry room (Jacob Appel, fig. 2); pp. 46–47: left wall, kitchen; p. 48: kitchen; p. 51: right wall, kitchen; pp. 58–59: best kitchen; pp. 64–65: ceiling painting, best kitchen (Amsterdam, c. 1690–1710); pp. 68–69: children's room; p. 74: storage attic; pp. 78–79: laundry attic; p. 94: library; p. 95: best kitchen; p. 96: collector's cabinet, tapestry room

1
Petronella Oortman's doll's house
Amsterdam, c. 1686–1710
Various materials, h. 255 × w. 190 × d. 78 cm
Amsterdam, Rijksmuseum
Inv. no. BK-NM-1010

2
Jacob Appel
Petronella Oortman's doll's house
C. 1710
Oil on parchment on canvas, 87 × 69 cm
Amsterdam, Rijksmuseum
Inv. no. SK-A-4245

3
Detail of one leg of the doll's house

4
Detail with one drawer of the doll's house open

5
Detail of the side of the doll's house with the monogram BO (Brandt–Oortman)

6
Hall bench
Amsterdam, c. 1690–1710
Olive, h. 9.7 × w. 17.1 × d. 3.8 cm
Inv. no. BK-NM-1010-140-B

7
Attributed to Johannes Voorhout (I)
Ceiling painting in the entrance hall
C. 1690–1710
Oil on panel, 35 × 24.3 cm (excl. frame)
Inv. no. BK-NM-1010-245

8
Grisaille in the entrance hall of the doll's house, attributed to Jan Cornelisz Hoogsaat

9
Comptoir in Petronella de la Court's doll's house (fig. 72)

10
Garden room in Petronella de la Court's doll's house (fig. 72)

11
Swaddled baby with *doopluier* ('baptismal nappy')
Amsterdam, c. 1690–1710
Mat rush, linen, wax, glass, silk, l. 9.2 cm
Inv. no. BK-NM-1010-357

12
Comfortable dressing gown
Northern Netherlands, c. 1690–1710
Silk, l. 20 × w. 23 cm
Inv. no. BK-NM-1010-92

13
Canopy bed with appurtenances
Amsterdam, c. 1690–1710
Walnut, silk, linen, cotton, down, jute(?), brass, iron, h. 27.5 × l. 28 × w. 12.5 cm
Inv. nos. BK-NM-1010-33, -34, -35-A, -B, -36-A, -B

14
Cradle with appurtenances
Amsterdam, c. 1690–1710
Osier, walnut, silk, linen, cotton, down, h. 9.8 × l. 10.8 × w. 5.3 cm
Inv. nos. BK-NM-1010-39-A, -39-B, -46-A, -B, -48-A, -B, -54, -55

15
Fire basket with cloth
Halle(?)/Amsterdam, c. 1675–1710
Osier, silk, h. 9 × diam. 7.2 cm
Inv. nos. BK-NM-1010-64, -219

16
Johannes Voorhout (I)
Chimney piece depicting Pharaoh's daughter finding Moses in the bulrush basket
Amsterdam, c. 1690–1710
Oil on canvas, 13.5 × 11.5 cm
Inv. no. BK-NM-1010-241

17
Attributed to Christian Warenberg (active 1696–1747)
Wall sconce with personification of autumn
Amsterdam, c. 1700–1710
Silver, h. 7 × w. 5.3 × d. 2.8 cm
Inv. no. BK-NM-1010-101-C

18
Three pipes, 'Gouda' type with long stem and heeled bowl
Amsterdam(?), c. 1690–1710
Milk glass (top), bone (middle and bottom), l. 5 and 3.6 cm resp.
Inv. nos. BK-NM-1010-354-A to -C

19
Game board (board for tric-trac on the inner side, boards for chess and nine men's morris on the outer sides) with discs and kopeks
Amsterdam, c. 1690–1710
Walnut, olive, ebony and palm wood, brass, bone, h. 1.9 × l. 5.8 × b. 5.8 cm
Inv. nos. BK-NM-1010-276, -277-A to -C

20
Two spittoons in Kakiemon style
Japan, c. 1690–1710
Porcelain, h. 2 × diam. 3.2 cm
Inv. nos. BK-NM-1010-115-A, -B

21
Attributed to Nicolas Piemont
Ceiling painting in the *zaal*
C. 1690–1709
Oil on canvas, 69 × 66 cm
Inv. no. BK-NM-1010-240-E

22
Tea table
Amsterdam, c. 1690–1710
Painting attributed to Willem Hendrik Wilhelmus van Royen
Softwood, h. 13 × w. 20.7 cm
Inv. no. BK-NM-1010-27

23
Ensemble of ten chairs, a table and a daybed
Amsterdam, c. 1690–1710
Walnut, silk, h. 14.5 cm (chairs), 10.1 cm (table), 7.5 cm (daybed)
Inv. nos. BK-NM-1010-7-A to -H, -8-A, -B, -20, -30, -41-A to -C

24
Collector's cabinet with shell collection
Amsterdam, c. 1690–1710
Fruitwood, shells, h. 28.2 × w. 23.2 × d. 9 cm
Inv. no. BK-NM-1010-2

25
Library
Various materials, h. 35.8 × w. 35.8 × d. 28 cm

26
Nine separate quires of 7–10 blank sheets each and two sets of loose sheets
Amsterdam, 1690–1710
Paper, h. 3.9 x w. 2.6 cm
Inv. nos. BK-NM-1010-181, -358

27
Kern des Bijbels
The Hague (A. de Groot en Zn), 1750
Clasps and mounts by Dirk Fortman (active 1736–1792)
Silk, gold, paper, h. 5 × w. 3.3 × d. 1.5 cm
Inv. no. BK-NM-1010-180

28
Several dishes with miniature fruits
Amsterdam(?), c. 1690–1710
Glass, wax, 2.3–3 cm
Inv. nos. BK-NM-1010-353 (fruits) on -207, -342, -347-A, -B, 350-A to -C (dishes)

29
Contents of the pewter cupboard
Amsterdam(?), c. 1675–1710
Pewter, glass, diam. 1.2–3.5 cm
Inv. nos. BK-NM-1010-104, -105, -106, -107-A, -B, -108-A to -P, -204, -206-A, -B, -209, -210, -349-A, -B, -351, -352

30
Three forks and three knives
Amsterdam, c. 1690–1710
Silver, iron, ivory, tortoiseshell/horn, l. 2.6–3.1 cm
Inv. nos. BK-NM-1010-109-A to -C, -269A, -B, -270

31
Candlestick
Amsterdam, c. 1690–1710
Brass, h. 3.3 × diam. 2.2 cm
Inv. no. BK-NM-1010-265

32
Snuffers with stand
Amsterdam, c. 1690–1710
Brass, l. 2.4 cm (snuffers), h. 2.3 cm (stand)
Inv. nos. BK-NM-1010-266-A, -B

33
Privy
Various materials, h. 26 × w. 12.5 × d. 12.5 cm

34
Cellar
Various materials, h. 20 × w. 37.5 × d. 42 cm

35
Pots, bottles and jugs from the cellar
Amsterdam, c. 1675–1710
Glass, cork, h. 1.1–3.8 cm
Inv. nos. BK-NM-1010-198, -199, -200-A, -201-A to -D, -203-A to -C, -211-A to -C, -212-A to -C, -214, -217

36
Cauldron
Amsterdam, c. 1690–1710
Tin-plated copper, h. 2.8 × diam. 5.5 cm
Inv. no. BK-NM-1010-257

37
Five beer and wine barrels with taps
Amsterdam, c. 1690–1710
Oak, rattan, brass, l. 5.7 × diam. 4.5 cm
Inv. nos. BK-NM-1010-302-A to -E

38
Whisk broom, broom, and scrubber
Amsterdam, c. 1690–1710
Wood, l. 4.4–18 cm
Inv. nos. BK-NM-1010-299, -300-A, -301

39
Contents of the porcelain cabinet
Amsterdam/Haarlem, China, Japan, c. 1670–1720
Porcelain, glass, various dimensions
Inv. nos. BK-NM-1010-110-A to -C, 111-F, -H, -I, -112-A to -L, -113-A to -E, -117, -118-A, -B, 119-A, -B, -120, -121-A to -E, -122-A, -B, -312-A to -H, -313-A, -B, -E, -I, -J, -314-A to -D, -315-A to -C, -319-A to -C, -320, -321, -322-A, -B, -327, -328-A, -C, 331, -333, -336, -337, -338, 340-A, -B, -341, -344, -346-A to -C, -E, -349-C, -D

40
Lacemaking pillow, sewing pillow, sewing kit and pair of scissors
Amsterdam, 1690–1710
Various types of wood, brass, silk, paper, silver thread, mirror glass, tortoiseshell, linen, h. 1.8–3.2 × w. 1.7–5.2 × d. 2.7–5.5 cm
Inv. nos. BK-NM-1010-67, 68, 267, 275

41
Potty chair with pillows and chamber pot
Amsterdam, c. 1675/1690–1710
Palm wood, oak, brass, wool, silk, glass, h. 12.4 × w. 6.5 × d. 6 cm
Inv. nos. BK-NM-1010-15-A to -C, -335

42
Glassware from the porcelain cabinet
Amsterdam(?), c. 1675–1710
Glass, h. 0.7–3.4 cm
Inv. nos. BK-NM-1010-182-A, -B, -183-A, -B, 184-A, -B, 185-A, -B, -186-A, -B, 187, -188-A, -B, 189-A, -B, -190-A, -B, -191-C, -192-A to -D, -193-A, -B, -194, -195

43
Parrot cage
Amsterdam(?), c. 1690–1710
Tin-plated iron, brass, ebony, h. 11.4 × diam. 5.6 cm
Inv. no. BK-NM-1010-280

44
Drop-leaf table
Amsterdam, c. 1690–1710
Olive, brass, h. 10 × w. 18.8 (leaves extended) × d. 13.1 cm
Inv. no. BK-NM-1010-19

45
Fire basket
Amsterdam, c. 1690–1710
Wrought iron, gilded brass, h. 5.5 × w. 8.6 × d. 5.2 cm
Inv. no. BK-NM-1010-259

46
Michiel Maenbeeck
Fireguard from Petronella Dunois's doll's house, 1676
Silver, 3.9 × 7.6 cm
Inv. no. BK-14656-107

47
Wicker chair
Halle(?), c. 1675–1710
Osier, glass, h. 6.4 × w. 4.6 × d. 3.5 cm
Inv. no. BK-NM-1010-224

48
Cradle with cradle cover
Amsterdam, c. 1690–1710
Osier, walnut, silk, h. 10 × l. 9.5 × w. 5 cm
Inv. nos. BK-NM-1010-40-A, -B

49
Canopy bed
Amsterdam, c. 1690–1710
Oak, silk, linen, cotton, jute, brass, down, h. 43 × l. 24.3 × w. 17.8 cm
Inv. nos. BK-NM-1010-37, -38, -44, -45, -56

50
In the style of Cornelis Dusart
The quack
C. 1690–1710
Oil on copper, in gilded bronze frame, 12 × 15 cm (with frame)
Inv. no. BK-NM-1010-244-A

51
In the style of Cornelis Dusart
The vendor
C. 1690–1710
Oil on copper, in gilded bronze frame, 12 × 15 cm (with frame)
Inv. no. BK-NM-1010-244-B

52
Mirror with frame
Amsterdam, c. 1690–1710
Gilded bronze, wood, amalgam, mirror glass, h. 21 × w. 12.3 × d. 1 cm
Inv. no. BK-NM-1010-94

53
Cabinet on stand with a garniture of vases
Amsterdam, c. 1690–1710
Oak, walnut, h. 25.3 × w. 19.4 × d. 8.6 cm
Inv. nos. BK-NM-1010-1, -325-A, -B, -326, -329, -330

54
Table with collapsible legs
Amsterdam, c. 1690–1710
Olive, silk, h. 8.9 × l. 11.7 × w. 9 cm
Inv. no. BK-NM-1010-22-A

55
Two stoves with fire pans
Amsterdam/Haarlem, c. 1675/1690–1700
Oak, glass, h. 2.3 × w. 2.8 × d. 2.8 cm
Inv. nos. BK-NM-1010-202-B, -213-A, -306-B, -306-E

56
Two covered jars and a storage jar
Amsterdam/Haarlem, c. 1675/1690–1700
Glass, chamois leather, linen, h. 1.4–2.5 × diam. 1.5–2.1 cm
Inv. nos. BK-NM-1010-205-A, -B, -208

57
Board stacked with peat briquettes
Northern Netherlands, c. 1690–1710
Peat, spruce, h. 10 × l. 16 × w. 3 cm
Inv. no. BK-NM-1010-362-A

58
Board stacked with firewood
Amsterdam, c. 1690–1710
Oak, beech, h. 9.7 × l. 16.5 × w. 4 cm
Inv. no. BK-NM-1010-361-B

59
Spinning wheel in Petronella Dunois's doll's house
Amsterdam, c. 1675–1700
Silver, h. 7.1 × w. 7.4 × d. 2.4 cm
Inv. no. BK-14656-3

60
Spinning wheel
Amsterdam, c. 1690–1710
Maple, ebony, linen, leather, h. 13.5 × w. 10 × d. 6.5 cm
Inv. no. BK-NM-1010-271

61
Wessel Jansen
Mouse trap with cat in Petronella Dunois's doll's house
Silver, h. 2.6 × l. 3 × w. 2.2 cm
After 1642–before 1696
Inv. no. BK-14656-104

62
Rat trap
Amsterdam, c. 1690–1710
Wood, brass, lead, h. 4 × l. 6.3 × w. 2.1 cm
Inv. no. BK-NM-1010-305

63
Hamper
Halle(?), c. 1690–1710
Osier, wood, brass, h. 10 × w. 10.9 × d. 7.8 cm
Inv. no. BK-NM-1010-221

64
Clothes basket
Halle(?), c. 1690–1710
Osier, h. 3.2 × w. 9.6 × d. 5.5 cm
Inv. no. BK-NM-1010-229

65
Bakermat (wicker cradle)
Halle(?), c. 1690–1710
Osier, h. 5 × l. 18 cm
Inv. no. BK-NM-1010-220

66
Box-bed with appurtenances and chamber pot
Amsterdam/India(?), Japan, c. 1690–1710
Wood, silk, cotton, linen, brass, down, porcelain, h. 23 cm (curtain)
Inv. nos. BK-NM-1010-42-A, -B, -43, -51-A, -C, -58-A to -C, -114-A

67
Napkin with central
embroidered monogram BO
Amsterdam/Haarlem, c. 1690–1710
Linen, 13 × 9 cm
Inv. no. BK-NM-1010-80-B

68
Trestle table with ironing cloth,
smock, napkin, and irons on racks
Amsterdam, c. 1690–1710
Wood, wool, linen, iron, brass,
h. 12.5 × l. 27.4 × w. 9.1 cm
Inv. nos. BK-NM-1010-23, -80A,
-83, -85, -260-A, -B, -261-A, -B

69
Linen press
Amsterdam, c. 1690–1710
Oak, walnut, brass, h. 25 × w. 16.3 ×
d. 11 cm
Inv. no. BK-NM-1010-4

70
Bench with linen basket
Amsterdam, c. 1690–1710
Wood, linen, h. 6.2 × w. 8.6 ×
d. 3.7 cm (bench), h. 1.3 × w. 8.1 ×
d. 5.4 cm (linen basket)
Inv. nos. BK-NM-1010-16, -82-A to -C,
-86-A, -B, -304

71
Doll's house
Nuremberg, 1673
Various materials, h. 107 ×
w. 1.5 × d. 45.6 cm
London, The Victoria
& Albert Museum
Inv. no. W.41-1922

72
Petronella de la Court's doll's house
Amsterdam, c. 1668–1690
Various materials, h. 206.5 ×
w. 182 × d. 74.5 cm
Utrecht, Centraal Museum
Inv. no. 5000

73
Petronella Dunois's doll's house
Amsterdam, c. 1676
Various materials, h. 200 ×
w. 150.5 × d. 56 cm
Amsterdam, Rijksmuseum
Inv. no. BK-14656
Gift of A.S.M. van Tienhoven-Hacke

74
Petronella Oortman's doll's house,
back (fig. 1)

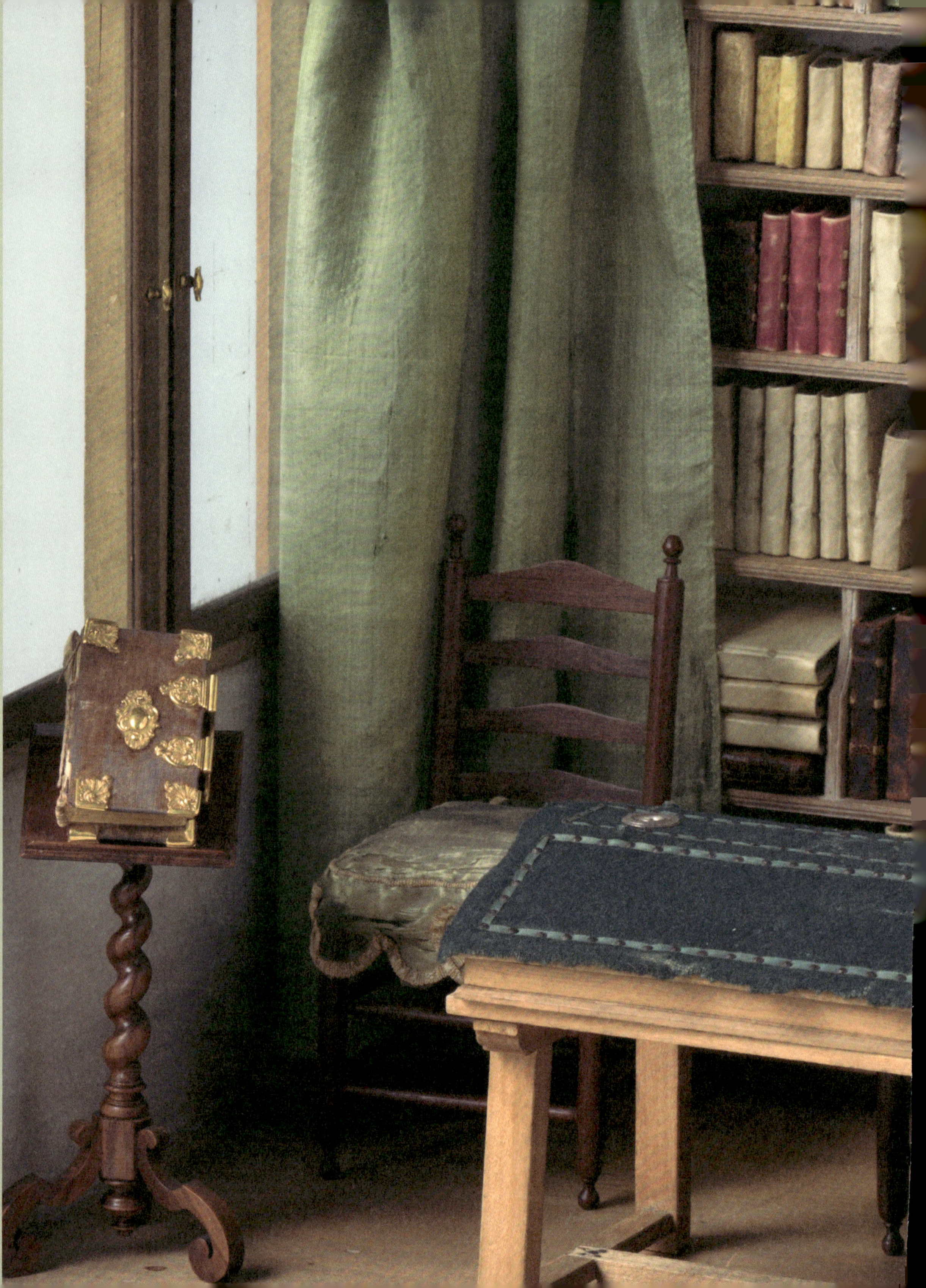

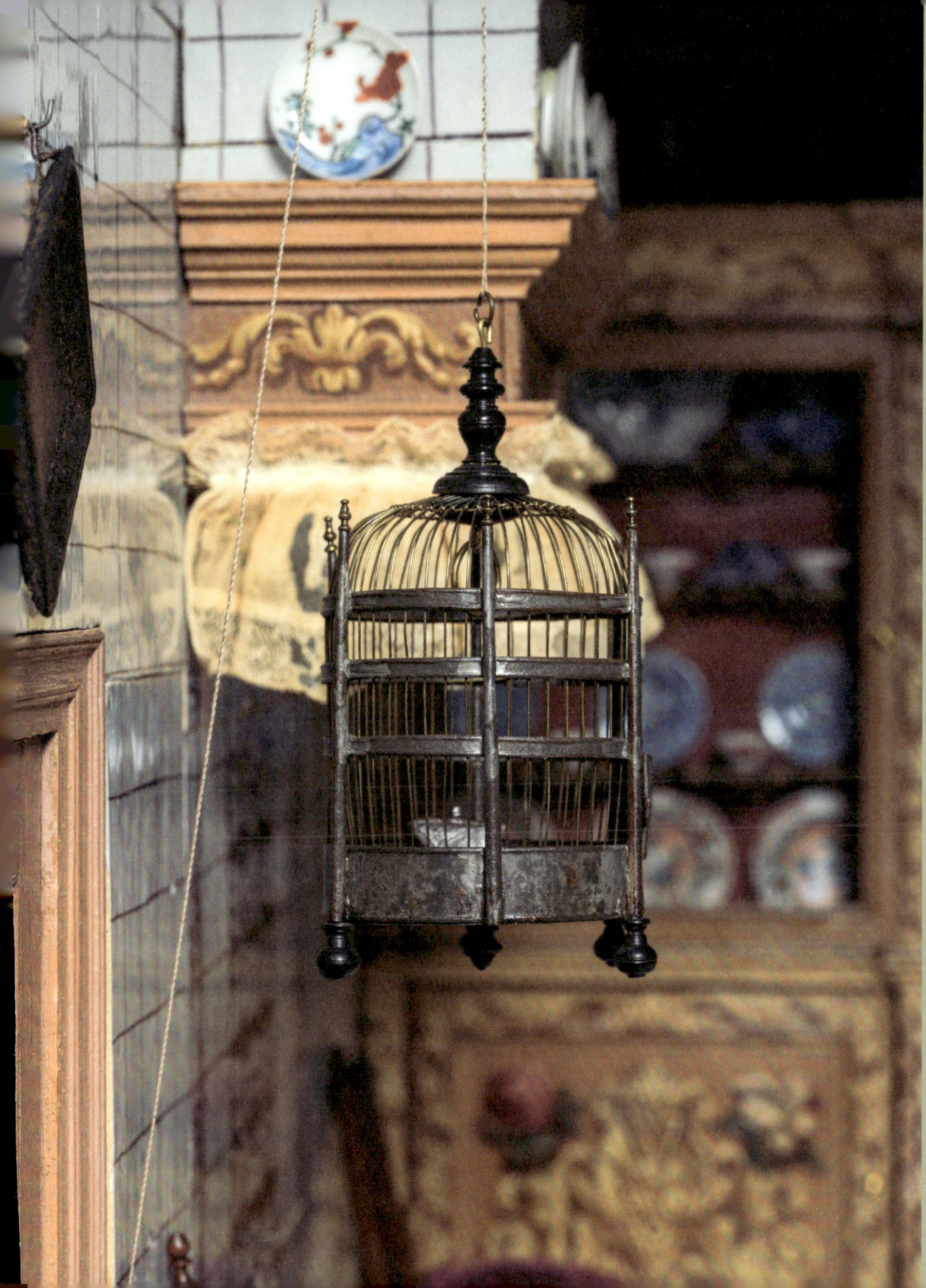

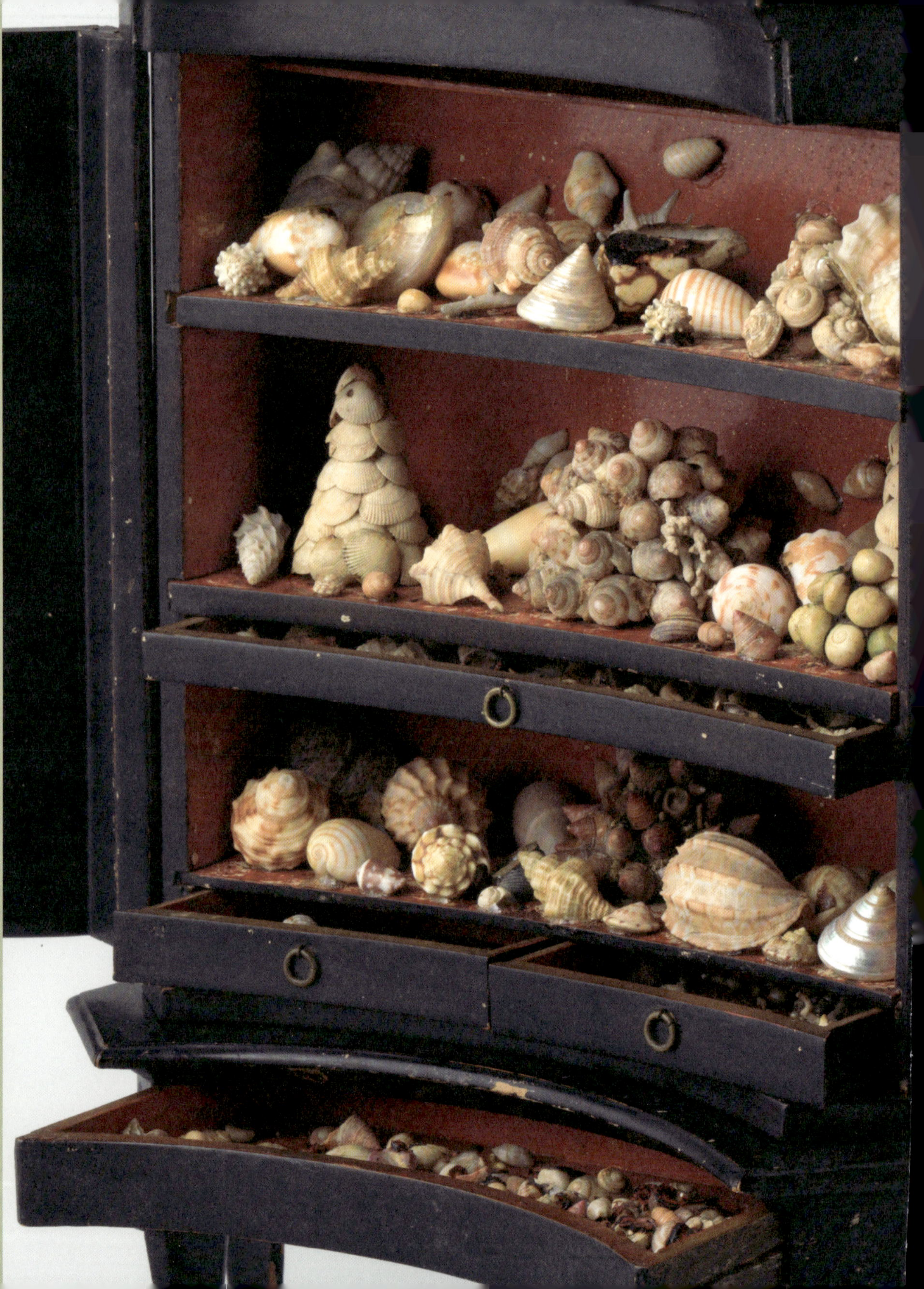